OXFORD STUDIES IN T
CULTURAL FORMS

General Editors
HOWARD MORPHY AND FRED MYERS

═══════

Anthropology, Art, and Aesthetics

OXFORD STUDIES IN THE ANTHROPOLOGY OF CULTURAL FORMS

Oxford Studies in the Anthropology of Cultural Forms is a series focusing on the anthropology of art, material culture, and aesthetics. Titles in the series will concentrate on art, music, poetry, dance, ritual form, and material objects studied as components of systems of knowledge and value, as they are transformed and reproduced over time. Howard Morphy is University Lecturer in Ethnology at the University of Oxford, and Curator at the Pitt Rivers Museum. Fred Myers is Associate Professor of Anthropology at New York University.

ANTHROPOLOGY
ART
AND
AESTHETICS

═══

EDITED BY

Jeremy Coote and Anthony Shelton

CLARENDON PRESS · OXFORD

Oxford University Press, Walton Street, Oxford OX2 6DP

Oxford New York
Athens Auckland Bangkok Bombay
Calcutta Cape Town Dar es Salaam Delhi
Florence Hong Kong Istanbul Karachi
Kuala Lumpur Madras Madrid Melbourne
Mexico City Nairobi Paris Singapore
Taipei Tokyo Toronto
and associated companies in
Berlin Ibadan

Oxford is a trade mark of Oxford University Press

Published in the United States
by Oxford University Press Inc., New York

British Library Cataloguing in Publication Data
Data available

Library of Congress Cataloging in Publication Data
Anthropology, art, and aesthetics/edited by Jeremy Coote and
Anthony Shelton.
Includes bibliographical references and index.
1. Art and anthropology. 2. Art and society. 3. Art, Primitive.
1. Coote, Jeremy. II. Shelton, Anthony.
N72.S6A65 1992 701'.03—dc20 91–34843

ISBN 0–19–827945–0 (Pbk)

Printed in Great Britain
on acid-free paper by
Biddles Ltd, Guildford and King's Lynn

ACKNOWLEDGEMENTS

The essays in this volume have their origins in two series of seminars and lectures organized by the editors and held in Oxford in 1985. The first series, entitled 'Anthropological Approaches to Non-Western Art', was held at the Oxford Institute of Social Anthropology. We are grateful to those members of the then staff and student body who helped to make the series such a success, and in particular to Christian McDonaugh, Merete Jakobsen, and the late Andrew Duff-Cooper, whose contributions to the series could not be included here.

The second series, of public lectures with the title 'Art and Anthropology', was held at Wolfson College, Oxford, under the joint auspices of the College and the Oxford University Anthropological Society. The Anthropological Society provided generous financial support through a grant from the University's Clubs Committee. As well as granting substantial funding, Wolfson College provided an informal and cordial ambience which contributed much to the sense of occasion of the lectures themselves. We are grateful to everyone who participated in the series, and in particular to Jonathan King, Jonathan Kingdon, Elizabeth Cowling, and Remo Guidieri, whose contributions could not be included in this collection. Thanks are also due to Adrian Gerbrands, who contributed much to the impact of the series with an entrancing talk to the departmental seminar of the Institute of Social Anthropology, given in association with the Wolfson series.

It seems now a long time since the plan for the original series was drawn up. We have been encouraged at various times since then by the support of numerous friends and colleagues. It would be excessive to mention them all, but we should like to thank in particular Godfrey Lienhardt, for his continual support, and Karel Arnaut, for practical assistance and for compiling the index.

We should also like to thank Oxford University Press for taking on the task of publishing the collection. We are pleased that the volume should be appearing in the Press's new series 'Oxford Studies in the Anthropology of Cultural Forms'. We must also thank, on our contributors' behalf and our own, the anonymous readers whose considered and constructive comments are reflected, we hope, in the book's final form. Wolfson College has provided more financial support in the form of a subsidy towards the cost of illustrations. Without it, the book would have been both less well illustrated and more expensive. Such generous support is greatly appreciated.

We are grateful to the following individuals and institutions for permission to reproduce illustrations: the American Museum of Natural History, New

York; the Auckland Museum, Auckland; the Museum für Völkerkunde und Schweizerisches Museum für Völkskunde, Basle; the Museum für Völkerkunde, Berlin; Shirley F. Campbell; the Hamburgisches Museum für Völkerkunde; the Hearst Museum of Anthropology, University of California at Berkeley; Richard A. Manoogian; the Museum of Modern Art, New York; Arnold T. Nelson; Papunya Tula Artists; the Pitt Rivers Museum, Oxford; the Sheldon Jackson Museum, Sitka, State of Alaska; and Survival Anglia, London.

Finally, we should like to thank our fellow contributors for their patience.

Jeremy Coote and Anthony Shelton

CONTENTS

MAPS

FIGURES

PLATES

(between pp. 114 and 115)

CONTRIBUTORS

RUTH BARNES is an art historian currently researching and cataloguing early Indian textile collections at the Ashmolean Museum, Oxford.

ROSS BOWDEN is Senior Lecturer in Anthropology at La Trobe University, Melbourne.

JEREMY COOTE is an Assistant Curator at the Pitt Rivers Museum, University of Oxford.

SIR RAYMOND FIRTH is Emeritus Professor of Anthropology, University of London.

ALFRED GELL is Reader in Social Anthropology at the London School of Economics and Political Science, University of London.

SUSANNE KÜCHLER is a Lecturer in Anthropology at University College London.

ROBERT LAYTON is Professor of Anthropology at the University of Durham.

HOWARD MORPHY is University Lecturer in Ethnology at the University of Oxford, and Curator at the Pitt Rivers Museum.

JARICH OOSTEN is Senior Lecturer in the Department of Anthropology at the State University, Leiden.

ANTHONY SHELTON is Keeper of Non-Western Art and Anthropology and Head of the Green Centre for Ethnography at the Royal Pavilion Art Gallery and Museums, Brighton.

Introduction

JEREMY COOTE and ANTHONY SHELTON

The essays in this volume provide an introduction to the anthropological study of art and aesthetics, reflecting the richness and variety that characterize the subject today. While most of the essays concentrate on a single theme and a single cultural tradition, together they cover a wide theoretical and cultural range. There is, however, an accidental bias towards Oceania: Firth discusses Tikopia head-rests, Gell reflects on Trobriand canoes, Bowden focuses on the men's houses of the Kwoma of New Guinea, and Küchler analyses the *malangan* of New Ireland. Elsewhere, Layton and Morphy discuss Australian Aboriginal art-forms and aesthetics, while Barnes on Lamalera textiles, Oosten on Inuit masks, Shelton on the Huichol of Mexico, and Coote on the Nilotes of the Southern Sudan discuss Indonesian, Arctic, Middle American, and African traditions respectively.

While all the essays discuss themes of general interest, the opening two essays are more directly concerned with the subject as a whole. Firth's account of the changing relationship between art and anthropology during the sixty years since he first wrote on the subject not only acts as an introduction to the anthropology of art but also provides the volume with a historical dimension. Following this, Gell's discussion of the methodological basis of the anthropology of art raises fundamental questions about the nature of the subject itself. While it is clear that there is such a thing as the anthropological study of art, Gell's essay throws doubt on the existence of 'the anthropology of art' as an intellectual enterprise. Whether they accept Gell's arguments or not, anthropologists who study art will be encouraged by them to reflect on what they are trying to do in their work.

Firth's account of the history of the anthropological study of art obviates the need for such an account here. Nevertheless, a few remarks may be in order.

The claim that in recent years there has been a resurgence in the anthropological study of art is by now a commonplace one. Since the late 1970s, three English-language introductory books (Anderson, 1979; Layton, 1981; Hatcher, 1985) have appeared, and a major new journal, *Res*, has been founded. Today, monographs and journal articles on topics in the anthropology of art abound. The reasons behind this resurgence are no doubt complex and will only be fully understood in years to come, though some factors relevant to any final explanation have been highlighted elsewhere (Stocking, 1985).

It is worth remembering, however, that the West's original recognition of aesthetic value in the material products of other societies was not a result of anthropological insight. It took the perception of artists, in particular the Fauves and Cubists, to open Western eyes to the aesthetic qualities of non-Western arts. As Firth relates below, he was one of those anthropologists for whom the changes wrought in modern art 'came as a liberating influence'. Suddenly, 'the painting and sculpture which anthropologists encountered in exotic societies could be regarded, not as a product of imperfect vision, technical crudity, or blind adherence to tradition, but as works of art in their own right, to be judged as expressions of artists' original conceptions in the light of their cultural endowment'. But as well as seeing the discovery of non-Western art by Picasso and others as the moment when the West began to take non-Western arts seriously, we might also regard this 'discovery' as a stumbling-block which has long held back the development of an anthropology of art (Firth, 1973: 5). While one could trace separate histories for the anthropological study of art and the aestheticization of non-Western arts, they are indissolubly linked through their shared subject-matter.

Much energy has gone into satisfying the growing taste for non-Western art through the production of non-specialist books and the mounting of popular exhibitions. In academic studies, extensive work has gone into the establishment of spatio-temporal provenances, styles, schools, and other such features of Western art-historical scholarship. It is not in question whether it is possible to analyse non-Western materials in such ways, nor whether it is useful to do so—it clearly is for collectors, dealers, and museum curators; it is, however, reasonable to ask what such analysis has to do with the anthropological study of art.

While the seminars and lectures which were the origin of this volume had as one aim among many to encourage communication between all those interested in art—artists, art historians, art critics, philosophers, museum curators, as well as anthropologists—this volume is wholly anthropological. In contrast to the important earlier edited collections of Otten (1971), Jopling (1971), and Greenhalgh and Megaw (1978), for example, with their contributions from ethologists, archaeologists, psychiatrists, artists, and art historians, this collection is designed to illustrate the distinctive contribution to our understanding of art that anthropologists can make. This is not to deny the intrinsic value of other approaches, but to stress the particular values of the anthropological approach.

The history of the anthropological study of art is not easily distinguished from the history of anthropology in general. The 'isms' have been the same and in the same order: evolutionism, diffusionism, functionalism, structural functionalism, structuralism, post-structuralism. Moreover, anthropologists concerned with art draw on other areas of anthropological concern in their studies. The analysis of myth, for example, plays a prominent part in much anthropological writing on art, and has a role in almost all the essays in this collection.

The anthropology of art, though, has hardly ever—if ever—taken the lead, following instead the directions taken by mainstream anthropology. This may also partly explain the lack to date of a unified theoretical approach in the anthropological study of art. Inspired by the mainstream, it reflects the mainstream's own diversity. Remarkably, it has yet to significantly influence that mainstream, let alone other disciplines—except, perhaps, to a limited extent, art history (Forge, 1973: p. xxii). Despite its resurgence in recent years, the anthropology of art continues in many ways to be marginal to the subject as a whole, as if art were considered of secondary importance. Anthropological students of politics, economics, or kinship rarely draw on studies of art in their work. The relationship between art and the rest of anthropology remains asymmetrical. The marginalization of art within anthropology continues despite the growing recognition that the very physicality of art offers a prime medium for beginning the intellectual exploration of other societies. For this (if for no other) reason, art should be at the forefront of anthropological studies, rather than (as was so often the case in the past), relegated to the final chapter tacked on to introductory books and monographs.

That art is rarely the starting-point may be at least partly due to the fact that anthropological studies of art have so often consisted of little more than the investigation of the role of art objects in maintaining the social structure, as in functionalist analyses, or of investigating the meanings such objects encode, as in structuralist analyses. In such approaches, the 'artness' of the objects sometimes seems to be of secondary importance after their political or symbolic roles. Why art objects should function as they are supposed to do, how in fact they do so, and why and how they are vehicles of meaning are questions more often ignored than asked, and more asked than answered. In the essays that follow, the importance of art objects as objects is considered, the way they are supposed to work is investigated, and the forms they take explained, as well as their functions and meanings explored.

It is tempting to see the anthropology of art's lack of a distinctive subject-matter as an explanation for its marginalization and slow development since the rise of functionalism. The importance of such practical matters as the division between museum and academic departments is not to be underrated, but Gell offers below a more profound explanation. The failure of anthropologists to develop a true anthropology of art, he argues, is a result of too great a respect for, indeed a 'religious' attitude to, art. As the development of the sociology and anthropology of religion depended upon the rise of atheism in society at large and the adoption of at least 'methodological atheism' on the part of its practitioners, so we have to stop 'believing' in art and become methodological philistines before we can start to deal with art properly as sociologists and anthropologists: 'the first step which has to be taken in devising an anthropology of art is to make a complete break with aesthetics'. As art-lovers we may wish to submit ourselves to the experiences of art, but as anthropologists we must take an objective stance. We can only begin to study how it works by not ourselves succumbing to it.

Anthropology has to date focused on the function and meaning of art objects, rather than on their essential power as objects. Traditionally it has been aesthetics (the 'theology' of art) which has striven 'to illuminate the specific objective characteristics of the art object as an object'. If we wish to establish an anthropology of art, it is these characteristics of the object as object (not its functions or the meanings it communicates) which we must make central to our practice. Unlike aesthetics, however, which deals in universals, the anthropology of art will deal in cultural particulars. This Gell goes on to do in his analysis of how the perceptual effects of Trobriand canoe-boards are conceived of as evidence of magical power.

Gell is surely correct in calling attention to the need for anthropologists to focus on the object as object. Demonstrating how objects 'work' in their cultures of origin must be a central feature of any anthropology of art. In this volume, for example, Morphy's account of the concept of *bir'yun* among the Yolngu of northern Australia illuminates how art objects work for them, and Küchler's account of 'making skins' in New Ireland demonstrates how the well-known *malangan* sculptures work.

Objects and Interpretations

In recent decades anthropology, along with other intellectual disciplines, has been overwhelmingly concerned with meaning, a topic which is likely to remain near the centre of the anthropological study of art for the foreseeable future. Questions of meaning inhere in all the contributions to this volume, but they are especially foregrounded in the essays by Bowden, Küchler, and Oosten, which are gathered together for this reason in Part II, 'Objects and Interpretations'.

A major advantage anthropologists often have over art historians is that they study living traditions. Through participant-observation field-work, they are able to study at first hand the workings of an art tradition and to enquire into its meanings. While, as Bowden points out, anthropologists may often be 'confronted by a seemingly insurmountable wall of silence', through prolonged observation and participation it is often possible to piece together complex meanings through the combined analysis of language, myth, and art.

In the case of the Kwoma of New Guinea described by Bowden, for example, myths associated with the timbers used for particular architectural features of the men's houses evoke ideals such as creativity and aggressiveness in terms of which Kwoma men think of themselves. In this way art and architecture can be seen to communicate about the society that produces them. The art of a society can provide a fruitful starting-point for the analyst's explication of its world-view.

In her contribution, Küchler explores the meanings of finished *malangan* objects, as well as those of the materials out of which they are constructed and which inhere in the objects. She builds up a picture of the complex set of meanings embodied in each sculpture, both as an instance of a particular type of *malangan* and as relating to a particular person at the centre of a particular social grouping. The wooden object is a container for the life force of a deceased clan member. Just as the bones of the body are covered with skin, so the sculpture's carved surfaces are covered with paint. The *malangan* sculpture channels the life force back from the dead to the living, and identifies the members of dispersed clans and subclans through their shared rights in the design and exchange of the sculpture.

Not all the traditions anthropologists choose to study are, however, amenable to participant-observation field-work. While Inuit still produce art, and very successfully for external markets, the meanings of Inuit masks collected in the nineteenth century and held in museum collections cannot be recovered simply by asking contemporary Inuit. As seen by Oosten, the anthropologist's task is to reconstruct the socio-cultural reality in which the masks functioned and had their meanings. This involves the reconstruction of Inuit religion, philosophy, metaphysics, and ontology. Once this is done, formal features of the masks identified by the analyst may be seen to correspond with formal features of the society's philosophical and social structure.

The significance of Inuit masquerade is understood with reference to the opposition between soul and body in Inuit thought. In the earliest times, humans and animals were one and possessed identical attributes. Although later they were divided, their primeval unity could be re-established momentarily through masquerade. Transformation masks expressed both the body and soul of the beings represented, as well as their relations to those of the performer, and constituted important instruments in the symbolic manipulation of identity.

Traditions and Innovations

The stereotypical picture of anthropology as concerned with traditional, unchanging societies is no longer realistic. The societies that anthropologists have studied traditionally, such as those of Australian Aborigines, are not isolated and unchanging, and anthropologists have had to learn to deal with the dynamics of artistic change. In art history there has been a growing and complementary recognition of the importance of socio-cultural context, so that much art history and much anthropology of art are beginning to resemble each other in everything but traditional subject-matter and research materials. In African studies, for example, it is difficult to distinguish anthropological from art-historical accounts of art traditions, as a glance at any recent issue of *African Arts* will confirm. The classic art-historical concern with spatio-temporal provenance and the anthropological concern with socio-cultural context are now but two poles between which researchers oscillate as they try to understand any art tradition. But while anthropologists concern themselves more with identification and stylistic analysis, it is still their concern with context which defines their work as anthropological. Classification and formal stylistic analysis are important tools for anthropologists working on art, but they are means to an end, not the end itself. So there are no essays in this volume on stylistic analysis, on the identification of schools or the œuvre of individual artists. While it is essential for anthropologists to recognize the balance between the dictates of tradition and the opportunities for individual creativity in any particular society, it is the social aspects rather than the individual ones which are the stuff of anthropology. There is in this collection, however, a clear concern with historical change, especially but not exclusively, in the essays paired in Part III, 'Traditions and Innovations'.

Artists work within traditions and introduce innovations to them. While this is often in response to changing conditions, which may be of international dimensions, the approach taken in the essays by Barnes and Layton is to focus on the innovative actions of groups of artists while understanding these in their wider historical, political, and economic contexts. Such studies help us to understand both the internal dynamics of societies which have produced the art and the art itself. It is, perhaps, in such first-hand studies of change in living traditions that anthropologists have most to offer art historians, revealing as they do the empirical complexities of situations which even the most sophisticated models of change can only approximate.

Layton's essay compares the different responses of two adjacent Australian Aboriginal communities to the arrival of an external market. Such close cultural comparison is a hallmark of anthropological studies but is relatively rare in studies of art. Layton's approach is comparative at another level, too: through his discussion of the different responses to external change of hunter-gatherer and peasant societies, he is able to show how the Aboriginal response fits into a wider pattern. This is not to deny the particularities of the individual case, however, as his discussion of Papunya and Pitjantjatjara clearly shows. The community of Pitjantjatjara, whose carvings less fulfilled external market expectations, was more successful at retaining the autonomy of its religious traditions. Its members developed an art style that only marginally encroached upon traditional artistic activities, and modified decorative elements so as to not compromise those owned by the clan. In contrast, the Papunya produced a near-traditional style of painting with general elements substituted for sacred patterns and conventions in an attempt to preserve the distinction between the traditional, culturally integrated art and that produced for the external market. Unlike Pitjantjatjara art, which was considered too crude for the Australian fine-art market, the Papunya works were institutionalized and marketed at a national level, creating an asymmetrical relationship between the community and the national society. This essay clearly illustrates how evaluation of the effects of change depends upon one's criteria: the Papunya produced fine art but suffered in traditional terms.

Through her analysis of an Indonesian textile tradition, Barnes is able to illustrate how, far from rejecting change, as non-Western communities are sometimes assumed to do, societies may selectively incorporate aspects of change into their art as into other areas of their lives. The people of Lamalera welcomed the missionaries and the educational opportunities they provided, and in general are ready to adopt new possibilities while simultaneously emphasizing the indigenous qualities of their culture. Barnes illustrates this aspect of Lamalera society through an analysis of the structure of the local textiles, in which imported foreign patterns, such as those of Gujurati *patola* and Christian and European motifs, are found alongside traditional Lamalera ones.

The Anthropology of Aesthetics

The universal existence of aesthetic taste and aesthetic impulse have been recognized since the beginnings of anthropology, but it was not until the 1950s and 1960s that anthropologists began seriously to study aesthetics in non-Western societies. Understanding 'aesthetics' as having to do with standards of beauty, American anthropologists in particular produced a corpus of literature on indigenous evaluative criteria for works of art, especially in Africa. Such approaches have been taken further in the work of Fernandez (e.g. 1971) and others, who have investigated aesthetic 'principles' rather than standards of beauty, and have seen these as reflecting wider social principles. Much of the earlier work was published in journal articles, but building on such work, full-length monographs have now begun to appear (e.g. Boone, 1986; O'Hanlon, 1989) testifying to what seems to be an emerging 'anthropology of aesthetics' within, or perhaps complementary to, the anthropological study of art.

Quite what form this emerging anthropology of aesthetics will take is not clear: however distinct it becomes from the anthropology of art, it will presumably be closely related to it. For a coherent sub-sub-discipline to emerge, though, there will have to be at least minimal agreement on what is meant by the term 'aesthetics'. Below, Morphy refers to it as 'a rubric term with no simple, universally acceptable, definition'. Rather than trying here to predict what a future anthropology of aesthetics might be like, we shall instead review the various ways in which the term is used by the authors in this collection. This will, we hope, forestall possible confusion and help to clear the ground for a future anthropology of aesthetics.

Firth summarizes the central aspects of what is generally meant by aesthetics. He points out that it is upon what are conventionally taken to be the fine arts that 'the discipline of aesthetics—the philosophy of taste or, in its broader sense, the study of the conditions of sensuous perception—has been focused'. It is Firth's first sense of aesthetics which Gell has in mind when he writes that 'the first step which has to be taken in devising an anthropology of art is to make a complete break with aesthetics'. He regards the philosophy of taste, which he takes to be a branch of moral discourse concerned with transcendence and the True and the Good, as a sort of theology of art. Aesthetics as a universal moral discourse about art has no place in anthropology. The investigation of particular aesthetic discourses, however, is within the purview of what might be called the anthropology of aesthetics. It is just this which Shelton sets out to do in his investigation into Huichol aesthetics, an investigation which draws him inexorably into a discussion of Huichol ethics and ontology.

As Shelton's essay shows, in describing an indigenous aesthetic system it may not be enough to give an account of the context in which the objects are made, have their meaning, and are used; it may also be necessary to examine fundamental ontological categories underlying the ascription of value. In the Huichol case, aesthetic evaluations are based on the recognition of essences which underlie material expressions and refer to ideal conditions exemplified in ancestral mythic themes. In referring to these conditions, Huichol aesthetics is concerned not so much with notions of beauty as with ethical ideals.

In this view of aesthetics, it is the subject of the evaluations which determines whether they are to be treated by the analyst as 'aesthetic'; the criteria themselves, however, are not pre-defined but to be discovered by anthropological investigation.

Another possible aim of the anthropology of aesthetics is, paradoxically, exemplified in Gell's own essay. He recognizes that there is one valuable aspect of aesthetic discourse which the anthropology of art, as he sees it, must somehow reproduce: 'the capacity of the aesthetic approach to illuminate the specific objective characteristics of the art object as an object, rather than as a vehicle for extraneous social and symbolic messages'. It is precisely this which he sees as fundamental to the anthropology of art, but it is—on a different definition—what an anthropology of aesthetics might be expected to achieve. There is no contradiction here, just a difference in terminology. This anthropology of aesthetics, then, would be concerned with how objects work, how they achieve what it is they are meant to achieve in their cultural context. This has nothing to do with universal qualities or standards of beauty, but with people's conceptualizations of the effects of their art works. From this perspective, the essays by Gell and Morphy can be seen as having much in common. As with Shelton's approach, it is the producer of the effects, i.e. the art objects, which determines that the effects are to be classified as 'aesthetic' by the analyst.

Reflecting on the example of Trobriand canoe-boards, Gell argues that the basis of art is a technically achieved level of excellence which a society misrepresents to itself as a product of magic. The function of Trobriand canoe-boards is to dazzle their owners' Kula trade partners, making them take leave of their senses and trade more of their valuables than they otherwise would have done. The designs on the canoe-boards identify the boat with the original flying canoe of Kula mythology, and symbolize slipperiness, flowing water, and wisdom, all of which help to attract the luxury goods the expedition hopes for. In this example, the form and content of the art work together to produce magical, aesthetic effects.

Morphy observes that what Westerners would interpret as aesthetic effect the Yolngu see as the manifestation of ancestral power. Yolngu paintings are not simple mirror-representations of external pheonemena, but part of the essence of 'sacred law'. While ancestral power is the main concern of the artist, this is dependent upon his producing the correct design; the final evaluation will also take into account his ability to enhance the material on which it is painted. The painting does not assume its sacred power until the last stages of execution, when cross-hatching is applied to its surface. This produces a brilliant shimmer which is described as the source of its power and beauty.

Coote advances yet another view of the anthropology of aesthetics, arguing that there is a stage of anthropological enquiry which is rarely made explicit but which should be fundamental to the study of any art tradition. Taking it as axiomatic that people from different cultures live in different visual worlds, he argues that it is a basic task of the anthropology of aesthetics to investigate how people from different cultures 'see' the world. This, he argues, could usefully be taken by anthropologists as the study of aesthetics, without straying far from everyday usage. From the perspective of the essays of Gell, Shelton, and Morphy, however, it could be conceived as the study of the perceptual bases of indigenous evaluative processes, without necessarily exhausting what is understood by aesthetics.

Coote attempts to show that, through the analysis of the language people use in their descriptions and discussions of the visual world, the way in which they manipulate that world in art and material culture, their dances and rituals, and indeed all areas of their cultural life, the analyst can build up a picture of the way people in another society see the world. This is essential if the anthropologist is to understand the art of that society, for to do so the analyst must try to see it as the members of that society see it. Unsurprisingly, in the case of the Nilotic-speaking cattle-keepers of the Southern Sudan, the analyst must start with cattle, the classification of their colour configurations, grooming practices, representations of cattle in material culture, and so on. Elements of this Nilotic 'bovine' aesthetic can be traced through Nilotic dance, gesture, poetry, and play.

The themes by which the essays are organized in this volume and those which we have discussed briefly here are by no means all those which readers will find for themselves. The theme of exchange, for example, so central to much anthropology, recurs many times in these essays. Specialists in the areas covered by the individual essays will, we trust, find much to interest them, as will the general reader interested in what anthropologists have to say about art.

We have not tried in this brief introduction to paint a picture of a coherent discipline called the anthropology of art, for that would not be a fair reflection of the current state of the subject. Conceptions of the subject vary, as the essays that follow make clear. For example, Gell argues that the anthropology of art does not yet exist! Moreover, it is at least arguable that the anthropology of art and the anthropology of aesthetics may take different directions in the future. What is not to be doubted, however, is the richness and variety of work currently being done by anthropologists in their studies of art and aesthetics.

It may be that, as a sub-discipline, the anthropological study of art and aesthetics is still far from re-entering the mainstream of anthropology: it may still remain marginalized. To paraphrase Anthony Forge (1973: p. xiii), the place of the arts in anthropology continues to be a curious one. We hope that this collection will help to secure its future closer to the centre of anthropological studies.

References

ANDERSON, RICHARD L. (1979). *Art in Primitive Societies*. Englewood Cliffs, NJ: Prentice-Hall.

BOONE, SYLVIA ARDYN (1986). *Radiance from the Waters: Ideals of Feminine Beauty in Mende Art*. New Haven, Conn.: Yale Univ. Press.

FERNANDEZ, JAMES W. (1971). 'Principles of Opposition and Vitality in Fang Aesthetics', in Jopling (1971), 356–73 (first published 1966).

FIRTH, RAYMOND (1973). Preface to Forge (1973), pp. v–vii.

FORGE, ANTHONY (ed.) (1973). *Primitive Art and Society*. London: Oxford Univ. Press.

GREENHALGH, MICHAEL, and MEGAW, VINCENT (eds.) (1978). *Art in Society: Studies in Style, Culture and Aesthetics*. London: Duckworth.

HATCHER, EVELYN PAYNE (1985). *Art as Culture: An Introduction to the Anthropology of Art* (with introd. by E. Adamson Hoebel). Lanham, Md.: Univ. Press of America.

JOPLING, CAROL F. (ed.) (1971). *Art and Aesthetics in Primitive Societies: A Critical Anthology*. New York: Dutton.

LAYTON, ROBERT (1981). *The Anthropology of Art*. London: Granada.

O'HANLON, MICHAEL (1989). *Reading the Skin: Adornment, Display and Society among the Wahgi*. London: British Museum.

OTTEN, CHARLOTTE M. (ed.) (1971). *Anthropology and Art: Readings in Cross-Cultural Aesthetics*. Austin: Univ. of Texas Press.

STOCKING, GEORGE W. (1985). 'Essays on Museums and Material Culture', in George W. Stocking (ed.), *Objects and Others: Essays on Museums and Material Culture*. History of Anthropology 3. Madison: Univ. of Wisconsin Press, 3–14.

PART I

The Anthropology of Art

1

Art and Anthropology

RAYMOND FIRTH

In a discussion on art and anthropology it is not easy to strike a balance between description and theory, to show the richness of anthropological studies of art without releasing a flood of detail, to point out how our analyses of exotic, so-called primitive art can be fitted with significance into the understanding of art and of society as a whole. So I think it appropriate to say something about art in general before discussing anthropological contributions to the subject.

Some Definitions of Art

The term 'art' in English (*Kunst* and other analogues can have different glosses) indicates a conventional category of great diffuseness. It can refer to almost any patterned application of skill, from cooking or public speaking (rhetoric) to a variety of graphic and plastic creations. Historically, painting, sculpture, architecture, music, and poetry (or literature generally) have been distinguished as 'fine arts'. Fine Art must indeed constitute a respectable separate subject since the ancient universities of England have had Slade Professors of it! Upon these fine arts in particular the discipline of aesthetics—the philosophy of taste or, in its broader sense, the study of the conditions of sensuous perception—has been focused. Prominent here has been examination of response to the formal characteristics of a work of art, largely of course in a Western environment. So where do anthropologists enter the field, since for them, as for sociologists, art is essentially to be viewed as a social product? To an anthropologist, the formal qualities of a piece of sculpture or of music are significant. But from an anthropological standpoint, even the simplest naming of an object—as mask, or anthropomorphic figure, or funeral song—indicates an awareness of a social, ritual, and economic matrix in which the object has been produced.

Anthropologists have looked upon art in many different ways. Robert Redfield, twenty-five years ago, saw art as an enlargement of experience. With a liking for vivid analogies and a familiarity with Spanish writings, he cited

José Ortega y Gasset's analogy of art as a window upon a garden, a transparency through which one sees interesting human affairs (an image probably derived from Leonardo da Vinci—Redfield, 1959: 18–19; cf. Gombrich, 1960: 299). But, said Redfield, with modern non-objective art there is no garden, and the viewer has to find his own aesthetic meanings in what is produced. (He might also have added that the concept of a *window* is not universal; it may be lacking, for example, in traditional African and Oceanic architecture.) With exotic, say African, art, it is a very strange garden, unknown to the Western viewer, and it is part of an anthropologist's job to interpret the intellectual and emotional experiences which moved the artist to create it. Gregory Bateson, in analysing the compositional structure of a Balinese painting of a cremation procession, used a communication model. He declared that art was fundamentally part of man's search for grace, borrowing from Aldous Huxley this term to indicate naïve simplicity or lack of self-consciousness and deceit, a fundamental integration of the self. His central question was: in what form is information about psychic integration, the union of head and heart, contained or coded in the work of art? And in line with a prevalent fashion when he wrote, nearly twenty years ago, he said bluntly that he would ask only about the meaning of the code, and not about the meaning of the message it conveyed. He saw the art code, then, as an exercise in communicating about the unconscious, a skilled message about the interface between conscious and unconscious thinking (Bateson, 1973: 235, 242–3). At a very general level, I find these acceptable ways of looking at art. But I myself tend to take a rather different stance, with less imagery than Redfield and less stress on code/message than Bateson—and perhaps more neutral than his as regards affect. Art as I see it is part of the result of attributing meaningful pattern to experience or imagined experience. It is primarily a matter of perception of order in relations, accompanied by a feeling of rightness in that order, not necessarily pleasurable or beautiful, but satisfying some inner recognition of values. This patterning attribution can vary from relatively quiet recognition to direct creative manipulation, but it is never purely a passive condition; it involves some degree of ideational and emotional engagement with the relations suggested by the object. A notion of iconic, even symbolic, form is central to the consideration of much art patterning, but this applies particularly to the visual arts, and even here examples in abstract painting or in architecture leave the degree of fusion between sign and object an open question. Code and message can be useful metaphors for much specifically created art, but, as Bateson himself has acknowledged, the significance of some art is too diffuse to bear any very definite communication, and for the artist the message may not be capable of articulation, of direct expression, in any other form than his own creation.

    In popular views, art is set off from other types of patterning of experience by contrasts between art, say, and science, or craft, or religion, or the conventional constraints of custom. Yet such contrasts can involve overlapping, often confusing criteria. Some modern architects would insist that the 'art of building' is really a science. Even in the heart of scientific theory a distinguished physicist can describe Niels Bohr's insights and discoveries in quantum theory as resulting in 'the creation of an aesthetically beautiful structure of understanding, of enormous power' (Feshbach, 1985: 4). Art is often depicted as high-minded, non-utilitarian, and so distinguished from craft, which is technical skill applied to useful ends. Yet historically, the line between art and craft is hard to draw; one need only cite examples from Benvenuto Cellini's autobiography, or the constructions of the Bauhaus group, or the 'utility music' of Hindemith. Anthropologists are very familiar with societies in which an artist is primarily a craftsman, judged by how appropriate his creation is to a social use. Even in the West, the distinction between art and craft may depend primarily upon social, not aesthetic, parameters.

The relation of art to religion is complex. Universally, art has seemed to serve religion functionally and, conversely, to have drawn upon it for themes. Indeed, for Eric Gill, for whom sculpture was one kind of skilled devotion to the rule of God, all art was perhaps rightly called religious art. On the other hand, I am unorthodox enough to hold that religion itself is a human art. It constructs symbolically on what is termed an extra-human plane ideas which reflect in massive patterning the desires, hopes, and fears which people experience on the human plane (Firth, 1964: 238; 1971: 248–50). Religious art, then, in my view is a reinforcing in other media of conceptual patterning of a mystical order. It is not a case of redundancy, but gives symbolic information by visual or aural means.

Art has also been associated with freedom from restraint. In Eric Gill's expression, 'a work of art is not an act of prudence' (1934: 258). It is true that a Western artist may express in symbolic form ideas of a challenging, even revolutionary, nature which his society would not otherwise tolerate—or he himself always consciously entertain. But in the West this may be partly linked with a popular image of the Bohemianism attributed to artists of the nineteenth and early twentieth centuries, and not correspond to the sober professionalism of many artists of today. An artist's own technical rules and the logic of his inspiration may also bind him strongly. Anthropologists and art historians alike are well aware of the power of tradition in art style. And anthropologists know, too, how elaborate mystical rules may constrain the art work and the general conduct of African or Oceanic artists.

Another common contrast is between art and nature, with a tendency to regard art as consisting only of man-made objects, created by the work of human hands. But as surrealists pointed out, more pervasive acts of aesthetic creation can arise in the recognition of a quality of meaningful form in natural fields. Materials for art are everywhere, in nature as well as in things made by man. Coherent forms in snow crystals, the song of birds, the delicate shades of bare soil in a ploughed field, provide what I would call incipient art. The patterning occurs naturally, but is converted to art by human recognition. Art is a product of human commitment, determined by man's social existence. It is essentially form; but only when the form is mobilized for human purposes, given meaning in human terms by comparative associations, can one properly speak of art. Hence, I would say, the opposition often assumed between natural beauty and artificial beauty (e.g. Collingwood, 1925: 46) is false— except as a superficial distinction between degrees of involvement with the relationship in the material.

Art and 'Beauty'

But the patterning of art ordinarily involves skill in use of resources, the ability to express an idea forcefully, with economy, giving an impression of authoritative control of the medium. So in any definition of art one tends to return to a central notion of an object evoking a diffuse kind of reaction often referred to as aesthetic sensibility. To analyse this is not within my competence, but I assume that some complex combination of cognitive and emotive elements is involved. The quality in the art object which provokes this reaction has been described in many ways since classical times, but for some centuries has been crystallized as 'beauty'. Half a century ago R. G. Collingwood, the philosopher, for instance, conceived the root of aesthetic sensibility as lying in imagination, exemplified in the pursuit and enjoyment of beauty. Art for him was an immediate bridge between thought and experience. What art says, he argued, is beautiful, and what art means but does not say, is true (1925: 96–7). A former Slade Professor of Fine Art at Oxford, H. S. Goodhart-Rendel, defined art, that is, fine art, as having a capacity to touch men's thoughts and emotions, a quality which he equated with giving pleasure (1934: 2, 43, 82). The appeal of such idiom is shown by the anthropologists who have used it. David Stout (1971) used aesthetics in its dictionary sense of theories of the essential character of the beautiful and tests whereby the beautiful can be judged; and Harold Schneider's interpretation of the visual art of a Kenyan group, the Pokot, focused on their standards of beauty (1971: 30, 55; cf. Forge, 1967: 66). Ugliness was admitted in the idealist position of Collingwood, but only as frustrated, incoherent beauty (1925: 19–21). Edmund Leach too, while recognizing 'beautiful'/'ugly' as culture-bound terms, has still regarded them as criteria for distinguishing art from craft (1973: 224).

Yet in some European circles of the mid-1920s such insistence on pleasurable reaction, on beauty, as the sole touchstone of art would have seemed outmoded. It was perhaps most tenable in the realm of music, which relies on fewer images of the external world than do painting, sculpture, or poetry. But even leaving aside the earlier grotesques of Hieronymus Bosch and the illustrations of the horrors of war by Goya, the twentieth-century 'conflict' pictures of Kandinsky, the *Rock Drill* of Jacob Epstein, the work of Cubists, Fauves, and Vorticists had all demonstrated the force of a vision of an alternative, novel kind. Not only had the search for direct 'literal' representation taken a much more analytical turn, but also the old scholarly canons of harmony had been abandoned. These tended to be looked upon as ideological constructs, not absolute criteria. In some cases the quality of violence was scarcely concealed (cf. Rutter, 1926: 114). It had even been claimed that in the red flowering of violence itself beauty can be perceived. But apart from this it is a fair assumption that 'beauty' in any ordinary sense of the word had become a meaningless term as an objective for those artists. To some extent they were preoccupied with technical problems, such as how to give a dynamic quality to the flat surface of a painting. But their main concern was to express some inner vision, some invention of the mind, in as forceful and economical a manner as possible. And one central idea which seemed to lie behind much of this art was to provide images of activity, of power in the relationships handled. Notions of coherence, of integration, might be involved, but so also might notions of disturbance, disorder, conflict, fear, threat, ferocity, danger. More modern developments have produced a range of art endeavours, each with its own package of justificatory theory. Surrealism, metaphysical art, action painting, pop art, and many other experimental movements have aimed variously at revealing the inner mysterious qualities of objects and actions, even by dream analogy, at expressing the realities of life in harsh images or the basic compulsions of the artist in abstract spontaneity, or at creating striking designs from banal depictions of common things. In their different ways, all such experimental movements have focused on challenging the more conventional, accepted views of the nature of aesthetic recognition and aesthetic standards.

All this can be fitted, if somewhat awkwardly, into the concern of anthropologists with the exotic, the historical 'primitive'. For some anthropologists, of whom I was one, the admission into the graphic and plastic arts of distortion, of change of form from the proportions given by ordinary vision, came as a liberating influence. It was significant, not only for an appreciation of the contemporary Western art, but also for a clearer understanding of much medieval and exotic art. Like Romanesque painting and sculpture, which have long captured my interest, the painting and sculpture which anthropologists encountered in exotic societies could be regarded, not as a product of imperfect vision, technical crudity, or blind adherence to tradition, but as works of art in their own right, to be judged as expressions of artists' original conceptions in the light of their cultural endowment. At the same time, most anthropologists interested in this field rejected as a parody those

concepts of 'primitivism' which Western artists might employ to align themselves with what they thought to be the directness and simplicity of 'savage'
art.

History of Anthropological Interest in Art

My own early involvement in the subject may illustrate some of this. It is now
more than sixty years since I published my first paper on Oceanic art—a
discussion of the work of Maori wood-carvers (1925). It dealt largely with
craft workmanship, but it made two sociological points. The first was that
Maori carving had generally been studied in museum show-cases, as an
element of material culture, but that in order to appreciate the full value of
the art it should be studied in its original setting in village life—in its social
aspect. The second point was that, while Maori sculpture of the human figure
was often said to lack correctness or proportion or grace, this was not because
the Maori carver was unable to represent the human form in recognized
bodily relationships, but because he wanted to express some other characteristics of his ancestors or mythic beings. Nowadays such thoughts are
commonplace, but then they had some novelty. A decade later, in *Art and Life
in New Guinea* (1936: 9), I stressed recognition of 'the worth of traditions of
art different from our own, to perceive in an apparent distortion of reality the
expression of a valid and interesting idea, of a formal and forceful design'.
The book even included a prophetic statement that 'to an unknown wood-
carver of the Ivory Coast may [some day] be given that admiration which
formerly was the prerogative of a Veit Stoss or a Tilman Riemenschneider'.
(What I did not foresee was that such admiration might be concretely expressed in what much modern judgement seems to regard as the acid test of
aesthetic value—high auction prices!)

Of course I was by no means the first anthropologist to write about art. In
New Zealand I had the example of Augustus Hamilton, a museum director of
imagination, who compiled a massive study of the 'art workmanship' of the
Maori, published in 1896. Professional anthropologists were also active then,
albeit few in number. A. C. Haddon of Cambridge had published works on
the decorative art of New Guinea (1894) and on evolution in art (1895), while
Franz Boas of Columbia had analysed the art of the Indians of the north-west
Pacific coast of America (1897). These studies, like others by European
scholars, were concerned mainly with problems of regional style and origin,
evolution and distribution of design. Before the First World War, and even
between the wars, anthropological interest in art was very limited, and the
development of public awareness in so-called primitive art was due primarily
to a combination of aesthetic and commercial, not ethnographic, concerns. By
the time that Boas had made a general survey in *Primitive Art* (1927), many

spectacular masks and figurines of exotic carvings had passed through the studios of the post-Impressionist painters into the drawing rooms of the great collectors—such as Paul Guillaume in Paris or the German Baron Eduard von der Heydt. For anthropologists, the rich holdings of museums provided data for formal study, and occasionally, as with Albert B. Lewis's little brochure on New Guinea masks (1922), some further material for interpretation. A spin-off from artists' and lay public interest came in such critical essays as that of Roger Fry, who pointed out what he called the 'complete plastic freedom' of African sculpture, and more systematic illus- trated reviews such as that by Paul Guillaume and Thomas Munro of what they termed 'primitive negro sculpture' in West Africa (1926). Meanwhile the exhibitions had begun. By 1920 the Chelsea Book Club in London had assembled some thirty pieces of African sculpture, in a show which led Roger Fry (1928) to credit the Negro sculptor with creative aesthetic impulse, imaginative understanding of form, and exquisite taste in handling material. Continental exhibitions of African sculpture included one in Paris and another in Brussels in 1930, while May 1933 saw over a hundred pieces shown in the Lefèvre Gallery, London, in what was described as the first comprehensive survey of primitive African sculpture in Britain. In 1935 what was termed the first important exhibition of African art in the United States was held at the Museum of Modern Art in New York, and in 1936 the famous Surrealist exhibition in London, organized by Roland Penrose at the Royal Academy, included examples of primitive art—described with caution simply as 'Objects'!

I give this outline of early history to show the commingling of anthropo- logical and other interests in art. Clearly, despite a somewhat undiscriminat- ing, even lyrical approach to primitive art, the genuine aesthetic reactions of a lay public were stimulated by these exotic products, and helped in the devel- opment of anthropological art experience. Meanwhile the role of anthropo- logists as systematizers and contextual interpreters continued unobtrusively. In 1940 Leonhard Adam, a German judge who foresaw no future under Hitler and had moved to England (later settling in Australia), published his synoptic study which linked prehistoric with modern primitive art and gave brief regional surveys with general observations on peasant art, children's art, and the relation of European artists to the primitive. Adam emphasized the significance of cultural background, especially of religion, for an under- standing of primitive art, but his treatment of 'social implications' was very superficial, concerned mainly with the artistic role of women, dancing, and property rights. Of very different order was the highly focused, ironic study of Julius E. Lips, another émigré from Germany in the same period. Entitled *The Savage Hits Back* (1937), with an introduction by Malinowski, this book depicts, with an immense range of illustration, how artists and craftsmen in non-Western societies have portrayed white people in their painting and sculpture, with results varying from bland description to wild caricature. An early critic of colonialism, Lips put forward a powerful argument for the interpretation of a particular genre of exotic art in its full cultural context.

Since the last war the strictly anthropological study of art has flowered. Field studies of exotic art have multiplied, and critical analysis has become more penetrating. Sensitive, sophisticated studies of the style and creativity of individual artists have emerged. Interest has developed in comparative aesthetics, and in art as a medium of communication, as a factor in the organization and transmission of knowledge. A glance at the critical anthology on *Art and Aesthetics in Primitive Societies* edited by Carol Jopling (1971), or the symposium on *Primitive Art and Society* edited by Anthony Forge (1973*b*), or the review of *The Anthropology of Art* by Robert Layton (1981) will indicate the richness of the modern anthropological contribution. Co-operation with practitioners of other disciplines has strengthened the anthropological approach, as could be seen from such conferences as that on 'The Artist in Tribal Society' held in 1957 at the Royal Anthropological Institute (see Smith, 1961), and the paradoxically named exhibition '40,000 Years of Modern Art', sponsored by the Institute of Contemporary Arts in 1948–9. A comparison of primitive and modern Western art, this exhibition drew heavily on ethnographic material and ideas, while the essay, in the accompanying publication, examining primitive influences on modern art, by W. G. Archer and Robert Melville (1949), was conceived primarily from an artist's point of view.

Anthropological Interpretations of Art

In the relation of anthropology to aesthetics, one problem is the nature of the response to an object from an exotic culture, classified as art by someone from another, say a Western, culture. This problem has been tackled in a characteristically bold way by Edmund Leach (1973). He has argued that all true artists tend to occupy themselves with themes containing elements of a sensory ambiguity. He held that these elements are subject to taboo, especially of a sexual kind, and that what the external observer is responding to in an alien work of art is this general human interest in the ambiguous nature of the sexual message. Leach stressed that he was not saying that all aesthetic appreciation can be reduced to the recognition of disguised sexual symbolism. Nor was he holding that all cross-cultural recognition of art is sexually motivated. But he did argue that the first stirrings of Western interest in exotic art are stimulated by confusions of a physiological order, between male and female, food and non-food, symbols of dominance and symbols of submission (1973: 234). I think his hypothesis is difficult to test, and in any case has validity only as one element in a much broader spectrum of identification. It is true that, historically, some of the great early collectors of primitive art seem to have been attracted by a component of sexual as well as religious and aesthetic interest—as Eckart von Sydow has frankly said of Baron von der Heydt's collection (1932: v). But it is significant that Leach's illustrations were from Oceanic sculpture—one being the well-known Sepik *mwai* ancestor-mask from the Bateson collection, which appeared in the Surrealist exhibition of 1936. If his illustrations had been taken from Chinese landscape painting, Japanese flower arrangement, or even Maori spiral patterns in canoe-stern wood-carving, his argument might well have been harder to maintain. Leach's view may well apply to much in the visual and tactile portrayal of the human figure, or to more general forms where the appeal of a sensuous curve may be given a connotation of sexual ambiguity. But in the acoustic field it would have to be more subtle. If Leach had been analysing Polynesian songs or Malaitan flute music, the interpretation might have broken down altogether. The problems of comparative aesthetics are complex, and anthropologists have as yet reached no consensus about them. But I would hold that aesthetic sensibility responds to a great range of patterning, in which a contrast between familiar and unfamiliar in itself may be highly significant, and the very effort to incorporate the unfamiliar into our 'thought packages' can be an important stimulus. Our Western aesthetic responses go far beyond the appeal of ambiguity in taboo. Tension or ambiguity in a work of art, from our own or an alien culture, there probably must be. But it can be of a very diffuse kind, concerned with the effort to grasp novel patterns of colour, line, mass, or sound, and relate them to our existing experience.

A somewhat sceptical view of the interpretation of a work of art has been put forward by M. H. Abrams (1985), a former professor of English literature at Cornell, in a way which parallels some anthropological approaches. Abrams has distinguished what he calls a construction model of art, the maker's stance to work in progress, from a contemplation model, the perceiver's stance to the finished product. The contemplation model, in which the paradigmatic situation is that of a lone perceiver confronting an isolated work, however it happened to get made or whatever purposes it served, Abrams would trace to early classical and theological inspiration in other contexts. On historical grounds he holds that the theory of art as concerned with disinterested contemplation of the form of the object for its own sake, as end and not as means, is a product of eighteenth-century aestheticism, with social and economic undertones. The earlier treatment of art, he argues, had reference to human beings, events, purposes, and effects which it could serve. Basically, then, far from the theory of 'art-as-such', as he calls it, producing timeless truths about a distinctive class of artefacts, it is actually a way of talking about art that emerged at a particular historical period in a changing form of social life. Connoisseurship and interest in non-utilitarian aesthetic culture gave prestige and became signs of upper-class status. No doubt this thesis is challengeable, on historical as well as on other grounds. But it has something in common with an anthropological postulate, in which features of social context have claims to relevance in line with aesthetic elements in any appreciation of primitive art.

In the anthropology of art, though, it is obvious that we are dealing with abstractions developed in what I would call an analytical tradition with a strong philosophical component. In the kinds of society anthropologists study, there are undoubtedly people with aesthetic sensibilities of considerable power, but a concept of art there is hard to disentangle from notions of technical skill on the one hand and mystical knowledge and control on the other. Pleasure in deft arrangement of formal qualities is not absent. But it tends to find expression in technical judgement. As Roy Sieber (1971: 130) illustrated, when an Igala tribesman carefully scrutinized a mask he issued his critique in two words: one identified the mask type; the other indicated it was well done. Any aesthetic judgement of it, as voiced, was laconic and obscured by pragmatic interest. Many of our more abstract conclusions about exotic art are hypotheses which it is difficult to test, since they are based upon analogies which may be alien to the producers of the art. For a working artist in Western society, this presents no problem; he can focus only on the form of the exotic art object, as an instrument to aid his own creative effort. So, for post-Impressionist artists, the context of the exotic sculpture they collected was irrelevant, as Picasso used 'negro' idioms by ignoring their associations and looking upon them simply as systems of forms conveying ideas about the human figure, such as ferocity (Archer and Melville, 1949: 22). But for an anthropologist the contrast between the analytical tradition—which by now has become internationalized—and the local pragmatic tradition has always to be kept in mind. So one may have reservations about some of the more ingenious interpretations of exotic art, such as Bateson's Balinese painting code (1973), Leach's Trobriand Medusa (a flying-witch design on a war shield) (1954), or Lévi-Strauss's opposed Kwakiutl mask types of generosity and avarice (1983). They are intellectually exciting and plausible up to a point; but in the absence of field testing their conclusions must remain open, as a stimulus to comparative enquiry.

How best is an anthropologist to handle this problem of interpretation? More than fifty years ago Roger Fry spoke of 'the extreme complexity of the message embodied in a work of art' (1933: 40), and Wittgenstein later stressed the 'inexact, open-textured character of most ordinary meanings' (Findlay, 1984: 207), a view reinforced by the recent volume *Semantic Anthropology* (Parkin, 1982). Much anthropological interpretation has relied upon explicit meanings. The simplest type here is the identification of, say, anthropomorphic or zoomorphic forms in the art, on the assumption of shared experience, granted the social conditioning of perception. But while paintings or sculptures of fish, crocodiles, or men can be so interpreted, this does not go for spirits, whose idiom of portrayal may be quite locally idiosyncratic.

Abstract concepts, such as clan proprietary rights, or totemic bonds, need more than visual clues to interpret; linguistic information is also required. Robert Layton (1981: 93–133) has underlined some of the differences between the structure of a system of visual communication and the structure of language itself. But an important series of explicit meanings for exotic art has resulted from studies in which an anthropologist consulted and even worked with indigenous artists. A. A. Gerbrands (1967) working with Asmat and Warren d'Azevedo (1973) with Liberian wood-carvers, and Anthony Forge (1966; 1967; 1973*a*) with Abelam painters, for example, have all been able to elucidate significant relationships in designs. They have also thrown light on questions of individual style in relation to traditional standards, and the position of the artist as conformer, arbiter, or rebel in respect of the major aesthetic and social values of his community. D'Azevedo, for instance, was impressed by the Liberian mask-carver's deviant position, as a kind of arbiter between male and female principles, maintaining his initiative by what was thought to be the institutionally expressed spirit manifestation of his technical virtuosity. By contrast, Forge found that Abelam artists were in tune with their society's major values, were expected to be good men, and indeed tended to be so, with fewer homicides, fewer adulteries, and less flamboyant quarrels with wives and clansmen (cf. also Sieber 1971: 128). But many anthropologists have had neither the good fortune nor the skill to work in this way, and have had to rely on more haphazard tapping of information about art meanings. Even then, this relatively unsystematic approach has produced a rich body of data for a wide range of cultures.[1]

Much modern anthropology of art has been concerned not only with explicit but also with implicit meanings—relationships which the people themselves do not, possibly cannot, formulate in words, but which are of prime importance for an understanding of the origin and maintenance of their art. One general theory of symbolic behaviour, including the creation of things classified as art, assumes the existence and operation of psychological processes of which the persons concerned are quite unaware in any conscious sense. To unravel the meaning of many symbols in exotic art, then, demands complicated, subtle analysis, which includes study of the symbols as a system, in relation to one another through the total art field and in relation also to the more general iconography of the society. This may also involve the recognition of transformations, the appearance of the same theme in different symbolic form, as by inversion, or of the same symbol in contrasted contexts. Probably the best known example of such structuralist interpretation of exotic art is the elegant study by Claude Lévi-Strauss (1983) of two contrasted styles of north-west-coast Indian face masks. By an intricate process of reasoning through art to myth and ideology about the use of copper, Lévi-Strauss identified masks with wide-open protruding eyes, slit mouth, and lolling tongue, and masks with recessed, half-closed eyes, and round open mouth with no tongue showing, as complementary symbolic presentations of attitudes towards riches and social status. According to context the two styles represented the opposition between generosity and avarice, in a complex strategy of ideas about social status and use of resources. Another challenging exercise in subliminal logic has come from Edmund Leach's structuralist comments upon Michelangelo's paintings on the Sistine chapel ceiling (1977). Using the concepts of binary opposition, transformation, boundary ambiguity, and the like, he has interpreted Michelangelo's iconography in terms of metaphor which, as Leach himself says, may have struck the critics as 'too clever by half', but which in his view offers a new set of clues to possible processes in the artist's thought. If the human figures in the paintings are seen in terms of their whole spacing and sequence, it is claimed, then their recurrent transformations reveal basic concepts of the artist about the major themes of sin and redemption, or the identification of mother Eve with the Virgin Mary. By now, elements of structuralist analysis have been built into many anthropological studies of art conducted in the field, to cite only Alfred Gell's (1975) examination of cassowary and fish masks and body paint styles among the Umeda of the Sepik.

Anthropologists dealing with iconography often face a problem of categorization: 'Is this really *art?*' I think two points are relevant here. First, the concept 'art' as such is alien to the practice and presumably the thought of many of the peoples studied by anthropologists, who try to present the people's own iconic classification as a whole. Then, many simple iconic forms can bear a strong semantic charge, which puts them alongside more elaborate ritual forms to which the designation of art would be given—for example, the cross in much Christian sculpture. Examples from my own experience in the Oceanic field will illustrate the need for a broad approach.

Contrasts in Art Forms: Tikopia, Maori

While so much of Oceanic graphic and plastic composition is of cultic significance, design for ornament, for decorative effect and enhancement, does occur, if one is to accept what seem to be plain sober expressions of indigenous opinion.[2] This is so in much Massim ornament where simple patterns of circles and curves, even when they seem to produce anthropomorphic figures, may be solely decorative devices (Firth, 1936: 50–7, 62–5, 69–70). But simplicity of design should not be equated with simplicity of interpretation. Nancy Munn (1973: 123–38) has demonstrated very clearly how Australian Warlpiri combinations of circle and line symbolically express basic ideas of relationship between past and present, going out and coming in on a time plane, in a cosmic model of world order. Other simple geometric forms such as triangles, pyramids, and allied angular developments can also vary in meaning according to context. Consider Tikopia wood carving. The Tikopia, unlike the Maori, and some other Polynesian people, have no high art of anthropomorphic type. Much of their traditional decorative patterning is triangular, as in male breast tattoo, or quadrangular pyramidal, as on wooden canoe-covers, food-bowls, or head-rests. But decoration may be closely allied to more purely ritual significance. While the patterning of one object may carry no particular associations other than those of *fakarākei*, ornamentation, a similar shaping of another object may express traditional religious symbolic characteristics of great sacredness.

A wooden head-rest, a male pillow, is a utilitarian object with a considerable variety of form (Firth, 1973) and simple decorative elaboration. A common though by no means general type of decoration is the shaping of downward-sloping lugs to the ends of the head platform of the pillow (Fig. 1.1). Traditional wooden pillows had a mild quality of personal taboo, associated with the head of the owner, but such taboo applied to all male pillows, irrespective of the lug ornamentation. An analogous simple geometrical shape, more angular and in which the lugs have been incorporated into the body of the design, is shown by the central figure in Fig. 1.2. But this is an object with a strong semantic charge of a mystical order. The whole carving (produced for me in 1929 but lost in the war) is an exemplar of types of figured ornamentation set traditionally on the most sacred canoes of one Tikopia chief, the Ariki Fangarere. The sculpture shows a naturalistic and an abstract treatment of the same bird theme—representations of a migrant wader, the *turi*, probably a turnstone (*Arenaria interpres*), which arrives in Tikopia at the onset of the monsoon season, the period of storms and occasional devastating tropical cyclones. The rounded avian supporting figures were described as the *turi*, the wader itself; the central angular branching shape was termed *manu tapu*, the sacred creature, and stated to be *turi* in another rendering. Now, it is interesting that while both these types of figure had mystical value—strong ritual sanctions inhibited their display on canoes other than those of the Fangarere chief or his chiefly sisters' sons—the bird of naturalistic form was of less ritual weight than its abstract presentation, the 'sacred creature'. The image of the bird in geometrical projection carried more emotional loading than the more 'literal' representation of it. And by contrast to the reverence accorded to these sculptures, the living wader itself was not respected, as when stones were thrown at the birds resting on the beach.

I could argue that such ritualization of the abstract constitutes a general principle in the emergence of art from craft. What it does in the present instance is to allow for the crystallization of a series of associations which it might be difficult to attach so easily to the naturalistic bird form. For related to *manu tapu* conceptually, and from a structural point of view apparently a transformation of it, was *iofā*. The name means literally 'four-cornered', but

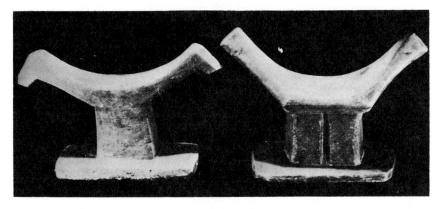

FIG. 1.1. Common types of Tikopia head-rest; collected 1952; wood; *c.*9 in. (23.0 cm.) high; author's collection.

FIG. 1.2. Naturalistic waders and abstract 'sacred bird'; carved by Pa Fenuatara in 1929; Tikopia; wood; *c.*12 in. (30.5 cm.) high; lost in Second World War.

was used traditionally as a descriptive term. Comparison of *iofā* (Fig. 1.4) with *manu tapu* (Figs. 1.2 and 1.3) shows that there is a close relationship in stylized form, both having central stem and dependent arms, but those of *iofā* reach down to the base platform, giving the 'four-cornered' space on each side of the stem. *Iofā* was even more sacred than *manu tapu*. Whereas the

FIG. 1.3. *Manu tapu*, 'sacred bird'; collected 1952; Tikopia; wood; $4\frac{1}{2}$ in. (11.5 cm.) high; author's collection.

FIG. 1.4. *Iofã*, 'four-cornered' constellation figure; carved by Pa Fenuatara in 1952; Tikopia; wood; $8\frac{1}{2}$ in. (21.5 cm.) high; author's collection.

'sacred creature' was set on several ritual canoe-covers and exposed to the accidents of sea use as well as being set on a temple ridge-pole (Firth, 1960: 27; 1967: 288–90, 369), the *iofā* was reserved for the highest-ranking sacred canoe of the Ariki Fangarere alone, as well as his temple in Marae.

Elucidation of the meaning of *iofā* was not easy. Indeed, I did not learn its full significance on my first visit to Tikopia; it was only on my return after more than twenty years that I induced my friend Pa Fenuatara to explain it to me. In 1929 I had been looking for a biological model for the design—some bird or marine creature, as with *manu tapu* and the *turi* wader. In fact, as my more persistent enquiry revealed, the identification was celestial. Tikopia constellations are, of course, very different from Western star groups, and they have constructed a constellation termed Manu from several bright stars. Manu, a creature generally, may be glossed here as Bird, with Rigel in Orion as the body, and Betelgeuse in Orion and Canopus in Carina as the northern and southern 'wings'.[3] The *iofā* design, with its central stem and dependent arms, was identified with this constellation Manu. But there was multiple linkage. In Tikopia myth the constellation Manu is glossed as a spirit personification in the heavens, protagonist in a struggle with the culture hero Metikitiki, and in reaction to this violence, author of hurricanes and allied devastation in Tikopia. So the *iofā* design is a symbol of power and a warning of disaster. Naturalistic bird sculpture, abstract bird sculpture, and abstract constellation spirit sculpture, all of very simple type, have been traditionally set in an ideational cluster associated with monsoon and potential tropical cyclone, heralded by the arrival of the migrant wader. Moreover, on the social scene, these representations were primarily the property of a single clan chief whose prime god in other myth sequences (Firth, 1961: 29; 1970: 167) was the apotheosis of the general concept of disease and death, worshipped in an elaborate religious cycle in which his temple with the *iofā* and *manu tapu* ornaments was a focal point. So, whether art or just plain iconography, the simple structured patterning has had powerful associations, which it is essential to know if the full meaning of the designs is to be understood.

The compression of natural features in the example just given produced two simple styles of conventionalization in contrast. The question of why such contrasting representations should arise has occupied many anthropologists studying exotic art. The problem of origins, or genesis of each individual type in differentiation, is unlikely ever to be solved completely; but what anthropologists have been able to do is to throw light on the meaning of the differentiation. As already mentioned, a classic study of this kind is of Kwakiutl and allied masks by Lévi-Strauss. A less-known analysis is the study of primitive Indian sculpture by W. G. Archer, *The Vertical Man* (1947). Among the cattle-keeping Ahir of Bihar, Archer found contrasted sculptural styles of representing the cattle god. One was a 'muscular guardian' style, with angular idioms and prominent club; the other was a 'benign hero' style, with softened curves and club reduced to a baton or omitted altogether. The geometric treatment of the figure enhances the notion of the god's super-human power, while the differentiation of the features has emphasized either the god's vigilant defence of the herds or his benevolent strength towards his people. This projection of contrasting aspects of a figure of power by differentiated images can be looked at as a kind of aesthetic prolixity, an urge to multiply images rather than try to compress all significant qualities into a single image. It can be related to the common north-west-coast Indian phenomenon of split representation of animal forms, with fragmentation and distortion of bodily parts. As Boas demonstrated (1927: 221–50; cf. Layton, 1981: 153–60), such style is not a failure of perspective portrayal, but an attempt by the artist to include all the significant symbolic features of the animal, with implications for totemic grouping and social status of persons involved. The north-west-coast artist crowds all the symbolic features on to the one plastic or graphic field, whereas the Ahir sculptor separated out into different images the two basic guardian elements he wished to emphasize. Yet the north-west-coast art also shows faithfulness to a natural model in lifelike human masks. As Layton points out, it seems likely that there is a tension between imitation of nature and reduction of motifs to a few regular forms, and that this tension is itself a stimulus to aesthetic creation.

Such interpretations are relevant over a wide range of exotic art objects. They would seem to point to a clearer understanding of contrasted styles of anthropomorphic figuration in Maori art, which has recently attracted much international attention—as exemplified by an impressive exhibition of Maori art at the Metropolitan Museum of New York (see Mead 1984*b*). In traditional Maori wood-carving, one style of depiction of anthropomorphic figures has been relatively naturalistic, with rounded body and face, mouth and nose in proportion, lips lightly closed, and some verisimilitude in male tattoo. (No female figure seems to have been rendered in this style.) The other style has been in flatter plane, with little bodily depth, gaping mouth, enlarged lips, and protruding tongue, and facial decoration of a curvilinear incised type, not closely imitative of personal tattoo. The contrast in treatment is illustrated by Figs. 1.5 and 1.6. Fig. 1.5 is a sculpture of Toroa, a noted ancestor of Tuhoe people, forming the base of the centre-post of a large carved and painted meeting-house known as Te Whai-a-te-motu at Mātātua (cf. Firth, 1929: pl. VIIIB). Fig. 1.6 shows a sculptured side-panel, believed to have been part of a house belonging to Hine Matioro of Ngati Porou of the east coast of New Zealand; it is a very old piece, having been carved with stone tools.[4] The figure is of a female.

The interpretation of such contrasted figures has been advanced greatly in recent years through more refined historical and archaeological studies of style, provenance, and context. Although comprehension of their significance is not yet fully clear, it seems that technical, social, and mystical factors are all

FIG. 1.5. Traditional Maori centre-post of 'memorial' type; nineteenth century; *c.*36 in. (90.0 cm.) high; photographer: Raymond Firth, 1924. The sculpture is an effigy of Toroa (from whom the Tuhoe people trace descent) at the base of the centre-post of the house Te Whai-a-te-Motu at Mātātua.

involved. Technically, the more 'naturalistic' figures, all male, and sometimes aggressively sexually so, seem to have served as bases to house centre-posts, fortress gateways, or palisade posts, whereas the flatter plane figures were commonly side-posts of houses or major motifs in lintel or threshold timbers. Socially, the bases to house centre-posts often represented fairly recent ancestors, whereas figures of the other type seemed to represent more remote ancestral figures of vague identification or mythic beings. Yet there have been cases in which a side-post in 'grotesque' form was identified as an early nineteenth-century ancestor (Mead 1984*b*: cat. no. 89). Regional and tribal variations, and the idioms of individual carvers, about which much is now being discovered by scholars, complicate the interpretation. But from the data already accumulated, there is a suggestion that we are dealing once again with conceptual selectivity of socially relevant qualities. The situation may be

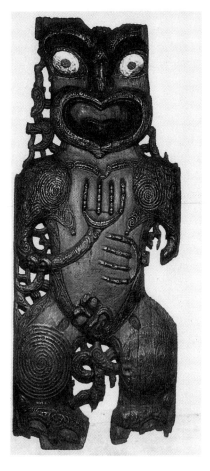

FIG. 1.6. Traditional Maori house side-panel (*poupou*) of 'mystical power' type; eighteenth century (recovered 1885); 44 in. (112.0 cm.) high; courtesy of the Auckland Museum, New Zealand (Ethnology 5017). A Ngati Porou carving from Whangara, possibly from the house Te Aitanga-a-Hauiti hapu of Hine Matioro.

looked at as analogous to that of map projection in geography. The choice of a particular projection depends upon the shape and size of the ground and the purpose for which it is needed; and some degree of distortion is to be tolerated according to the major aim. The dichotomy in Maori anthropomorphic styles seems, then, to be not between human beings and mythic figures—the former being 'naturalistic' and the latter 'grotesque'—but between human and superhuman attributes in the same traditional world of beings who belong both to the past and the present, in different senses. A 'realistic' rendering in a sculpture represents a person from the past in a domestic, social, political world; a 'grotesque' rendering, with protruding tongue, represents a personalized phase or aspect of mystical power and relation with the world of spirits. Within a 'grotesque' rendering, in particular, specific symbols often appear, linking such mystical power of the past with present-day people by genealogical connection or traditional tale. For example, a sculptured projection of the basic Arawa ancestor Tamatekapua sometimes portrays him with a pair of stilts. These serve as sign to identify the figure, and also as marker for a traditional tale of clever theft of bread-fruit which provided the rationale for an ancestral migration, with all its symbolic implications. But however 'naturalistic' a Maori anthropomorphic sculpture may be termed, it is so in only a relative way, by comparison with the more flattened 'grotesque' treatment. Even in what is regarded as a self-portrait of an artist, carved in his own house (Kernot, 1984: 155, fig. 33), the head alone is relatively lifelike, and the body follows highly stylized conventions, as a field for decorative display of incised spiral ornament, and the symbolic presentation of a ceremonial chief's adze. As Bernie Kernot remarks of the figure, it is not a portrait in the ordinary sense of the term. Throughout this whole area of Maori anthropomorphic sculpture there is still room for speculative interpretation. But it seems clear that the problem of aesthetic creation has been complicated by the drive for cultural allusion of a symbolic kind.

Modern Developments in 'Exotic' Art

Most anthropological studies of art have been concerned with traditional art—or what has passed for such. Exotic art has often been regarded as fixed by convention, unalterable in style. But modern studies have revealed that the alleged 'traditional' has often been a product of an early contact with Western industrial influences, including steel tools. Anthropological studies, too, have demonstrated that considerable initiative has been shown by individual artists, initiative which, fed into the stream of local art production, has given significant potentiality for change. Anthony Forge (1967), for instance, has shown how Abelam artists exercised a good deal of enterprise within the ancestral style. Much of an artist's work was specially commissioned, even by enemy villages, and he was expected to produce appropriate designs for cult occasions without copying, that is, as an original contribution. So innovation inevitably occurred, backed by a critical interest in novelty, though the social demand was based primarily on a concept of the potential ritual power of a painting. Yet in Abelam views, though an individual modification in style might be perceptible to an outside observer, such a gradual change in style by cumulative effect could still be claimed to be within the ancestral tradition.

The greatest influence for change in exotic art has, of course, been the impact of industrial society from the West. In the nineteenth and early twentieth centuries, Oceanic art, for example, lost much of its dynamic quality: its forms were flattened, its design impoverished, its inspiration faded. Imitation at a commercial level has often occurred, with development of tourist art, souvenir art, airport art. Nelson Graburn, who has edited an excellent summary of the modern development of exotic art under the title *Ethnic and Tourist Arts* (1976*b*), has pointed out how the symbolic content of such art is often reduced and popular notions of ethnicity reinforced; he has called such material 'ethno-kitsch' (Graburn, 1976*a*: 6).

But what Graburn and many other commentators have also pointed out (e.g. Layton, 1981: 202–11) is the more positive character of many modern developments. Industrial society has not only offered a new market for indigenous art work, it has also given new opportunities for artistic enterprise. In the Australian Aboriginal field, for instance, one has only to mention the landscape paintings of Albert Namatjira and his imitators and the bark paintings of Yirrkala to realize the complex relationship in production between traditional design, modern techniques, commercial motives, ritual and symbolic associations, pedagogical stimulus, and individual artistic creativity. In Inuit soapstone carving, Pueblo pottery, Navaho weaving, British Columbian totem poles, Kelantan Malay silverware, Benin ebony sculpture—to cite only a few examples—distinctive syntheses have been developed. In many cases schools of training in the arts have been set up, combining modern with traditional influences in novel ways.

Significant also are the conceptual changes, including changes in indigenous interpretation, that have occurred. This may be illustrated by the modern history of Maori wood-carving. Nowadays Maori artists still acquire reputation by producing sculpture for Maori purposes, in particular the meeting-houses which are the centre of so much Maori formal social life. But increasingly their work, and the great body of historic Maori sculpture on site in villages and preserved in museums, is regarded as a cultural symbol. It is not merely a statement of Maori nostalgic concern for a retrospective traditional order; it is an expression of faith in a new order. It can even be an instrument in a cultural and political struggle, part of the assertion of the unique place of the Maori people in claims to share the resources of New Zealand, redress the past to some degree, and yet preserve a recognizably separate role in New Zealand society. An anthropologist of Maori descent, Sidney Mead, has argued in reference to the Metropolitan Museum exhibition (which was opened ritually in New York by Maori elders flown over for the purpose) that Maori art is part of *mana Maori*, a symbolic display of the power and authority of a growing Maori nationalism (Mead, 1984*a*: 20–36). Such indigenous reinterpretations of art call for sympathetic appraisal in any anthropological study of the field.

More generally, political statement through the medium of art is not novel. Historically there are many examples, especially perhaps in literature and music, of art which had a deliberate purpose of incitement to understand and change the social order. Such expressions have involved not merely an individual talent and creative impulse but also a response to some collective norms of judgement. The results of such political art have not been easy to assess— even leaving aside the depressing examples of Soviet realism or Chinese murals of peasant struggle. But for anthropological interpretation it is a relevant question how far the exotic art we study has been a product of tension, not just in the personality of the artist or in his overall relation to his society, but also between conflicting forces in the political system. Much exotic art, when contextualized, clearly relates to concepts of power. But is it the political power, backed by physical force, of discrepant social elements in disproportionate control of resources? Such art is often sectionalized, emblematic of contrasted social groups such as clans, villages, or other local populations, and paying homage to the position, if not the persons, of leaders in rank and wealth. But is it an expression of protest and threat against exploitation, or only of respect for claim, status, and privilege? The powers it suggests are often mystical rather than secular, though their symbolic character may tend to reinforce the secular structure. Does a Marxist distinction between realistic art, reflecting productive intercourse between man and nature, and idealistic art, attempting to conceal relations of exploitation by ritual or allied types of delusive presentation, find backing from the classless or proto-class societies where anthropologists often work? Or is such a distinction too bland and simplistic to help our analysis? In so far as art objects may embody reflective comment on the nature of political authority, what degree of flexibility can they entertain as a carrier of challenging values and a stimulus to change? Such questions may be answerable in a definite way neither by anthropology nor by art history; but to ask them may suggest closer analytical enquiry, and anticipate a closer co-operation between the disciplines.

Notes

1 A representative example is shown by the synoptic account of Indian art in the USA by Frederic Douglas and René d'Harnoncourt (1941).

2 Frederick Dockstader, an American professional silversmith from Arizona, who became Director of the Museum of the American Indian, has stated (1973: 114) that in his own experience a silversmith, potter, or weaver will usually create a design purely for the decorative aspect, wholly ignoring 'symbolic' features.

3 Richard Feinberg (1988: 100) has, from an Anutan source, identified the body of Manu as Sirius, with the southern wing also as Canopus. Earlier, I also identified Manu tentatively as Sirius (1961: 21).

4 It is now in the Auckland Museum; see Mead (1984*b*); Simmons (1984: 104).

References

ABRAMS, M. H. (1985). 'Art-As-Such: The Sociology of Modern Aesthetics', *Bulletin of the American Academy of Arts and Sciences*, 38/6: 8–33.

ADAM, LEONHARD (1940). *Primitive Art.* Harmondsworth, Middx.: Allen Lane/ Penguin.

ARCHER, W. G. (1947). *The Vertical Man: A Study in Primitive Indian Sculpture.* London: Allen & Unwin.

—— and MELVILLE, ROBERT (1949). 'Primitive Influences in Modern Art', in *40,000 Years of Modern Art.* London: Institute of Contemporary Arts, 9–46.

BATESON, GREGORY (1973). 'Style, Grace and Information in Primitive Art', in Forge (1973*b*), 235–55.

BOAS, FRANZ (1897). 'The Decorative Art of the Indians of the North Pacific Coast', *Bulletin of the American Museum of Natural History*, 9: art. 10, 123–76.

—— (1955). *Primitive Art.* New York: Dover (first published 1927).

COLLINGWOOD, R. G. (1925). *Outlines of a Philosophy of Art.* London: Oxford Univ. Press.

D'AZEVEDO, WARREN L. (1973). 'Mask Makers and Myth in Western Liberia', in Forge (1973*b*), 126–50.

DOCKSTADER, FREDERICK J. (1973). 'The Role of the Individual Indian Artist', in Forge (1973*b*), 113–25.

DOUGLAS, FREDERIC H., and D'HARNONCOURT, RENÉ (1941). *Indian Art of the United States.* New York: Museum of Modern Art.

FEINBERG, R. (1988). *Polynesian Seafaring and Navigation: Ocean Travel in Anutan Culture and Society.* Kent, OH: Kent State Univ. Press.

FESHBACH, HERMAN (1985). 'Niels Bohr Symposium', *Bulletin of the American Academy of Arts and Sciences*, 38/5: 4–6.

FINDLAY, J. N. (1984). *Wittgenstein: A Critique.* London: Routledge & Kegan Paul.

FIRTH, RAYMOND (1925). 'The Maori Carver', *Journal of the Polynesian Society*, 34/4: 277–91.

—— (1929). *Primitive Economics of the New Zealand Maori.* London: Routledge.

—— (1936). *Art and Life in New Guinea.* London: Studio.

—— (1960). 'Tikopia Woodworking Ornament', *Man*, 60: art. 27, 17–20 and pls. C and D between pp. 16 and 17.

—— (1961). *History and Traditions of Tikopia.* Wellington: Polynesian Society.

—— (1964). *Essays on Social Organization and Values.* LSE Monographs on Social Anthropology, No. 28. London: Athlone (first published 1959).

—— (1967). *The Work of the Gods in Tikopia*, 2nd edn. LSE Monographs on Social Anthropology, Nos. 1 and 2. London: Athlone.

—— (1970). *Rank and Religion in Tikopia.* London: Allen & Unwin.

—— (1971). *Elements of Social Organization.* London: Tavistock.

—— (1973). 'Tikopia Art and Society', in Forge (1973*b*), 25–48.

FORGE, ANTHONY (1966). 'Art and Environment in the Sepik', *Proceedings of the Royal Anthropological Institute for 1965.* London: Royal Anthropological Institute, 23–31.

—— (1967). 'The Abelam Artist', in M. Freedman (ed.), *Social Organization: Essays Presented to Raymond Firth.* London: Frank Cass, 65–84.

—— (1973*a*). 'Style and Meaning in Sepik Art', in Forge (1973*b*), 169–92.

—— (ed.) (1973*b*). *Primitive Art and Society.* London: Oxford Univ. Press.

FRY, ROGER (1928). 'Negro Sculpture', in *Vision and Design.* London: Chatto & Windus, 99–103 (first published 1920).

—— (1933). *Art-History as an Academic Study.* Cambridge: Cambridge Univ. Press.

GELL, ALFRED (1975). *Metamorphosis of the Cassowaries: Umeda Society, Language and Ritual.* LSE Monographs on Social Anthropology, No. 51. London: Athlone.

GERBRANDS, A. A. (1967). *Wow-Ipits: Eight Asmat Woodcarvers of New Guinea.* Studies in Ethno-Aesthetics, Field Report 3. The Hague: Mouton.

GILL, ERIC (1934). *Art-Nonsense and Other Essays,* 2nd edn. London: Cassell.

GOMBRICH, E. H. (1960). *Art and Illusion: A Study in the Psychology of Pictorial Representation.* London: Phaidon.

GOODHART-RENDEL, H. S. (1934). *Fine Art.* Oxford: Clarendon Press.

GRABURN, NELSON H. H. (1976*a*). 'Introduction: Arts of the Fourth World', in Graburn (1976*b*), 1–32.

—— (ed.) (1976*b*). *Ethnic and Tourist Arts: Cultural Expressions from the Fourth World.* Berkeley: Univ. of California Press.

GUILLAUME, PAUL, and MUNRO, THOMAS (1926). *Primitive Negro Sculpture.* London: Cape.

HADDON, A. C. (1894). *The Decorative Art of British New Guinea.* Cunningham Memoir 10. Dublin: Royal Irish Academy.

—— (1895). *Evolution in Art: As Illustrated by the Life-History of Designs.* London: Walter Scott.

HAMILTON, AUGUSTUS (1896). *The Art Workmanship of the Maori Race in New Zealand.* Wellington: New Zealand Institute.

JOPLING, CAROL F. (ed.) (1971). *Art and Aesthetics in Primitive Societies.* New York: Dutton.

KERNOT, BERNIE (1984). 'Nga Tohunga Whakairo o Mua: Maori Artists of Time Before', in Mead (1984*b*), 138–55.

LAYTON, ROBERT (1981). *The Anthropology of Art.* London: Granada.

LEACH, EDMUND (1954). 'A Trobriand Medusa?', *Man,* 54: art. 158, 103–5.

—— (1973). 'Levels of Communication and Problems of Taboo in the Appreciation of Primitive Art', in Forge (1973*b*), 221–34.

—— (1977). 'Michelangelo's Genesis: Structuralist Comments on the Paintings on the Sistine Chapel Ceiling', *The Times Literary Supplement,* 18 Mar., 311–13.

LÉVI-STRAUSS, CLAUDE (1983). *The Way of the Masks,* trans. S. Modelski. London: Cape.

LEWIS, ALBERT B. (1922). *New Guinea Masks.* Field Museum of Chicago Leaflet 4. Chicago: Field Museum of Chicago.

LIPS, JULIUS E. (1937). *The Savage Hits Back or The White Man through Native Eyes.* London: Lovat Dickson.

MEAD, SIDNEY MOKO (1984*a*). 'Ka Tupu te Toi Whakairo ki Aoteroa: Becoming Maori Art', in Mead (1984*b*), 63–75.

—— (ed.) (1984*b*). *Te Maori: Maori Art from New Zealand Collections.* New York: Abrams.

MUNN, NANCY (1973). *Walbiri Iconography: Graphic Representation and Cultural Symbolism in a Central Australian Society.* Ithaca, NY: Cornell Univ. Press.

PARKIN, DAVID (ed.) (1982). *Semantic Anthropology.* ASA Monographs, No. 22. London: Academic Press.

REDFIELD, ROBERT (1959). 'Art and Icon', in *Aspects of Primitive Art.* New York: Museum of Primitive Art.

RUTTER, FRANK (1926). *Evolution in Modern Art.* London: Harrap.

SCHNEIDER, HAROLD K. (1971). 'The Interpretation of Pakot Visual Art', in Jopling (1971), 55–63 (first published 1956).

SIEBER, ROY (1971). 'The Aesthetics of Traditional African Art', in Jopling (1971), 127–31 (first published 1959).

SIMMONS, DAVID R. (1984). 'Nga Taonga o Nga Waka: Tribal Art Styles', in Mead (1984*b*), 76–108.

SMITH, MARIAN W. (ed.) (1961). *The Artist in Tribal Society: Proceedings of a Symposium Held at the Royal Anthropological Institute.* London: Routledge & Kegan Paul.

STOUT, DAVID B. (1971). 'Aesthetics in Primitive Societies', in Jopling (1971), 30–4 (first published 1960).

SYDOW, ECKART VON (1932). *Kunst der Naturvölker: Sammlung Baron Eduard von der Heydt.* Berlin: Cassirer.

2

The Technology of Enchantment and the Enchantment of Technology

===

ALFRED GELL

Introduction: Methodological Philistinism

The complaint is commonly heard that art is a neglected topic in present-day social anthropology, especially in Britain. The marginalization of studies of primitive art, by contrast to the immense volume of studies of politics, ritual, exchange, and so forth, is too obvious a phenomenon to miss, especially if one draws a contrast with the situation prevailing before the advent of Malinowski and Radcliffe-Brown. But why should this be so? I believe that it is more than a matter of changing fashions in the matter of selecting topics for study; as if, by some collective whim, anthropologists had decided to devote more time to cross-cousin marriage and less to mats, pots, and carvings. On the contrary, the neglect of art in modern social anthropology is necessary and intentional, arising from the fact that social anthropology is essentially, constitutionally, anti-art. This must seem a shocking assertion: how can anthropology, by universal consent a Good Thing, be opposed to art, also universally considered an equally Good Thing, even a Better Thing? But I am afraid that this is really so, because these two Good Things are Good according to fundamentally different and conflicting criteria.

When I say that social anthropology is anti-art, I do not mean, of course, that anthropological wisdom favours knocking down the National Gallery and turning the site into a car park. What I mean is only that the attitude of the art-loving public towards the contents of the National Gallery, the Museum of Mankind, and so on (aesthetic awe bordering on the religious) is an unredeemably ethnocentric attitude, however laudable in all other respects.

Our value-system dictates that, unless we are philistines, we should attribute value to a culturally recognized category of art objects. This attitude of aestheticism is culture-bound even though the objects in question derive from many different cultures, as when we pass effortlessly from the contemplation of a Tahitian sculpture to one by Brancusi, and back again. But this willingness to place ourselves under the spell of all manner of works of art, though it contributes very much to the richness of our cultural experience, is paradoxically the major stumbling-block in the path of the anthropology of art, the ultimate aim of which must be the dissolution of art, in the same way that the dissolution of religion, politics, economics, kinship, and all other forms under which human experience is presented to the socialized mind, must be the ultimate aim of anthropology in general.

Perhaps I can clarify to some degree the consequences of the attitude of universal aestheticism for the study of primitive[1] art by drawing a series of analogies between the anthropological study of art and the anthropological study of religion. With the rise of structural functionalism, art largely disappeared from the anthropological bill of fare in this country, but the same thing did not happen to the study of ritual and religious belief. Why did things happen this way? The answer appears to me to lie in an essential difference between the attitudes towards religion characteristic of the intelligentsia of the period, and their attitudes towards art.

It seems to me incontrovertible that the anthropological theory of religion depends on what has been called by Peter Berger 'methodological atheism' (Berger, 1967: 107). This is the methodological principle that, whatever the analyst's own religious convictions, or lack of them, theistic and mystical beliefs are subjected to sociological scrutiny on the assumption that they are not literally true. Only once this assumption is made do the intellectual manœuvres characteristic of anthropological analyses of religious systems become possible, that is, the demonstration of linkages between religious ideas and the structure of corporate groups, social hierarchies, and so on. Religion becomes an emergent property of the relations between the various elements in the social system, derivable, not from the condition that genuine religious truths exist, but solely from the condition that societies exist.

The consequences of the possibility that there are genuine religious truths lie outside the frame of reference of the sociology of religion. These consequences—philosophical, moral, political, and so on—are the province of the much longer-established intellectual discipline of theology, whose relative decline in the modern era derives from exactly the same changes in the intellectual climate as have produced the current efflorescence of sociology generally and of the sociology of religion in particular.

It is widely agreed that ethics and aesthetics belong in the same category. I would suggest that the study of aesthetics is to the domain of art as the study of theology is to the domain of religion. That is to say, aesthetics is a branch of moral discourse which depends on the acceptance of the initial articles of faith: that in the aesthetically valued object there resides the principle of the True and the Good, and that the study of aesthetically valued objects constitutes a path toward transcendence. In so far as such modern souls possess a religion, that religion is the religion of art, the religion whose shrines consist of theatres, libraries, and art galleries, whose priests and bishops are painters and poets, whose theologians are critics, and whose dogma is the dogma of universal aestheticism.

Unless I am very much mistaken, I am writing for a readership which is composed in the main of devotees of the art cult, and, moreover, for one which shares an assumption (by no means an incorrect one) that I too belong to the faith, just as, if we were a religious congregation and I were delivering a sermon, you would assume that I was no atheist.

If I were about to discuss some exotic religious belief-system, from the standpoint of methodological atheism, that would present no problem even to non-atheists, simply because nobody expects a sociologist of religion to adopt the premises of the religion he discusses; indeed, he is obliged not to do so. But the equivalent attitude to the one we take towards religious beliefs in sociological discourse is much harder to attain in the context of discussions of aesthetic values. The equivalent of methodological atheism in the religious domain would, in the domain of art, be *methodological philistinism*, and that is a bitter pill very few would be willing to swallow. Methodological philistinism consists of taking an attitude of resolute indifference towards the aesthetic value of works of art—the aesthetic value that they have, either indigenously, or from the standpoint of universal aestheticism. Because to admit this kind of value is equivalent to admitting, so to speak, that religion is true, and just as this admission makes the sociology of religion impossible, the introduction of aesthetics (the theology of art) into the sociology or anthropology of art immediately turns the enterprise into something else. But we are most unwilling to make a break with aestheticism—much more so than we are to make a break with theology—simply because, as I have been suggesting, we have sacralized art: art is really our religion.

We can not enter this domain, and make it fully our own, without experiencing a profound dissonance, which stems from the fact that our method, were it to be applied to art with the degree of rigour and objectivity which we are perfectly prepared to contemplate when it comes to religion and politics, obliges us to deal with the phenomena of art in a philistine spirit contrary to our most cherished sentiments. I continue to believe, none the less, that the first step which has to be taken in devising an anthropology of art is to make a complete break with aesthetics. Just as the anthropology of religion commences with the explicit or implicit denial of the claims religions make on believers, so the anthropology of art has to begin with a denial of the claims which objects of art make on the people who live under their spell, and also on ourselves, in so far as we are all self-confessed devotees of the Art Cult.

But because I favour a break with the aesthetic preoccupations of much of the existing anthropology of art, I do not think that methodological philistinism is adequately represented by the other possible approaches: for instance, the sociologism of Bourdieu (e.g. 1968), which never actually looks at the art object itself, as a concrete product of human ingenuity, but only at its power to mark social distinctions, or the iconographic approach (e.g. Panofsky, 1962) which treats art as a species of writing, and which fails, equally, to take into consideration the presented object, rather than the represented symbolic meanings. I do not deny for an instant the discoveries of which these alternative approaches are capable; what I deny is only that they constitute the sought-for alternative to the aesthetic approach to the art object. We have, somehow, to retain the capacity of the aesthetic approach to illuminate the specific objective characteristics of the art object as an object, rather than as a vehicle for extraneous social and symbolic messages, without succumbing to the fascination which all well-made art objects exert on the mind attuned to their aesthetic properties.

Art as a Technical System

In this essay, I propose that the anthropology of art can do this by considering art as a component of technology. We recognize works of art, as a category, because they are the outcome of technical process, the sorts of technical process in which artists are skilled. A major deficiency of the aesthetic approach is that art objects are not the only aesthetically valued objects around: there are beautiful horses, beautiful people, beautiful sunsets, and so on; but art objects are the only objects around which are *beautifully made*, or *made beautiful*. There seems every justification, therefore, for considering art objects initially as those objects which demonstrate a certain technically achieved level of excellence, 'excellence' being a function, not of their characteristics simply as objects, but of their characteristics as *made* objects, as products of techniques.

I consider the various arts—painting, sculpture, music, poetry, fiction, and so on—as components of a vast and often unrecognized technical system, essential to the reproduction of human societies, which I will be calling the technology of enchantment.

In speaking of 'enchantment' I am making use of a cover-term to express the general premiss that human societies depend on the acquiescence of duly socialized individuals in a network of intentionalities whereby, although each individual pursues (what each individual takes to be) his or her own self-interest, they all contrive in the final analysis to serve neccessities which cannot be comprehended at the level of the individual human being, but only at the level of collectivities and their dynamics. As a first approximation, we can suppose that the art-system contributes to securing the acquiescence of individuals in the network of intentionalities in which they are enmeshed. This view of art, that it is propaganda on behalf of the status quo, is the one taken by Maurice Bloch in his 'Symbols, Song, Dance, and Features of Articulation' (1974). In calling art the technology of enchantment I am first of all singling out this point of view, which, however one refines it, remains an essential component of an anthropological theory of art from the standpoint of methodological philistinism. However, the theoretical insight that art provides one of the technical means whereby individuals are persuaded of the necessity and desirability of the social order which encompasses them brings us no closer to the art object as such. As a technical system, art is orientated towards the production of the social consequences which ensue from the production of these objects. The power of art objects stems from the technical processes they objectively embody: the *technology of enchantment* is founded on the *enchantment of technology*. The enchantment of technology is the power that technical processes have of casting a spell over us so that we see the real world in an enchanted form. Art, as a separate kind of technical activity, only carries further, through a kind of involution, the enchantment which is immanent in all kinds of technical activity. The aim of my essay is to elucidate this admittedly rather cryptic statement.

Psychological Warfare and Magical Efficacy

Let me begin, however, by saying a little more about art as the technology of enchantment, rather than art as the enchantment of technology. There is an obvious prima-facie case for regarding a great deal of the art of the world as a means of thought-control. Sometimes art objects are explicitly intended to function as weapons in psychological warfare; as in the case of the canoe prow-board from the Trobriand Islands (Fig. 2.1)—surely a prototypical example of primitive art from the prototypical anthropological stamping-ground. The intention behind the placing of these prow-boards on Kula[2] canoes is to cause the overseas Kula partners of the Trobrianders, watching the arrival of the Kula flotilla from the shore, to take leave of their senses and offer more valuable shells or necklaces to the members of the expedition than they would otherwise be inclined to do. The boards are supposed to dazzle the beholder and weaken his grip on himself. And they really are very dazzling, especially if one considers them against the background of the visual surroundings to which the average Melanesian is accustomed, which are much more uniform and drab than our own. But if the demoralization of an opponent in a contest of will-power is really the intention behind the canoe-board, one is entitled to ask how the trick is supposed to work. Why should the sight of certain colours and shapes exercise a demoralizing effect on anybody?

The first place one might seek an answer to such a question is in the domain of ethology, that is, in innate, species-wide dispositions to respond to particular perceptual stimuli in predetermined ways. Moreover, were one to show such a board to an ethologist, they would, without a doubt, mutter 'eye-

F IG. 2.1. Trobriand canoe-prow; Kitava Island, Milne Bay Province, Papua New Guinea; photographer: Shirley F. Campbell, May 1977. The prow assembly is adorned with Kula shell valuables (see Campbell 1984). See also Pl. I.

spots!' and immediately start pulling out photographs of butterflies' wings, likewise marked with bold, symmetrical circles, and designed to have much the same effect on predatory birds as the boards are supposed to have on the Trobrianders' Kula partners, that is, to put them off their stroke at a critical moment. I think there is every reason to believe that human beings are innately sensitive to eye-spot patterns, as they are to bold tonal contrasts and bright colours, especially red, all of them features of the canoe-board design. These sensitivities can be demonstrated experimentally in the infant, and in the behavioural repertoire of apes and other mammals.

But one does not have to accept the idea of deep-rooted phylogenetic sensitivity to eye-spot patterns and the like to find merit in the idea that the Trobriand canoe-board is a technically appropriate pattern for its intended purpose of dazzling and upsetting the spectator. The same conclusion can follow from an analysis of the *Gestalt* properties of the canoe-board design. If one makes the experiment of attempting to fixate the pattern for a few moments by staring at it, one begins to experience peculiar optical sensations due to the intrinsic instability of the design with its opposed volutes, both of which tend to lead the eye off in opposite directions.

In the canons of primitive art there are innumerable instances of designs which can be interpreted as exploiting the characteristic biases of human visual perception so as to ensnare us into unwitting reactions, some of which might be behaviourally significant. Should we, therefore, take the view that the significance of art, as a component of the technology of enchantment, derives from the power of certain stimulus arrays to disturb normal cognitive functioning? I recall that Ripley's *Believe It Or Not* (at one time my favourite book) printed a design which was claimed to hypnotize sheep: should this be considered the archetypal work of art? Does art exercise its influence via a species of hypnosis? I think not. Not because these disturbances are not real psychological phenomena; they are, as I have said, easily demonstrable experimentally. But there is no empirical support for the idea that canoe-boards, or similar kinds of art objects, actually achieve their effects by producing visual or cognitive disturbances. The canoe-board does not interfere seriously, if at all, with the intended victim's perceptual processes, but achieves its purpose in a much more roundabout way.

The canoe-board is a potent psychological weapon, but not as a direct consequence of the visual effects it produces. Its efficacy is to be attributed to the fact that these disturbances, mild in themselves, are interpreted as evidence of the magical power emanating from the board. It is this magical power which may deprive the spectator of his reason. If, in fact, he behaves with unexpected generosity, it is interpreted as having done so. Without the associated magical ideas, the dazzlingness of the board is neither here nor there. It is the fact that an impressive canoe-board is a physical token of magical prowess on the part of the owner of the canoe which is important, as is the fact that he has access to the services of a carver whose artistic prowess is also the result of his access to superior carving magic.

The Halo-Effect of Technical 'Difficulty'

And this leads on to the main point that I want to make. It seems to me that the efficacy of art objects as components of the technology of enchantment— a role which is particularly clearly displayed in the case of the Kula canoe—is itself the result of the enchantment of technology, the fact that technical processes, such as carving canoe-boards, are construed magically so that, by enchanting us, they make the products of these technical processes seem enchanted vessels of magical power. That is to say, the canoe-board is not dazzling as a physical object, but as a display of artistry explicable only in magical terms, something which has been produced by magical means. It is the way an art object is construed as having come into the world which is the source of the power such objects have over us—their becoming rather than their being.

Let me turn to another example of an art object which may make this point clearer. When I was about eleven, I was taken to visit Salisbury Cathedral. The building itself made no great impression on me, and I do not remember it at all. What I do remember, though, very vividly, is a display which the cathedral authorities had placed in some dingy side-chapel, which consisted of a remarkable model of Salisbury Cathedral, about two feet high and apparently complete in every detail, made entirely out of matchsticks glued together; certainly a virtuoso example of the matchstick modeller's art, if no great masterpiece according to the criteria of the salon, and calculated to strike a profound chord in the heart of any eleven-year-old. Matchsticks and glue are very important constituents of the world of every self-respecting boy of that age, and the idea of assembling these materials into such an impressive construction provoked feelings of the deepest awe. Most willingly I deposited my penny into the collecting-box which the authorities had, with a true appreciation of the real function of works of art, placed in front of the model, in aid of the Fabric Fund.

Wholly indifferent as I then was to the problems of cathedral upkeep, I could not but pay tribute to so much painstaking dexterity in objectified form. At one level, I had perfect insight into the technical problems faced by the genius who had made the model, having myself often handled matches and glue, separately and in various combinations, while remaining utterly at a loss to imagine the degree of manipulative skill and sheer patience needed to complete the final work. From a small boy's point of view this was the ultimate work of art, much more entrancing in fact than the cathedral itself, and so too, I suspect, for a significant proportion of the adult visitors as well.

Here the technology of enchantment and the enchantment of technology come together. The matchstick model, functioning essentially as an advertisement, is part of a technology of enchantment, but it achieves its effect via the enchantment cast by its technical means, the manner of its coming into being, or, rather, the idea which one forms of its coming into being, since making a matchstick model of Salisbury Cathedral may not be as difficult, or as easy, as one imagines.

Simmel, in his treatise on the *Philosophy of Money* (1979: 62 ff.), advances a concept of value which can help us to form a more general idea of the kind of hold which art objects have over us. Roughly, Simmel suggests that the value of an object is in proportion to the difficulty which we think we will encounter in obtaining that particular thing rather than something else. We do not want what we do not think we will ever get under any set of circumstances deemed realizable. Simmel (ibid. 66) goes on to say:

We desire objects only if they are not immediately given to us for our use and enjoyment, that is, to the extent to which they resist our desire. The content of our desire becomes an object as soon as it is opposed to us, not only in the sense of being impervious to us, but also in terms of its distance as something not yet enjoyed, the subject aspect of this condition being desire. As Kant has said: the possibility of experience is the possibility of objects of experience—because to have experiences means that our consciousness creates objects from sense-impressions. In the same way, the possibility of desire is the possibility of objects of desire. The object thus formed, which is characterised by its separation from the subject, who at the same time establishes it and seeks to overcome it by his desire, is for us a value.

He goes on to argue that exchange is the primary means employed in order to overcome the resistance offered by desired objects, which makes them desirable, and that money is the pure form of the means of engaging in exchange and realizing desire.

I am not here concerned with Simmel's ideas about exchange value and money; what I want to focus on is the idea that valued objects present themselves to us surrounded by a kind of halo-effect of resistance, and that it is this resistance to us which is the source of their value. Simmel's theory, as it stands, implies that it is difficulty of access to an object which makes it valuable, an argument which obviously applies, for example, to Kula valuables. But if we suppose that the value which we attribute to works of art, the bewitching effect they have on us, is a function, at least to some extent, of their characteristics as objects, not just of the difficulties we may expect to encounter in obtaining them, then the argument cannot be accepted in un-modified form. For instance, if we take up once again the instance of the matchstick model of Salisbury Cathedral, we may observe that the spell cast over me by this object was independent of any wish on my part to gain possession of it as personal property. In that sense, I did not value or desire it, since the possibility of possessing could not arise: no more am I conscious today of any wish to remove from the walls and carry away the pictures in the National Gallery. Of course, we do desire works of art, the ones in our price bracket, as personal property, and works of art have enormous significance as items of exchange. But I think that the peculiar power of works of art does not reside in the objects *as such*, and it is the objects as such which are bought and sold. Their power resides in the *symbolic* processes they provoke in the beholder, and these have *sui generis* characteristics which are independent of the objects themselves and the fact that they are owned and exchanged. The value of a work of art, as Simmel suggests, is a function of the way in which it resists us, but this 'resistance' occurs on two planes. If I am looking at an old master painting, which, I happen to know, has a saleroom value of two million pounds, then that certainly colours my reaction to it, and makes it more impressive than would be the case if I knew that it was an inauthentic reproduction or forgery of much lesser value. But the sheer incommen-surability between my purchasing power and the purchase price of an authentic old master means that I cannot regard such works as significant exchange items: they belong to a sphere of exchange from which I am excluded. But none the less such paintings are objects of desire—the desire to possess them in a certain sense, but not actually to own them. The resistance which they offer, and which creates and sustains this desire, is to being possessed in an intellectual rather than a material sense, the difficulty I have in mentally encompassing their coming-into-being as objects in the world accessible to me by a technical process which, since it transcends my understanding, I am forced to construe as magical.

The Artist as Occult Technician

Let us consider, as a step up from the matchstick model of Salisbury Cathedral, J. F. Peto's *Old Time Letter Rack* (Fig. 2.2), sometimes known as *Old Scraps*, the notoriously popular *trompe-l'œil* painting, complete with artfully rendered drawing-pins and faded criss-cross ribbons, letters with still-legible, addressed envelopes to which lifelike postage stamps adhere, newspaper cuttings, books, a quill, a piece of string, and so on. This picture is usually discussed in the context of denunciations of the excesses of illusionism in nineteenth-century painting; but of course it is as beloved now as it ever was, and has actually gained prestige, not lost it, with the advent of photography, for it is now possible to see just how photographically real it is, and all the more remarkable for that. If it was, in fact, a colour photograph of a letter rack, nobody would give tuppence for it. But just because it is a painting, one which looks as real as a photograph, it is a famous work, which, if popular votes counted in assigning value to paintings, would be worth a warehouse full of Picassos and Matisses.

The popular esteem in which this painting is held derives, not from its aesthetic merit, if any, since nobody would give what it represents (that is, a letter rack) a second glance. The painting's power to fascinate stems entirely from the fact that people have great difficulty in working out how coloured pigments (substances with which everybody is broadly familiar) can be applied to a surface so as to become an apparently different set of substances, namely, the ones which enter into the composition of letters, ribbons, drawing-pins, stamps, bits of string, and so on. The magic exerted over the beholder by this picture is a reflection of the magic which is exerted inside the picture, the technical miracle which achieves the transubstantiation of oily pigments into cloth, metal, paper, and feather. This technical miracle must be distinguished from a merely mysterious process: it is miraculous because it is achieved both by human agency but at the same time by an agency which transcends the normal sense of self-possession of the spectator.

Thus, the letter rack picture would not have the prestige it does have if it were a photograph, visually identical in colour and texture, could that be managed. Its prestige depends on the fact that it is a painting; and, in general, photography never achieves the popular prestige that painting has in societies

Alfred Gell

FIG. 2.2. John F. Peto, *Old Time Letter Rack*; 1894; oil on canvas; 30 × 25 in. (76.2 × 63.5 cm.); Manoogian Collection.

which have routinely adopted photography as a technique for producing images. This is because the technical processes involved in photography are articulated to our notion of human agency in a way which is quite distinct from that in which we conceptualize the technical processes of painting, carving, and so on. The alchemy involved in photography (in which packets of film are inserted into cameras, buttons are pressed, and pictures of Aunt Edna emerge in due course) are regarded as uncanny, but as uncanny processes of a natural rather than a human order, like the metamorphosis of caterpillars into butterflies. The photographer, a lowly button-presser, has no prestige, or not until the nature of his photographs is such as to make one start to have difficulties conceptualizing the processes which made them achievable with the familiar apparatus of photography.

In societies which are not over-familiar with the camera as a technical means, the situation is, of course, quite different. As many anthropologists who have worked under such conditions will have occasion to know, the ability to take photographs is often taken to be a special, occult faculty of the photographer, which extends to having power over the souls of the photographed, via the resulting pictures. We think this a naïve attitude, when it comes to photography, but the same attitude is persistent, and acceptable, when it is expressed in the context of painting or drawing. The ability to capture someone's likeness is an occult power of the portraitist in paint or bronze, and when we wish to install an icon which will stand for a person— for example, a retiring director of the London School of Economics—we insist on a painted portrait, because only in this form will the captured essence of the no-longer-present Professor Dahrendorf continue to exercise a benign influence over the collectivity which wishes to eternalize him and, in so doing, derive continuing benefit from his *mana*.

Let me summarize my point about Peto's *Old Scraps* and its paradoxical prestige. The population at large both admire this picture and think that it emanates a kind of moral virtue, in the sense that it epitomizes what painters 'ought' to be able to do (that is, produce exact representations, or rather, occult transubstantiations of artists' materials into other things). It is thus a symbol of general moral significance, connoting, among other things, the fulfilment of the painter's calling in the Protestant-ethic sense, and inspiring people at large to fulfil their callings equally well. It stands for true artistry as a power both in the world and beyond it, and it promotes the true artist in a symbolic role as occult technician. Joined to this popular stereotype of the true artist is the negative stereotype of the false ('modern') artist of cartoon humour, who is supposed not to know how to draw, whose messy canvases are no better than the work of a child, and whose lax morality is proverbial.

Two objections can be made to the suggestion that the value and moral significance of works of art are functions of their technical excellence, or, more generally, to the importance of the fact that the spectator looks at them and thinks, 'For the life of me, I couldn't do that, not in a million years.' The first objection would be that *Old Scraps*, whatever its prestige among *hoi polloi*, cuts no ice with the critics, or with art-cultists generally. The second objection which might be raised is that, as an example of illusionism in art, the letter rack represents not only a particular artistic tradition (our own) but also only a brief interlude in that tradition, and hence can have little general significance. In particular, it cannot provide us with any insight into primitive art, since primitive art is strikingly devoid of illusionistic trickery.

The point I wish to establish is that the attitude of the spectator towards a work of art is fundamentally conditioned by his notion of the technical processes which gave rise to it, and the fact that it was created by the agency of another person, the artist. The moral significance of the work of art arises from the mismatch between the spectator's internal awareness of his own powers as an agent and the conception he forms of the powers possessed by the artist. In reconstructing the processes which brought the work of art into existence, he is obliged to posit a creative agency which transcends his own and, hovering in the background, the power of the collectivity on whose behalf the artist exercised his technical mastery.

The work of art is inherently social in a way in which the merely beautiful or mysterious object is not: it is a physical entity which mediates between two beings, and therefore creates a social relation between them, which in turn provides a channel for further social relations and influences. This is so when, for instance, the court sculptor, by means of his magical power over marble, provides a physical analogue for the less easily realized power wielded by the king, and thereby enhances the king's authority. What Bernini can do to marble (and one does not know quite what or how) Louis XIV can do to you (by means which are equally outside your mental grasp). The man who controls such a power as is embodied in the technical mastery of Bernini's bust of Louis XIV is powerful indeed. Sometimes the actual artist or crafts-man is quite effaced in the process, and the moral authority which works of art generate accrues entirely to the individual or institution responsible for commissioning the work, as with the anonymous sculptors and stained-glass artists who contributed to the glorification of the medieval church. Sometimes the artists are actually regarded with particular disdain by the power élite, and have to live separate and secluded lives, in order to provide ideological camouflage for the fact that theirs is the technical mastery which mediates the relation between the rulers and the ruled.

I maintain, therefore, that technical virtuosity is intrinsic to the efficacy of works of art in their social context, and tends always towards the creation of asymmetries in the relations between people by placing them in an essentially asymmetrical relation to things. But this technical virtuosity needs to be more carefully specified; it is by no means identical with the simple power to represent real objects illusionistically: this is a form of virtuosity which belongs, almost exclusively, to our art tradition (though its role in securing the prestige of old masters, such as Rembrandt, should not be underestimated). An example of virtuosity in non-illusionistic modern Western art is afforded by Picasso's well-known *Baboon and Young* (Fig. 2.3), in which an ape's face is created by taking a direct cast from the body-shell of a child's toy car. One would not be much impressed by the toy car itself, nor by the verisimilitude of Picasso's ape just as a model of an ape, unless one were able to recognize the technical procedure Picasso used to make it, that is, commandeering one of his children's toys. But the witty transubstantiation of toy car into ape's face is not a fundamentally different operation from the transubstantiation of artists' materials into the components of a letter rack, which is considered quite boring because that is what artists' materials are for, generically. No matter what avant-garde school of art one considers, it is always the case that materials, and the ideas associated with those materials, are taken up and

FIG. 2.3. Pablo Picasso, *Baboon and Young*; 1950, Vallauris; bronze (cast 1955); $21\frac{1}{8} \times 14\frac{1}{8} \times 7\frac{3}{8}$ in. ($53.6 \times 35.7 \times 18.8$ cm.); collection, The Museum of Modern Art, New York (Mrs Simon Guggenheim Fund).

transformed into something else, even if it is only, as in the case of Duchamp's notorious urinal, by putting them in an art exhibition and providing them with a title (*Fountain*) and an author ('R. Mutt', alias M. Duchamp, 1917). Amikam Toren, one of the most ingenious contemporary artists, takes objects like chairs and teapots, grinds them up, and uses the resulting substances to create images of chairs and teapots. This is a less radical procedure than Duchamp's, which can be used effectively only once, but it is an equally apt means of directing our attention to the essential alchemy of art, which is to make what is not out of what is, and to make what is out of what is not.

The Fundamental Scheme Transfer between Art Production and Social Process

But let us focus our attention on art production in societies without traditions and institutions of 'fine art' of the kind which nurtured Picasso and Duchamp. In such societies art arises particularly in two domains. The first of these is ritual, especially political ritual. Art objects are produced in order to be displayed on those occasions when political power is being legitimized by association with various supernatural forces. Secondly, art objects are produced in the context of ceremonial or commercial exchange. Artistry is lavished on objects which are to be transacted in the most prestigious spheres of exchange, or which are intended to realize high prices at market. The kind of technical sophistication involved is not the technology of illusionism but the technology of the radical transformation of materials, in the sense that the value of works of art is conditioned by the fact that it is difficult to get from the materials of which they are composed to the finished product. If we take up the example of the Trobriand canoe-board once more, it is clear that it is very difficult to acquire the art of transforming the root-buttress of an ironwood tree, using the rather limited tools which the Trobrianders have at their disposal, into such a smooth and refined finished product. If these boards could be simply cast in some plastic material, they would not have the same potency, even though they might be visually identical. But it is also clear that in the definition of technical virtuosity must be included considerations which might be thought to belong to aesthetics.

Let us consider the position of a Trobriand carver, commissioned to add one more to the existing corpus of canoe-boards. The carver does not only have the problem of physically shaping rather recalcitrant material with in-adequate tools: the problem is also one of visualizing the design which he mentally follows in carving, a design which must reflect the aesthetic criteria appropriate to this art genre. He must exercise a faculty of aesthetic judge-ment, one might suppose, but this is not actually how it appears to the artist in the Trobriands who carves within a cultural context in which originality is not valued for its own sake, and who is supposed by his audience, and himself, to follow an ideal template for a canoe-board, the most magically efficacious one, the one belonging to his school of carving and its associated magical spells and rites. The Trobriand carver does not set out to create a new type of canoe-board, but a new token of an existing type; so he is not seeking to be original, but, on the other hand, he does not approach the task of carving as merely a challenge to his skill with the materials, seeing it, instead, primarily as a challenge to his mental powers. Perhaps the closest analogy would be with a musician in our culture getting technically prepared to give a perfect perform-ance of an already existing composition, such as the 'Moonlight' Sonata.

Carvers undergo magical procedures which open up the channels of their minds so that the forms to be inscribed on the canoe-board will flow freely both in and out. Campbell, in an unpublished study of Trobriand (Vakuta) carving (1984), records that the final rite of carving initiation is the ingestion of the blood of a snake famed for its slipperiness. Throughout the initiation the emphasis is placed on ensuring free flow (of magical knowledge, forms, lines, and so on) by means of the metaphoric use of water and other liquids, especially blood and bespelled betel-juice. It is, of course, true that the Melanesian curvilinear carving style is dominated by an aesthetic of sinuous lines, well-represented in the canoe-board itself; but what for us is an aesthetic principle, one which we appreciate in the finished work, is from the carver's point of view a series of technical difficulties (or blockages of the flow) which he must overcome in order to carve well. In fact, one of the carver's initiatory rites represents just this: the master carver makes a little dam, behind which sea-water is trapped. After some magical to-do, the dam is broken and the water races back to the sea. After this, the initiate's mind will become quick and clear, and carving ideas will flow in similarly unimpeded fashion into his head, down his arms, out through his fingers, and into the wood.

We see here that the ability to internalize the carving style, to think up the appropriate forms, is regarded as a matter of the acquisition of a kind of technical facility, inseparable from the kind of technical facility which has to be mastered in order for these imagined forms to be realized in wood. Trobriand carving magic is technical-facility magic. The imaginative aspect of the art and the tool-wielding aspect of the art are one and the same. But there is a more important point to be made here about the magical significance of the art and the close relationship between this magical significance and its technical characteristics.

It will be recalled that these boards are placed on Kula canoes, their purpose being to induce the Kula partners of the Trobrianders to disgorge their best valuables, without holding any back, in the most expeditious fashion. Moreover, these and the other carved components of the Kula canoe (the prow-board, and the wash-board along the side) have the additional purpose of causing the canoe to travel swiftly through the water, as far as possible like the original flying canoe of Kula mythology.

Campbell, in her iconographic analysis of the motifs found on the carved components of canoes, is able to show convincingly that slipperiness, swift movement, and a quality glossed as 'wisdom' are the characteristics of the real and imaginary animals represented, often by a single feature, in the canoe art. A 'wise' animal, for instance, is the osprey, an omnipresent motif: the osprey is wise because it knows when to strike for fish, and captures them with unerring precision. It is the smooth, precise efficiency of the osprey's fish-getting technique which qualifies it to be considered wise, not the fact that it is knowledgeable. The same smooth and efficacious quality is desired for the Kula expedition. Other animals, such as butterflies and horseshoe bats, evoke swift movement, lightness, and similar ideas. Also represented are waves, water, and so on.

The success of the Kula, like the success of the carving, depends on unimpeded flow. A complex series of homologies, of what Bourdieu (1977) has called 'scheme transfers', exists between the process of overcoming the technical obstacles which stand in the way of the achievement of a perfect 'performance' of the canoe-board carving and the overcoming of the technical obstacles, as much psychic as physical, which stand in the way of the achievement of a successful Kula expedition. Just as carving ideas must be made to flow smoothly into the carver's mind and out through his fingers, so the Kula valuables have to be made to flow smoothly through the channels of exchange, without encountering obstructions. And the metaphoric imagery of flowing water, slippery snakes, and fluttering butterflies applies in both domains, as we have seen.

We saw earlier that it would be incorrect to interpret the canoe-board ethologically as an eye-spot design or, from the standpoint of the psychology of visual perception, as a visually unstable figure, not because it is not either of these things (it is both) but because to do so would be to lose sight of its most essential characteristic, namely, that it is an object which has been made in a particular way. That is, it is not the eye-spots or the visual instabilities which fascinate, but the fact that it lies within the artist's power to make things which produce these striking effects. We can now see that the technical activity which goes into the production of a canoe-board is not only the source of its prestige as an object, but also the source of its efficacy in the domain of social relations; that is to say, there is a fundamental scheme transfer, applicable, I suggest, in all domains of art production, between technical processes involved in the creation of a work of art and the production of social relations via art. In other words, there exists a homology between the technical processes involved in art, and technical processes generally, each being seen in the light of the other, as, in this instance, the technical process of creating a canoe-board is homologous to the technical processes involved in successful Kula operations. We are inclined to deny this only because we are inclined to play down the significance of the technical domain in our culture, despite being utterly dependent on technology in every department of life. Technique is supposed to be dull and mechanical, actually opposed to true creativity and authentic values of the kind art is supposed to represent. But this distorted vision is a by-product of the quasi-religious status of art in our culture, and the fact that the art cult, like all other cults, is under a stringent requirement to conceal its real origins, as far as possible.

The Enchantment of Technology: Magic and Technical Efficacy

But just pointing to the homology between the technical aspect of art production and the production of social relations is insufficient in itself, unless we can arrive at a better understanding of the relation between art and magic, which in the case of Trobriand canoe art is explicit and fundamental. It is on the nature of magical thought, and its relation to technical activity, including the technical activity involved in the production of works of art, that I want to focus in the last part of this essay.

Art production and the production of social relations are linked by a fundamental homology: but what are social relations? Social relations are the relations which are generated by the technical processes of which society at large can be said to consist, that is, broadly, the technical processes of the production of subsistence and other goods, and the production (reproduction) of human beings by domesticating them and breeding them. Therefore, in identifying a homology between the technical processes of art production and the production of social relations, I am not trying to say that the technology of art is homologous to a domain which is not, itself, technological, for social relations are themselves emergent characteristics of the technical base on which society rests. But it would be misleading to suggest that, because societies rest on a technical base, technology is a cut-and-dried affair which everybody concerned understands perfectly.

Let us take the relatively uncontentious kind of technical activity involved in gardening—uncontentious in that everybody would admit this is technical activity, an admission they might not make if we were talking about the processes involved in setting up a marriage. Three things stand out when one considers the technical activity of gardening: firstly, that it involves knowledge and skill, secondly, that it involves work, and thirdly, that it is attended by an uncertain outcome, and moreover depends on ill-understood processes of nature. Conventional wisdom would suggest that what makes gardening count as a technical activity is the aspect of gardening which is demanding of knowledge, skill, and work, and that the aspect of gardening which causes it to be attended with magical rites, in pre-scientific societies, is the third one, that is, its uncertain outcome and ill-understood scientific basis.

But I do not think things are as simple as that. The idea of magic as an accompaniment to uncertainty does not mean that it is opposed to knowledge, i.e. that where there is knowledge there is no uncertainty, and hence no magic. On the contrary, what is uncertain is not the world but the knowledge we have about it. One way or another, the garden is going to turn out as it turns out; our problem is that we don't yet know how that will be. All we have are certain more-or-less hedged beliefs about a spectrum of possible outcomes, the more desirable of which we will try to bring about by following procedures in which we have a certain degree of belief, but which could equally well be wrong, or inappropriate in the circumstances. The problem of uncertainty is, therefore, not opposed to the notion of knowledge and the pursuit of rational technical solutions to technical problems, but is inherently a part of it. If we consider that the magical attitude is a by-product of uncertainty, we are thereby committed also to the proposition that the magical attitude is a by-product of the rational pursuit of technical objectives using technical means.

Magic as the Ideal Technology

But the relationship between technical processes and magic does not only come about because the outcome of technical endeavours is doubtful and results from the action of forces in nature of which we are partially or wholly ignorant. Work itself, mere labour, calls into being a magical attitude, because labour is the subjective cost incurred by us in the process of putting techniques into action. If we return to Simmel's ideas that 'value' is a function of the resistance which has to be overcome in order to gain access to an object, then we can see that this 'resistance' or difficulty of access can take two forms: (i) the object in question can be difficult to obtain, because it has a high price at market or because it belongs to an exalted sphere of exchange; or (ii) the object can be difficult to obtain because it is hard to produce, requiring a complex and chancy technical process, and/or a technical procedure which has high subjective opportunity costs, i.e. the producer is obliged to spend a great deal of time and energy producing that particular product, at the expense of other things he might produce or the employment of his time and resources in more subjectively agreeable leisure activities. The notion of 'work' is the standard we use to measure the opportunity cost of activities such as gardening, which are engaged in, not for their own sake, but to secure something else, such as an eventual harvest. In one sense, gardening for a Trobriander has no opportunity cost, because there is little else that a Trobriander could conceivably be doing. But gardening is still subjectively burdensome, and the harvest is still valuable because it is difficult to obtain. Gardening has an opportunity cost in the sense that gardening might be less laborious and more certain in its outcome than it actually is. The standard for computing the value of a harvest is the opportunity cost of obtaining the resulting harvest, not by the technical, work-demanding means that are actually employed, but effortlessly, by magic. All productive activities are measured against the magic-standard, the possibility that the same product might be produced effortlessly, and the relative efficacy of techniques is a function of the extent to which they converge towards the magic-standard of zero work for the same product, just as the value to us of objects in the market is a function of the relation between the desirability of obtaining those objects at zero opportunity cost (alternative purchases forgone) and the opportunity costs we will actually incur by purchasing at the market price.

If there is any truth in this idea, then we can see that the notion of magic, as a means of securing a product without the work-cost that it actually entails, using the prevailing technical means, is actually built into the standard evaluation which is applied to the efficacy of techniques, and to the computation of the value of the product. Magic is the baseline against which the concept of work as a cost takes shape. Actual Kula canoes (which have to be sailed, hazardously, laboriously, and slowly, between islands in the Kula ring) are evaluated against the standard set by the mythical flying canoe, which achieves the same results instantly, effortlessly, and without any of the normal hazards. In the same way, Trobriand gardening takes place against the background provided by the litanies of the garden magician, in which all the normal obstacles to successful gardening are made absent by the magical power of words. Magic haunts technical activity like a shadow; or, rather, magic is the negative contour of work, just as, in Saussurean linguistics, the value of a concept (say, 'dog') is a function of the negative contour of the surrounding concepts ('cat', 'wolf', 'master').

Just as money is the ideal means of exchange, magic is the ideal means of technical production. And just as money values pervade the world of commodities, so that it is impossible to think of an object without thinking at the same time of its market price, so magic, as the ideal technology, pervades the technical domain in pre-scientific societies.[3]

It may not be very apparent what all this has got to do with the subject of primitive art. What I want to suggest is that magical technology is the reverse side of productive technology, and that this magical technology consists of representing the technical domain in enchanted form. If we return to the idea, expressed earlier, that what really characterizes art objects is the way in which they tend to transcend the technical schemas of the spectator, his normal sense of self-possession, then we can see that there is a convergence between the characteristics of objects produced through the enchanted technology of art and objects produced via the enchanted technology of magic, and that, in fact, these categories tend to coincide. It is often the case that art objects are regarded as transcending the technical schemas of their creators, as well as those of mere spectators, as when the art object is considered to arise, not from the activities of the individual physically responsible for it, but from the divine inspiration or ancestral spirit with which he is filled. We can see signs of this in the fact that artists are not paid for 'working' for us, in the sense in which we pay plumbers for doing so. The artists' remuneration is not remuneration for his sweat, any more than the coins placed in the offertory plate at church are payments to the vicar for his praying on behalf of our souls. If artists are paid at all, which is infrequently, it is as a tribute to their moral ascendancy over the lay public, and such payments mostly come from public bodies or individuals acting out the public role of patrons of the arts, not from selfishly motivated individual consumers. The artist's ambiguous position, half-technician and half-mystagogue, places him at a disadvantage in societies such as ours, which are dominated by impersonal market values. But these disadvantages do not arise in societies such as the Trobriands, where all activities are simultaneously technical procedures and bound up with magic, and there is an insensible transition between the mundane activity which is necessitated by the requirements of subsistence production and the most overtly magico-religious performances.

The Trobriand Garden as a Collective Work of Art

The interpenetration of technical productive activity, magic, and art, is wonderfully documented in Malinowski's *Coral Gardens and Their Magic* (1935). Malinowski describes the extraordinary precision with which Trobriand gardens, having been cleared of scrub, and not only scrub, but the least blade of grass, are meticulously laid out in squares, with special structures called 'magical prisms' at each corner, according to a symmetrical pattern which has nothing to do with technical efficiency, and everything to do with achieving the transcendence of technical production and a convergence towards magical production. Only if the garden looks right will it grow well, and the garden is, in fact, an enormous collective work of art. Indeed, if we thought of the quadrangular Trobriand garden as an artist's canvas on which forms mysteriously grow, through an occult process which lies partly beyond our intuition, that would not be a bad analogy, because that is what happens as the yams proliferate and grow, their vines and tendrils carefully trained up poles according to principles which are no less 'aesthetic' than those of the topiarist in the formal gardens of Europe.[4]

The Trobriand garden is, therefore, both the outcome of a certain system of technical knowledge and at the same time a collective work of art, which produces yams by magic. The mundane responsibility for this collective work of art is shared by all the gardeners, but on the garden magician and his associates more onerous duties are imposed. We would not normally think of the garden magician as an artist, but from the point of view of the categories operated by the Trobrianders, his position is exactly the same, with regard to the production of the harvest, as the carver's position is with regard to the canoe-board, i.e. he is the person magically responsible, via his ancestrally inherited *sopi* or magical essence.

The garden magician's means are not physical ones, like the carver's skill with wood and tools, except that it is he who lays out the garden originally and constructs (with a good deal of effort, we are told) the magic prisms at the corners. His art is exercised through his speech. He is master of the verbal poetic art, just as the carver is master of the use of visual metaphoric forms (ospreys, butterflies, waves, and so on). It would take too long, and introduce too many fresh difficulties, to deal adequately with the tripartite relationship between language (the most fundamental of all technologies), art, and magic. But I think it is necessary, even so, to point out the elementary fact that Trobriand spells are poems, using all the usual devices of prosody and metaphor, about ideal gardens and ideally efficacious gardening techniques. Malinowski (1935: i. 169) gives the following ('Formula 27'):

I

Dolphin here now, dolphin here ever!
Dolphin here now, dolphin here ever!

Dolphin of the south-east, dolphin of the north-west.
Play on the south-east, play on the north-west, the dolphin plays!
The dolphin plays!

II

The dolphin plays!
About my *kaysalu*, my branching support, the dolphin plays.
About my *kaybudi*, my training stick that leans, the dolphin plays.
About my *kamtuya*, my stem saved from the cutting, the dolphin plays.
About my *tala*, my partition stick, the dolphin plays.
About my *yeye'i*, my small slender support, the dolphin plays.
About my *tamkwaluma*, my light yam pole, the dolphin plays.
About my *kavatam*, my strong yam pole, the dolphin plays.
About my *kayvaliluwa*, my great yam pole, the dolphin plays.
About my *tukulumwala*, my boundary line, the dolphin plays.
About my *karivisi*, my boundary triangle, the dolphin plays.
About my *kamkokola*, my magical prism, the dolphin plays.
About my *kaynutatala*, my uncharmed prisms, the dolphin plays.

III

The belly of my garden leavens,
The belly of my garden rises,
The belly of my garden reclines,
The belly of my garden grows to the size of a bush hen's nest,
The belly of my garden grows like an ant-hill,
The belly of my garden rises and is bowed down,
The belly of my garden rises like the iron-wood palm,
The belly of my garden lies down,
The belly of my garden swells,
The belly of my garden swells as with a child.

and comments (1935: ii. 310–11):

the invocation of the dolphin . . . transforms, by a daring simile, the Trobriand garden, with its foliage swaying and waving in the wind, into a seascape . . . Bagido'u [the magician] explained to me . . . that as among the waves the dolphin goes in and out, up and down, so throughout the garden the rich garlands at harvest will wind over and under, in and out, of the supports.

It is clear that not only is this hymn to superabundant foliage animated by the poetic devices of metaphor, antithesis, arcane words, and so on, all meticulously analysed by Malinowski, but that it is also tightly integrated with the catalogue of sticks and poles made use of in the garden, and the ritually important constructions, the magic prisms and boundary triangles which are also found there. The garden magician's technology of enchantment is the reflex of the enchantment of technology. Technology is enchanted because the ordinary technical means employed in the garden point inexorably towards magic, and also towards art, in that art is the idealized form of production. Just as when, confronted with some masterpiece, we are fascinated because we are essentially at a loss to explain how such an object comes to exist in the world, the litanies of the garden magician express the fascination of the Trobrianders with the efficacy of their actual technology which, converging towards the magical ideal, adumbrates this ideal in the real world.

Notes

1 'Non-Western' has been suggested to me as a preferable alternative to 'primitive' in this context. But this substitution can hardly be made, if only because the fine-art traditions of Oriental civilizations have precisely the characteristics which 'primitive' is here intended to exclude, but cannot possibly be called 'Western'. I hope the reader will accept the use of 'primitive' in a neutral, non-derogatory sense in the context of this essay. It is worth pointing out that the Trobriand carvers who produce the primitive art discussed in this essay are not themselves at all primitive; they are educated, literate in various languages, and familiar with much contemporary technology. They continue to fabricate primitive art because it is a feature of an ethnically exclusive prestige economy which they have rational motives for wishing to preserve.

2 The Kula is a system of ceremonial exchanges of valuables linking together the island communities of the Massim district, to the east of the mainland of Papua New Guinea (see Malinowski, 1922; Leach and Leach, 1983). Kula participants (all male) engage in Kula expeditions by canoe to neighbouring islands, for the purpose of exchanging two types of traditional valuable, necklaces and arm-shells, which may only be exchanged for one another. The Kula system assumes the form of a ring of linked island communities, around which necklaces circulate in a clockwise direction. Kula men compete with other men from their own community to secure profitable Kula partnerships with opposite numbers in overseas communities in either direction, the object being to maximize the volume of transactions passing through one's own hands. Kula valuables are not hoarded; it is sufficient that it should become public knowledge that a famous valuable has, at some stage, been in one's possession. A man who has succeeded in 'attracting' many coveted valuables becomes famous all around the Kula ring (see Munn, 1986).

3 In technologically advanced societies where different technical strategies exist, rather than societies like the Trobriands where only one kind of technology is known or practicable, the situation is different, because different technical strategies are opposed to one another, rather than being opposed to the magic-standard. But the technological dilemmas of modern societies can, in fact, be traced to the pursuit of a chimera which is actually the equivalent of the magic-standard: ideal 'costless' production. This is actually not costless at all, but the minimization of costs to the corporation by the maximization of social costs which do not appear on the balance sheet, leading to technically generated unemployment, depletion of unrenewable resources, degradation of the environment, etc.

4 In the Sepik, likewise, the growing of long yams is an art-form, and not just metaphorically, because the long yam can be induced to grow in particular directions by careful manipulation of the surrounding soil: it is actually a form of vegetable sculpture (see Forge, 1966).

References

BERGER, PETER (1967). *The Social Reality of Religion*. Harmondsworth, Middx.: Penguin.

BLOCH, MAURICE (1974). 'Symbols, Song, Dance, and Features of Articulation: Is Religion an Extreme Form of Traditional Authority?', *Archives Européennes de Sociologie*, 15/1: 55–81.

BOURDIEU, PIERRE (1968). 'Outline of a Sociological Theory of Art Perception', *International Social Science Journal*, 20/4: 589–612.

—— (1977). *Outline of a Theory of Practice*. Cambridge: Cambridge Univ. Press.

CAMPBELL, SHIRLEY (1984). 'The Art of the Kula'. Ph.D. thesis, Australian National Univ., Canberra.

FORGE, ANTHONY (1966). 'Art and Environment in the Sepik', *Proceedings of the Royal Anthropological Institute for 1965*. London: Royal Anthropological Institute, 23–31.

LEACH, JERRY W., and LEACH, EDMUND (1983). *The Kula: New Perspectives on Massim Exchange*. Cambridge: Cambridge Univ. Press.

MALINOWSKI, BRONISLAW (1922). *Argonauts of the Western Pacific: An Account of Native Enterprise and Adventure in the Archipelagoes of Melanesian New Guinea*. London: Routledge.

—— (1935). *Coral Gardens and their Magic: A Study of the Methods of Tilling the Soil and of Agricultural Rites in the Trobriand Islands*. 2 vols. London: Allen & Unwin.

MUNN, NANCY (1986). *The Fame of Gawa: A Symbolic Study of Value Transformation in a Massim (Papua New Guinea) Society*. Cambridge: Cambridge Univ. Press.

PANOFSKY, ERWIN (1962). *Studies in Iconology: Humanistic Themes in the Art of the Renaissance*. New York: Harper & Row.

SIMMEL, GEORG (1979). *The Philosophy of Money*. Boston: Routledge & Kegan Paul.

PART II

Objects and Interpretations

3

Art, Architecture, and Collective Representations in a New Guinea Society

ROSS BOWDEN

Art and the Communication of Symbolic Values

The assertion that art 'communicates' is one that is very commonly made about painting, sculpture, and other visual art-forms in both Western and tribal societies. But establishing with any degree of certainty what a particular painting or sculpture might 'say' about the society which produces it is no easy matter. And teasing the 'meaning' out of art objects is made all the more difficult by the fact that artists generally (including writers and composers) typically show little interest in, or even aptitude for, translating into ordinary discourse what their creations are 'about'—something that has been noted since at least the time of Plato (Plato, 1984: 51; see also Blocker, 1979: 57–9, 67, 324). This lack of concern, or even ability, on the part of the artist to interpret what he has created for the benefit of an observer means that when the anthropologist sets out to enquire into the 'meaning' of a particular visual art-form, more often than not he or she is confronted by a seemingly insurmountable wall of silence. It is largely for this reason, I believe, that so much of the anthropological literature on art is distinguished more by what it does not say than by what it does. As Anthony Forge (1979: 280) has remarked: 'It is a truism that art communicates, but what does it communicate? Here the philosophers and historians, and indeed all students of art, seem to become evasive, trivial or unintelligible. . . .'

Notwithstanding the formidable methodological and other problems involved, my own research, together with that of Forge (1966), Gell (1975), and others in the Sepik River region of Papua New Guinea, indicates that, in this area of Melanesia at least, plastic art-forms can be seen to communicate significant information about the societies that produce them—information that is expressed in somewhat different ways in many other contexts as well: in myth, ritual, and so on. To illustrate this I examine the architecture and sculpture of Kwoma ceremonial men's houses (*korombo*; 'haus tambarans' in New Guinea Pidgin). Kwoma men's houses, when fully decorated, are lavishly embellished with paintings and carvings and represent some of the most outstanding contemporary art-forms in Oceania; like vernacular architecture generally in Papua New Guinea, however, they have been largely ignored by students of art (but see Behrmann, 1950–1; Forge, 1966; Schuster, 1985). The specific aim of the present analysis is to illustrate the way in which such buildings provide a symbolic focus for two distinct sets of ideas. First, I show that men's houses embody in their architecture and decorative art ideals which men hold in relation to themselves. These are the apparently contra-dictory but related beliefs that men ideally are killers (i.e. hunters of animals and killers of other people in warfare) and creators: horticulturally, through their capacity to plant and grow yams—the most highly prized cultivated crop in this society—and, in human terms, through their potent and fecund sexuality. I have indicated elsewhere (Bowden, 1983*a*) that the beliefs that men ideally are both killers and creators horticulturally are actually related in Kwoma thought, for only men who have killed in battle are thought capable of cultivating yams. It is believed (or at least was until recently) that if a non-homicide were to plant yams, the seed tubers would not germinate but simply rot in the ground. As far as the reproductive capacities of homicides are concerned, there is no belief that men need to be killers before they can father offspring; but homicides are the persons of highest prestige in the society and they are the men whom women aspire above all to marry, monogamously or polygynously. Homicides consequently tend to have more wives, and children, than other men.

I stated above that the architecture and art of Kwoma men's houses embody or express certain ideals which men hold in relation to themselves. The same point could be put more strongly by saying that Kwoma actually attribute to men's houses qualities which they admire in men, notably the attributes of homicidal aggressiveness and creativity in the contexts of yam cultivation and human reproduction. One consequence of this is that in Kwoma collective representations men are tacitly identified with ceremonial buildings.

The second set of ideas I wish to consider concerns the way in which myths associated with the art in men's houses advance models or explanations for the origin of culture. The particular idea I wish to isolate concerns the belief that culture originated in (or what amounts to the same thing in this context, consists in) exchange: the exchange of various kinds of thing between different individuals and groups. The idea that exchange is central to the constitution of society is by no means a new one, of course, though in my opinion it has still not received the attention it deserves in studies of Papua New Guinea social organization (Bowden, 1982; 1983*b*; 1988). The idea that Kwoma culture originated in (and by implication consists in) exchange, furthermore, occurs over and over again in both art and myth. Because the notion of exchange in Kwoma thought is so pervasive, I make no attempt to examine it here in detail. All I will do is briefly allude to it—and especially to the idea that exchange is synonymous with the origin of culture—in connection with the myths associated with two prominent sets of sculptures in the men's house Waypanal in Bangwis[1] village, my field base. But one point that should be emphasized in passing, because of its wider implications for the study of Kwoma art and myth, is that the two distinct sets of ideas I have isolated—of men as killers and creators, and of exchange—are actually closely related at a more abstract level in Kwoma thought (see also Whitehead, 1986). In Kwoma collective representations, killing in the context of warfare, the creativity that it entails, and exchange are transformations or analogues of each other. Kwoma believe that in the act of killing the slayer acquires the victim's soul—an entity which thereafter resides in, or remains attached to, the distinctive shell and feather ornaments that a homicide wears (Bowden, 1983a, pl. 19). It is through the acquisition of an enemy's soul that a homicide is actually endowed with creativity, especially horticulturally. For Kwoma, in other words, killing in battle, and consequently the creativity it entails, consists in the exchange of fertility between enemy groups. More particularly, it consists in the exchange of fertility between groups of men, since warfare in this society, like hunting, is exclusively a man's activity.

The fact that Kwoma conceptualize killing in battle as an exchange of fertility is also the explanation (or at least partly so) of the fact that the military enemy is so often represented in myth and other contexts as an affine, especially a wife. This in turn can be related to the fact that outside the context of warfare the major occasion on which Kwoma consciously and deliberately exchange fertility between independent political groups is marriage; in this society marriage is explicitly conceptualized as the exchange of women with active reproductive capacities between groups of men who are actual or potential military enemies (Bowden, 1982; 1983b).[2] The fact that Kwoma conceptualize both warfare and marriage as exchanges of fertility between 'enemies' also suggests that killing in battle (the exchange of imaginary fertility) can be regarded as a metaphor for, or analogue of, the marriage system (the exchange of real fertility between groups). Both institutions in any case are different manifestations of the more basic concept of exchange.

The Cultural Setting

Kwoma are a Papuan-speaking people (Wurm and Hattori, 1981) numbering approximately 2,000 who live in the Washkuk Hills in the East Sepik Province of Papua New Guinea (Bowden, 1983a: 8–14). The population is divided into four named, politically autonomous tribes: Honggwama, Koriyasi, Worimbach, and Tonggwinjamb. Traditionally (before about 1940), warfare among these tribes, and with neighbouring groups, was common. Formerly, each tribe comprised a large but discrete settlement group located for defensive purposes on the top of a high ridge; today, all four groups have relocated to sites lower down the hills near waterways. Two of the tribes (Tonggwinjamb and Worimbach) still constitute discrete settlement groups, but the other two have divided into a number of distinct villages. Tribes are composed of numerous patrilineal and patrilocal clans. Clans rather than tribes are the basic social units. Each separately owns an estate in land which it manages in its own interests; independently organizes the prestations of wealth that surround puberty, marriage, and death (Bowden, 1983*b*; 1988); and owns a set of sculptures and other ritual paraphernalia which it displays in ceremonies.

Structurally a men's house consists of nothing more than a steeply pitched, saddle-backed roof supported by several rows of posts (Figs. 3.1–3.3; see also Bowden, 1983*a*: 44 ff.; Newton, 1971; Kaufmann, 1979). In contrast to their better-known Iatmul and Abelam counterparts (Schuster, 1985; Forge, 1966), Kwoma ceremonial buildings are open at both ends and have no walls; the sides of the roof, however, reach so close to the ground that these effectively serve as side-walls. The top of the roof at both the front and back of the building extends several metres beyond the sides, creating a pair of long overhanging porches. The central ridge-pole is supported by a line of four (or, in smaller men's houses, two) posts (Fig. 3.2). The sides of the roof are each supported by two pairs of longitudinal beams resting on shorter posts (Fig. 3.3). (Small men's houses may have only one longitudinal beam on each side.) The structure is given added lateral stability by a pair of struts at each end that extend out from roughly its central line to the middle of the ceiling on each side. The size of a men's house varies according to the numerical strength and energy of the clan, or group of clans, that builds it. At present, the largest of the four fully decorated buildings in the tribe in which I have done the bulk of my work—the Honggwama—measures 41 metres in length, 13 in width, and approximately 10 in height. The others range from 32 to 20 metres in length. The only furnishings in a men's house consist of eight to ten large wooden slit-gongs measuring from four to six metres in length, distributed around the sides and centre of the building (Fig. 3.7), and a number of wooden stools and slabs on which men either sit around small, smouldering fires or stretch out to sleep. In contrast to Abelam men's houses, which Forge (1966: 25) reports are conceptually 'female', Kwoma buildings, including all of their major structural components, such as the ridge-pole, longitudinal side-beams, central posts, and slit-gongs, are grammatically, and symbolically, male. In plan, *korombo* are symmetrical laterally and longitudinally (see Bowden, 1983*a*: 48). In style and method of construction, they are identical to those of Mayo-speakers immediately to the west (see Newton, 1971), to whom Kwoma are closely related historically and linguistically.

A men's house need not be decorated in any way to be used ritually, and many are not; but the largest are usually elaborately decorated with paintings and sculptures (see Figs. 3.1–3.6). The paintings (*mbi*) on sago bark that line the upper halves of the ceiling on each side represent for the most part

FIG. 3.1. The front of the men's house Waypanal, Bangwis village; photographer: Ross Bowden, January 1987. A meeting is in progress.

FIG. 3.2. View of the interior of men's house Waypanal, Bangwis village, from the front; photographer: Ross Bowden, January 1987. The main central upright shown is the front 'mother' (*nokwapa*) post.

FIG. 3.3. Bark-paintings, decorated beams, and carvings; front left side of the men's house Waypanal, Bangwis village; photographer: Ross Bowden, January 1987.

totemic plants and animals (Figs. 3.2, 3.3, and 3.4). Only clans that 'own' the totemic species in question have an automatic right to depict them in paintings; others may do so only with permission. The majority of the sculptures either depict well-known figures from myths (see Figs. 3.5 and 3.6) or are thinly disguised copies of secret ceremonial figures. Like totems, myths and spirits are owned by particular clans and men may only carve or paint depictions of figures from myths, or spirits, in which their clans hold copyright. A minority of carvings consist of 'meaningless' decorative designs. Sculptures depicting the most well-known mythological and ceremonial figures tend to be concentrated in the front half of a building; less well-known figures and 'purely decorative' designs tend to be concentrated at the back. In fully decorated structures, several lavishly carved and painted horizontal beams run across the main axis of the building roughly half way up the ceiling (Figs. 3.2); these serve aesthetic rather than structural purposes, for they are not found in undecorated buildings. The carvings on the lower sides of such cross-beams, looking directly down on the men who sit below them, are predominantly copies of *yena* and *minja* figures displayed during the two yam harvest rituals of the same names (Bowden, 1983*a*). These sculptures, like their ceremonial prototypes, are thought to be vivified by the spirits they

FIG. 3.4. Detail of ceiling paintings on sago-bark, front right corner of the men's house Waypanal, Bangwis village; photographer: Ross Bowden, January 1987. See also Pl. II.

FIG. 3.7. Detail of a carved and painted slit-gong in men's house Wambon, Washkuk village; photographer: Ross Bowden, January 1982. The finial is decorated in the form of a crocodile's head, the crocodile being a well-known totem of one of the clans that participated actively in the construction of the building. See also Pl. III.

FIG. 3.5. Portrait sculpture of the culture hero Naluwen, men's house Waypanal, Bangwis village; photographer: Ross Bowden, January 1987.

FIG. 3.6. The mythical figure Mandiikapames, men's house Waypanal, Bangwis village; photographer: Ross Bowden, January 1987.

depict; the spirits, men say, watch over proceedings in the building and sanction the conventions that govern behaviour within it. One basic convention is that no person may strike or otherwise aggressively lay hands on another within the confines of the building. Kwoma acknowledge that this enables people to debate matters of clan or wider village concern in men's houses, including such potentially explosive subjects as sorcery (Bowden, 1987), without fear of violence from opponents. If a person were to breach

FIG. 3.8. Women dancing outside the ceremonial men's house Wiiny Bogur ('fork in a *wiiny* tree'), Washkuk village; photographer: Ross Bowden, December 1972. The occasion is a performance of Minja, one of three yam harvest rituals performed annually. The women are separated physically and visually from the men inside the building, and from the ceremonial sculptures displayed, by a tall screen of sago-palm fronds and other decorative plant materials. For ceremonies, women decorate according to their husbands' ritual status. The wives of homicides wear many of the same homicidal shell and feather decorations as their husbands; and the wives of men who have not achieved homicidal status wear appropriate lower-prestige decorations. Today, women also don new dresses and other items of Western apparel that are valued for their bright colours.

this supernaturally sanctioned taboo, they would be required forthwith to provide a large pig for sacrifice in the building. Like many other Sepik peoples, Kwoma do not keep domesticated pigs, and to obtain a suitable animal might take several weeks of hunting. Failure to provide a pig within a reasonable time would result in the spirits that inhabit the cross-beams afflicting the offender with a potentially fatal wasting disease.

Any adult male member in a community in which a ceremonial house is being constructed may make bark paintings and have them incorporated into the ceiling decorations. The owners also welcome contributions of paintings (and carvings) by members of other tribes, for this lightens the immense burden of fully decorating such a structure. Only paintings by the most knowledgeable and highly respected artists, however, are displayed lower down the ceilings, in the most visually prominent positions. The carving and painting of major architectural features such as the main beams and posts is similarly done only by the most skilled artists; less skilled men, and youths 'in training', limn minor posts and beams. The most talented artists are termed *woyi siipiikwiina neekitawa yikapwa*, 'adze- and brush-holding children'. In this society only men are bark-painters and sculptors. Women's visual art consists principally of utilitarian string bags with dyed abstract designs, and their own ceremonial body decorations.[3]

Each clan is formally entitled to construct and reside around its own ceremonial house. However, Kwoma clans are small,[4] and normally several contiguous exogamous groups, or a village as a whole, communally construct and use a single building. Bangwis village presently has three fully decorated *korombo*. The oldest, named Waypanal (Fig. 3.1), is located at the physical centre of the village on the top of Bangwis hill. For a decade after it was built (in the late 1960s) this was the only men's house in Bangwis, and was used communally by all of the village's nine clans. Another, named Geyasatuk, is situated at the extreme northern edge of the village, and the third, Minjawular, on the western side of Bangwis hill. Both of the latter were constructed in the late 1970s. Performances of ceremonies are initiated by individual clans; the initiating group determines when performances will take place and which sculptures will be displayed. All ceremonies, however, are attended by members of a tribe as a whole. Occasionally members of other tribes, and neighbouring language groups, also attend. Unlike Iatmul buildings (Schuster, 1985), Kwoma men's houses are not divided into distinct areas where the members of different clans sit and place their fires. Men sit and make small fires wherever they wish.

The Structure of Settlements

I begin this discussion of the way in which the architecture and art of Kwoma ceremonial buildings communicate information about the society in which they are found by considering in general terms the relationship between these buildings and the men who construct and occupy them. Like men's houses elsewhere in the Sepik, Kwoma ceremonial buildings are located (whenever possible) at the physical centre and highest points of clan settlements. As well as being at the physical centre of settlements, they provide (as elsewhere in the Sepik) the focus of the social and ceremonial lives of the adult male members of the communities in which they are located. They are the buildings in which men (and only men) spend part of almost every day of their lives either sitting quietly chewing betel-nut, dozing after a hard day's work, or in conversation with other men; they are the buildings in which men publicly debate matters of clan and village concern and in which, formerly, they prepared for war; and they are the buildings in which men perform the rituals that are believed to be of vital importance for the economic and political well-being of the communities in which they are located (Bowden, 1983a).

As is the case generally in the Sepik, Kwoma women have no equivalent structures in which to congregate for social or ceremonial purposes. Formerly, moreover, women were prohibited from entering men's houses and even from approaching them except on specific ritual occasions. Today, the rule excluding women from such buildings has been relaxed to the extent that they may enter them during village meetings; but on these occasions they must enter from the back and sit at the back, in marked spatial contrast to the men, who sit at the front. On ritual occasions women are still rigorously prohibited from entering a ceremonial building, and may only approach it, to dance and sing outside at the front, after men have erected a tall screen to prevent them from observing, and hence learning about, what is going on inside (Fig. 3.8).

Men rationalize the exclusion of women from ceremonial buildings with reference to alleged differences between the natures of the two sexes. Men say that they as a category are 'hot' (*hi uwuto*) whereas women as a category are 'cold' (*neekiireyawa*). The 'coldness' of women, however, is not a passive or negative quality but an active one, for if a cold object were to come into contact with a hot object, the former would drain the heat out of the latter and destroy its physical, mental, or ritual potency. Since men believe that all ritual objects are 'hot' like themselves, and must be so to be ritually efficacious, they must be protected from women. For instance, men believe that if a woman were to see a *yena* or *minja* figure being carved or displayed ceremonially, it would immediately fracture, the spirit it embodies would flee the scene, and the ritual in which it is displayed would be rendered ineffectual. Women potentially have an equally destructive effect on men's houses themselves and men. Thus, if a woman were to enter a building and sit on one of the slit-gongs, the drum would immediately cease to produce a powerful, far-carrying sound and would be ineffective as a musical and signalling instrument. Such an action, people say, would also gravely weaken the men who customarily occupy the building, preventing them from carrying out their ritual duties or (as they were required traditionally to do) from militarily defending their community. To preserve the integrity of a men's house and the political viability of the community in which it is located, therefore, men believe that they are duty-bound rigorously to restrict women's access to these buildings.

The preceding remarks indicate that, in the context of ceremonial houses and the rituals performed within them, Kwoma women are very much 'on the outer', spatially and symbolically. The 'peripheral' or 'outside' position that women occupy *vis-à-vis* men in relation to men's houses can be correlated with the structure of villages. Each of the localized clans which compose Kwoma villages contains a residentially stable core of agnatically related men.

Normatively, and with few exceptions in practice, men reside throughout their lives with their agnates at their place of birth (unless their group as a whole moves) and live in stable, solidary groups: physically, genealogically, and socially. Because clans are exogamous and patrilocal, women born into them (unlike the men) do not remain resident members, but leave on marriage to take up residence with their husbands in other clan settlements. Women, in other words, move between groups. Since divorce in Kwoma society occurs relatively frequently, and many women marry more than once, adult females are even conceptualized as being continually on the move, shifting from one clan to another throughout their adult lives as they enter or leave marriages. Unlike men, therefore, who constitute the residential and social cores of the groups of which the society is composed, women link groups, occupying, as it were, the spaces between them (cf. Strathern, 1972). To phrase the matter slightly differently, from the point of view of the resident members of any one clan, men are the insiders, while adult women (in the form of wives) are the outsiders (cf. Meggitt, 1964).

This opposition between male insiders and female outsiders can be developed even further. Kwoma men regard the members of *all* clans other than their own, including those in the same village, as potential enemies. Traditionally, warfare only took place between tribes, but clans belonging to the same tribe were (and still are) thought to kill each other not by fighting but by sorcery (Bowden, 1987). Since clans are exogamous, men by definition obtain their wives from 'enemy' groups—'we marry our enemies', as they say. Furthermore, in marked contrast to their attitudes to out-marrying clan sisters, with whom they maintain warm, solidary relations, men are highly ambivalent about their wives. Not only do the latter derive from outside, or 'enemy', groups, but they remain permanently identified with those groups. For instance, married women receive regular visits from their brothers— 'enemies' of their husbands—and men believe that if they seriously alienate or persistently antagonize their wives the latter will not hesitate to leave them to marry someone else, or secretly pass some of their leavings, such as food scraps, to their brothers with instructions to 'poison' them.[5] A clan settlement or larger village, therefore, is composed of a group (or several groups) of closely related men and married women who both derive from and are identified with outside or 'enemy' groups.

The important differences socially and structurally between the adult men and women who compose clan settlements can also be correlated symbolically with the physical layout of villages. Ceremonial houses, I have indicated, are normally located at the centre of clan settlements. Being the structures that men build and occupy to the effective exclusion of women, they form a clear spatial counterpart to the central position that men occupy, structurally, in clan communities. The dwelling houses which in-marrying wives occupy (in which men actually sleep with their wives at night) are, by contrast, scattered around the clan's ceremonial house, occupying, literally, the margins or periphery of the settlement (see Whiting, 1941: 10).[6] But more than this, resident females not only occupy peripheral positions spatially in settlements, unlike men they never form solidary groups. Physically, in-marrying wives remain permanently divided among themselves in their separate and often widely scattered dwellings (Whiting, 1941: 5–6; Mead, 1972: 211),[7] and socially they neither constitute a single kin group (the marriage rules specifically prevent this; see Bowden, 1983*b*) nor ever act as a group. In fact, the only occasion on which the adult women resident in a clan settlement (or larger village) ever physically come together is when they dance outside a men's house during a ceremony, and then they only form a group (and an extremely ephemeral one at that) in relation to the men whose wives they are (cf. Strathern and Strathern, 1971: 153). Spatially, socially, and symbolically, therefore, men are at the centre of a community, as is a men's house. Women, on the other hand, are on the periphery, their peripheral position symbolically and structurally corresponding both to the fact that the houses in which they live are on the margins of a clan settlement and to the fact that they are generally excluded from ceremonial houses.[8]

The Identification of Men with Ceremonial Houses

The discussion thus far has indicated that there is a clear correlation between the central position that men's houses occupy spatially in clan settlements and the central position that men occupy structurally in clan communities. I now take the argument a step further by considering one of the ways in which men are tacitly identified in Kwoma collective representations with ceremonial houses. This relates to the rules governing the kinds of timber that must be used for different parts of these buildings. Customarily, the longitudinal side-beams and the ridge-pole, both of which are elaborately carved and painted, are made of a timber named *mes* (New Guinea Pidgin 'malas'). Similarly, the central uprights, which are again lavishly decorated with carvings and are painted (Figs. 3.1, 3.2, and 3.4), are conventionally made from a hardwood named *nyembi* (Pidgin 'garamut'). Through the use of *mes* and *nyembi* timbers for the main beams and posts in ceremonial houses, men can be seen to be attributing to these buildings qualities which they admire in themselves. These are the two superficially different but related ideas mentioned earlier, notably of homicidal aggressiveness on the one hand and masculine creativity, in the context of both yam cultivation and human reproduction, on the other. By attributing to men's houses attributes or qualities which they greatly admire in themselves, men may thereby be seen to be tacitly identifying themselves with these structures.

The two timbers, *mes* and *nyembi*, give prominence to ideas relating to fertility and homicidal aggression in several ways. First, the *mes* species of tree provides the wood from which yam-planting dibbles are conventionally made. It is thought that if any other type of wood were to be used, the growth of the yams would be jeopardized. *Mes* wood, that is, is directly associated with garden fertility in the context of yam cultivation. But more than this, in a myth titled 'The Song of Mes',[9] the eponymous hero of which is a magical tree of this species, yam-planting dibbles are explicitly associated with masculine sexuality and procreativity. The narrative begins by describing how a gardener makes a clearing in the forest and plants yams. At the end of the day, when the work has been completed, the man throws the dibble into the bush at the side of the swidden. Shortly afterwards a female python finds the freshly cut dibble and ingests some of the sap that is still exuding from it, whereupon she becomes pregnant and gives birth to a male human child. In this myth, therefore, *mes* timber is directly associated with masculine sexuality and fertility, for the sap impregnates the female snake. Implicitly, the myth is also equating the dibble with the penis. Although the narrative only makes this association implicitly, it is made explicitly in art associated with men's houses. For instance, in Waypanal at Bangwis there is a slit-gong with a carving on its finial depicting this very incident in the myth of the *mes* tree (see Bowden, 1983*a*: pl. 32). The carving shows the snake ingesting sap from the digging stick and simultaneously giving birth to a human child, the head of which can be seen emerging from the snake. The salient feature of the sculpture in this context, however, is the fact that the artist has carved the dibble in the form of a penis, for the head of the penis can be seen quite clearly at the end from which the snake ingests sap.

Later in the same narrative the myth dramatically reinforces the symbolic association between *mes* wood and masculine procreativity. It tells how the child who is born to the snake, and adopted by the gardener and his wife, is eventually killed (for reasons not made clear in the narrative) when he is found in the forest by members of a neighbouring, 'enemy' tribe who have been visiting the boy's village to participate in a ceremony. The boy's killers secretly bury his body beside a forest track; following this, a huge *mes* tree emerges from the grave. Some of the tree's thick roots lie across the track, and whenever a woman passing by steps over them she immediately becomes pregnant. So great in fact are the tree's masculine procreative powers that it impregnates even tiny, prepubescent girls, all of whom, because of their physical immaturity, die in childbirth. So in the myth the timber that is customarily used for the ridge-pole and side-beams of men's houses is unambiguously associated with masculine sexuality and procreativity, and also fertility in the context of yam cultivation.

The myth concludes by describing how the tree temporarily transforms into a man and visits a nearby village. There it 'tricks' a married women into following it out into the forest. When it reaches the spot beside the track where it normally stands, it transforms back into a tree and carries the woman high up into its branches. There, permanently stranded, the woman metamorphoses into the bulbous woody growths that are often seen on the branches of this species of tree. Kwoma associate the tree's capture of a woman through subterfuge with the philandering for which outstanding big men (*hisawa ma*) are known; such men are thought to be more energetic sexually than others, and not above resorting to trickery and even force to attract and hold women. For instance, a major Honggwama big man boasted to me how he had acquired one of his three wives by literally taking hold of her one day when her then husband was out of the village and marching her back to his house. Her apparent acceptance of the situation, combined with her 'captor's' declaration that he would defend his new possession with force if need be, dissuaded her former husband from attempting to retrieve her. Relations between the two men and their respective clans returned to normal when the big man in question made the conventionally required bridewealth payment to her former husband. In addition to the symbolic values already noted, therefore, *mes* timber is associated with another masculine ideal, the capacity to attract and hold women—a capacity identified pre-eminently with major big men. Notice also how this and the other masculine ideals identified above are all associated in the myth with warfare and homicidal aggression; for the tree which epitomizes them emerges from the grave of a victim of an intertribal killing.

The timber that is used for the central uprights in these buildings is associated more than anything else with the idea of homicidal aggressiveness, but also with superabundant masculine sexuality and fertility in the context of yam cultivation. There is a myth—one of several dealing with the origin of men's houses—that tells how a group of villagers construct a huge ceremonial building named Dowamu. Unbeknown to them, the men's house they construct is a violent homicidal and cannibal spirit. Whenever the adult members of the village go hunting or gardening, Dowamu collapses on any unattended children who wander into it, and kills and eats them. The villagers at first are completely baffled by the disappearance of their children, but soon discover the reason why and decide to retaliate. They reason that they cannot kill the building by spearing it, for it is not a person; they decide therefore to burn it down. But when men surround it and put torches to the thatch, the spirit Dowamu, who is the men's house, magically escapes underground in the form of the front central *nyembi* post and hides in a nearby stream. Women and girls from the same village later discover it there while fishing with hand-nets. The myth tells how the women while wading in the stream feel the post darting around under the water like a large fish; in some versions of the narrative it prods the women phallically between the legs, as a result of which they all become pregnant. As in the case of the *mes* tree, the post's masculine procreative powers are so great it impregnates even sexually immature girls, all of whom subsequently die in childbirth. The women immediately inform their husbands that they have found the post that escaped from the burning building, and with their assistance the following day catch it in their large round nets and drag it up on to the bank. There the men vent their anger on the cannibal spirit Dowamu by hacking at the post with their adzes. Splinters of wood fly in all directions. Some fall into the adjacent stream and there transform into the first bamboo flutes.[10] Another splinter that falls into the stream metamorphoses into a *yena* sculpture, i.e. of the type displayed during the yam harvest ceremonies, and which actually depicts the spirits responsible for the continuing fertility of yam gardens. Splinters that fall on to the ground around the post grow into the *nyembi* trees that men use today for the central posts of ceremonial buildings. After venting their anger on it, the men drag what remains of the post far off into the forest where they abandon it. They have not killed Dowamu, however, for, although the myth does not say so explicitly, it implies that he lives on in the form of the *nyembi* posts in men's houses.

The mythological identification of *nyembi* timber with the homicidal and cannibal spirit Dowamu underlies the respect with which men treat the central uprights in ceremonial buildings. In contrast to the shorter side-posts, people may not sit against or casually touch them. A breach of this taboo requires a pig sacrifice. Failure to make a sacrifice entails supernatural retaliation from Dowamu and the other spirits that inhabit these structures in the form of a wasting disease. The symbolic association between the central uprights and masculine aggression is underscored by the fact that when a men's house is being constructed, the owners bury the skulls and right arm-bones of kinsmen who were notable warriors or aggressive and forceful debaters beside these posts, a practice which is now illegal but continues covertly. Men say that placing such bones beside the posts adds to the 'strength' and 'aggressiveness of disposition' of the building—qualities which are otherwise greatly admired in men. Through the use of *mes* and *nyembi* timbers in the construction of ceremonial buildings, therefore, men give expression to ideas both of creativity, in the context of yam cultivation and human reproduction, and of homicidal aggressiveness.[11]

Exchange, the Origin of Culture, and Other Themes

Up to this point I have been concerned to illustrate some of the ways in which the architecture (and art) of men's houses express certain ideas and values which men hold in relation to themselves. I now comment briefly on some of the other ideas that emerge from myths associated with two very prominent sets of sculptures in the men's house named Waypanal (Figs. 3.5 and 3.6). The first consists of portraits of the two youthful culture heroes, Naluwen and

Moyichey, and other members of their natal family. A full-length, larger-than-life sculpture of Naluwen stands at the front of Waypanal against the front central post (Figs. 3.1 and 3.5), and an equally large, full-length sculpture of his brother Moyichey stands against the central post third from the front. A smaller, full-length portrait sculpture of the two men's younger brother, Mambor, decorates the right central side-post, and one of their mother stands directly opposite on the left side. Two other sculptures depicting Naluwen and Moyichey, under their alternative names of Kambiiriinay and Nipiisil, stand on top of the first and third cross-beams from the front of the building respectively. Originally the sculpture of Naluwen (Fig. 3.5) had a black-palm spear tucked under its right arm, but this is now missing. Moyichey holds a dagger in his raised right hand. The carvings on the cross-beams show the two men facing each other holding spears in throwing positions.

Naluwen and Moyichey are the two persons credited in myth with constructing the first men's house named Waypanal. A myth titled 'Waley' tells how the two brothers go hunting in the forest and come across a wide, newly cleared track that was previously unknown to them. They follow it and eventually find themselves at a village in the land of the dead. Save for the shades of two decrepit old women, the village is deserted, for the ghosts who normally occupy it have travelled to Naluwen and Moyichey's settlement (along the track the boys found) to collect the soul of a man who has just died. The brothers enter the village and there discover a magnificent, fully decorated men's house named Waypanal. The building's design and splendid decorative art-work so impress them that they resolve immediately to build an identical one when they return home. To ensure that they reproduce it exactly, they use lengths of split vine carefully to record its dimensions, and commit to memory the style and placement of its hundreds of paintings and sculptures. The boys then cautiously test one of its huge slit-gongs. As with all of the most expertly crafted drums, this emits a powerful, resonating sound even when only lightly struck. The sound disturbs the ghosts of the two old women who are sitting at their house nearby, and they aggressively call to the boys, demanding to know who is there. Naluwen and Moyichey nervously give their names. Appeased, the women invite them down to their house. The women manifest themselves to the boys as beautiful young girls. They engage in flirtatious banter with the brothers and provide them with a meal, acts which for Kwoma have explicitly sexual (and matrimonial) overtones. Later that day, worried that the other ghosts will return and kill the boys if they find them in the village, the girls urge Naluwen and Moyichey to leave; but first they instruct them how to steal a magical adze blade from the returning ghosts that will materially assist them to construct a replica of Waypanal. As instructed, the boys lie in wait beside the forest track, and at the appropriate moment pelt the band of psychopomps with aromatic plants and other missiles. Temporarily panic-stricken, the ghosts drop the large wooden 'hook' on which they are transporting the soul of the dead man, and from which the adze blade the boys seek is suspended in a small net bag. In the confusion they quickly seize the adze blade, and head for home. Back at their own village, in the land of the living, the two culture heroes construct an exact replica of Waypanal, including every detail of its decorative art-work. After completing the building, Naluwen and Moyichey decide not to remain in their community to enjoy the immense prestige and status of 'big men' (*hisawa ma*) they have now acquired by contributing so spectacularly to its cultural life, but return permanently to the land of the dead to marry the two girls they met there. But the only way they can do this is by dying. Kwoma have no tradition of dying 'by one's own hand', and to bring about their deaths the boys agree to kill each other. They fabricate a quarrel, begin fighting, and then spear each other. Ironically, when they get back to the land of the dead, this time as ghosts, the brothers discover that the two women they met, far from being beautiful young girls, are in reality wizened old hags, and that the latter appeared to them as young girls only to trick them into killing each other. Kwoma believe that ghosts, being former people, bitterly resent being dead, and from sheer spite will do everything in their power to trick the living into joining them in the land of the dead.

The men's house named Waypanal at Bangwis, like all previous buildings of the same name, is thought to replicate exactly the one constructed by Naluwen and Moyichey. One distinctive, copyrighted architectural feature of this class of buildings is the vaulted arches covered with bark paintings above the front and rear central posts (Fig. 3.1). The men who constructed this building told me that, to commemorate Naluwen and Moyichey themselves, they decided to embellish it with the set of portrait sculptures described above. Both sets of sculptures depicting Naluwen and Moyichey show the brothers armed with weapons and about to kill each other after completing their building. The sculptures of their brother Mambor and their mother similarly depict incidents in the myth. The narrative describes how Mambor from a distance hears his brothers fighting and goes to investigate. Discovering their suicide pact, he attempts to intervene. To prevent him from doing so the older brothers tie him to one of the building's side-posts. Mambor's portrait sculpture depicts him bound to the same side-post; he is calling frantically to others in the village to prevent Naluwen and Moyichey from killing each other. The sculpture of their mother depicts her weeping inconsolably after she has learned that her two oldest sons have died. It is worth remarking that these and other sculptures in the same building strikingly contradict Forge's (1979: 279) generalization that in the art of New Guinea as a whole 'there is no portrayal of any scene from a myth ... or indeed any "action" scene'.

Several other aspects of the myth 'Waley' deserve comment. First, it provides a classic 'charter' for the existence and design of men's houses named Waypanal. In contrast to such other elements of Kwoma culture as certain styles of ceremonial carvings which men acknowledge have been obtained in recent generations from neighbouring language groups, the narrative represents men's houses named Waypanal and their decorative art-work as primordial features of the society, as old as Kwoma culture itself. Second, the myth explicitly represents men's houses named Waypanal as supernatural in origin.[12] By attributing a supernatural origin to such buildings the myth can be seen to invest them, and the social values they express, with a sanctity and authority in social and ritual life that people (especially women) cannot question. Men's houses, that is, form part of the divine order of things. Third, the myth unambiguously, but indirectly, depicts Culture, in the form of men's houses named Waypanal, as a 'gift' of the gods, even if the gift in this case, like the fire of Prometheus, had to be stolen. But gifts, however acquired, must be repaid, and the myth indicates that Naluwen and Moyichey—who represent humanity *vis-à-vis* the ghosts (or spirits) from whom they steal the designs—'pay' for it with their own lives. (Men commenting on the myth make clear that the ghostly owners of Waypanal, being spirits, know in advance that Naluwen and Moyichey intend to 'steal' the design of their building, and to ensure that they 'pay' for it set a trap for them in the shape of the two beautiful but illusory young girls.) The narrative, in other words, equates the origin of Culture in the form of men's houses named Waypanal with gift exchange—in this case with the exchange of gifts between the mundane and supernatural worlds.

Fourth, the myth advances a model or theory of creativity in art which accords with the way people think in everyday life. In common with many other pre-industrial peoples (see e.g. Sutton, 1988: 19), Kwoma attribute aesthetic creativity—visual and verbal—to supernatural inspiration. In contrast to the contemporary Western paradigm of the artistic process, that is, inspiration derives not from within the person but from without. 'Waley' expresses this by representing the men's house constructed by Naluwen and Moyichey, including every detail of its lavishly decorated interior, as a simple replica of a building seen in the spirit world. Since the sculptures and paintings that decorate ceremonial buildings constitute by far the greater part of all Kwoma art, people accordingly think of the bulk of their traditional repertoire of visual motifs as copies of ancient supernatural prototypes. Kwoma acknowledge that change and innovation in art do occur, but they explain these in ways that are consistent with the belief that the supernatural world is the source of aesthetic inspiration. For instance, motifs which Kwoma have borrowed from other cultures (including European) are assumed to form part of the ancient visual patrimonies of their cultures of origin, and, like their own, to be ultimately of supernatural origin. Innovations introduced by outstanding individual artists are typically attributed to supernatural inspiration received in dreams. For Kwoma, dream experiences, including the entities seen in them, are the creations of clan spirits (Bowden, 1983*a*: 99–100).

One outstanding contemporary example of artistic innovation resulting from supernatural inspiration received in a dream is the new men's house named Wambon at Washkuk village. In basic structure Wambon is identical to all other Kwoma ceremonial houses, but the man principally responsible for designing and building it (in the late 1970s), Marak of the Cheembireekii Wanyi clan, decorated its ceiling in a distinctive, entirely original way. Un-like the three other fully decorated Honggwama *korombo*, in which totemic paintings cover the whole of the upper halves of the ceilings, in Wambon the uppermost section on each side of the central ridge-pole is painted jet black. The black is broken only intermittently by limned depictions of aquatic creatures and objects of material culture found among neighbouring river groups. The lower edges of this huge black expanse are decorated with painted low-relief sculptures of tilapia fish, an introduced species that has proliferated to the point where it is now the most commonly seen fish in the Sepik (and adjacent lagoons), and the major source of animal protein for people throughout this region.

In the course of a discussion with me about the ceiling's iconography, Marak described how he had been inspired to construct Wambon by a dream he had had several years earlier. In that dream he found himself in a strange village. There, like Naluwen and Moyichey in Waley, he discovered a huge and lavishly decorated men's house. He walked into the building and there found several (long dead) clan 'fathers' sitting on slit-gongs joking amongst themselves. He noticed his (long dead) father's personal net bag hanging from a rope from the ceiling, and wondered why his father (who he dreamed was still alive) would have left the building and not taken it with him. He then cast his eyes over the striking but highly unusual ceiling decorations. He pointed to the sculptures of tilapia fish and asked one of the men what these were. The man replied, 'Spirits'. After this Marak woke up. He said that the decorative work in the building had so impressed him that he had decided to replace the undecorated men's house then standing in Washkuk with one painted and decorated in exactly the same way. Marak stated that the dream, and the image of the men's house he had seen in it, was the creation of one of his clan's spirits (*sikiyawas*). He was uncertain as to which spirit, but on the basis of the sculptures of tilapia fish and the limned depictions of aquatic creatures and objects of material culture from neighbouring river groups he had con-cluded that it was a water spirit (*pa sikiyawas*) located in one of the ox-bow lagoons at the southern end of the Washkuk Hills, adjacent to the Sepik. The large black expanse running down the centre of the ceiling in the building seen in the dream he interpreted as representing the jet-black water found in such lagoons. Marak replicated all of these features in Wambon.

The second set of sculptures in Waypanal that I wish to comment on stands at the front of the building against the major left side-post (Fig. 3.6), and consists of a full-length portrait of the mythological figure Mandiikapames, and a small free-standing sculpture of his dog Nukowur. Mandiikapames suffers from elephantiasis of the scrotum; his portrait sculpture accordingly depicts him with greatly enlarged testicles (*mandii*). This grotesque male figure is one of the most well-known characters in Kwoma mythology. One of the two narratives in which he figures tells how he lives on his own in a clearing deep in the forest. His only permanent companions are the fierce man-eating hunting dog named Nukowur and an equally fierce tusked boar named Womonggweya. Because of his condition Mandiikapames is unable to stand for long, and he spends his days seated outside his house with his huge testicles resting in a hole he has dug in the groud. Mandiikapames possesses a continuously burning fire, and when people from nearby villages are out hunting in the forest and find themselves in need of fire for cooking, they turn to him for this precious artefact of culture. Like the spirit Dowamu, Mandiikapames is a homicide and a cannibal, and whenever possible he kills the people who visit his house by bludgeoning them with a heavy stick he keeps beside him when they bend down to get a brand from his fire. The sculpture of Mandiikapames in Waypanal depicts him holding this stick under his right arm.

Mandiikapames's importance mythologically, and the prominence of the position he occupies visually in Waypanal, is to be explained, I believe, by the fact that he is a symbolic 'mediator'. To borrow a phrase from Lévi-Strauss (1975: 188), Mandiikapames is a 'master of fire': he possesses cooking fire, and as Lévi-Strauss (1975: 64–5, 335–6 and *passim*) has amply demonstrated, fire is an important symbolic marker of the transition from Nature to Culture—a leitmotiv in Kwoma myth and ritual. As a master of fire Mandiikapames can be seen as a mediator between Nature and Culture, and also between the raw and the cooked, unambiguous metaphors in Kwoma thought for Nature (or non-Culture) and Culture respectively. He can also be viewed as a mediator between a whole range of other culturally significant oppositions: between life and death—he is alive like a living human being, but being diseased is symbolically 'dead' (Lévi-Strauss, 1975: 61); between this world and the subterranean region from which, through various holes, the chthonian ancestors of the Kwoma are thought to have emerged—unlike normal people who walk on the surface of the earth, Mandiikapames sits on the ground with his grotesquely swollen testicles resting in a large hole; between the forest which is the realm of non-humans (ghosts, spirits, and animals and plants which humans exploit for food) and villages, literal clearings in the forest, in which humans live in groups (unlike Mandiikapames, who dwells quasi-culturally in antisocial isolation); and so on.[13]

Mandiikapames's role as a symbolic mediator and symbol of the transition from Nature to Culture is emphasized even more starkly in another myth where he appears transmogrified half as a man (his front) and half as a log of rotting wood (his back). The story tells how Mandiikapames, now known as Apunyowkunggu, lies immobilized and face down across a forest track. People who clamber over him assume that he is a lifeless, decaying tree trunk and thoughtlessly hack at his posterior with their adzes. Small boys grievously aggravate his tormented condition by using him as a target for their toy arrows and spears. Eventually the long-suffering Apunyowkunggu speaks to two men passing by and asks them to carry him far away, to a site to the north of the Washkuk Hills. On the way, with the two men's assistance, he ruthlessly avenges himself on the people who so mercilessly hacked him about by causing a giant tree they are felling during a village working bee to fall on and either kill or horribly mutilate them. In return for their assistance in this regard, and for removing him from the track, Mandiikapames provides the men with all the food they require on their long journey by vomiting up dishes of hot, freshly cooked food of kinds which Kwoma now enjoy, but of which they were previously ignorant. When the party reaches its destination the two men decide to stay with Apunyowkunggu, marry and raise families. However, the site at which they settle lacks the majority of the forest plants and animals which Kwoma now exploit for food, and as a further expression of gratitude to the men for the services they rendered him Apunyowkunggu vomits these into existence. Among the numerous food plants and game animals he vomits up are the various species of sago palm on which Kwoma now rely for their staple. The men live amicably with their half-human, half-rotting log bene-factor for a number of years, with Apunyowkunggu acting as baby-sitter when they and their wives go out to work in the forest. But in time Apunyowkunggu decides that his human companions are not sufficiently appreciative of the great gifts he has given them, including knowledge of such useful arts as the correct method of processing sago, and, to qualify somewhat the untroubled life of leisure they have been leading under his tutelage, he provides them with the negative gifts of theft and conflict between kinsmen: he teaches the two men to steal from each other, and causes the son of one to kill the son of the other in a quarrel. In revenge for introducing these evils, which now plague humankind as a whole, the two men attempt to kill Apunyowkunggu by burning him alive in his house; but like all spirits he is ultimately invulnerable, and escapes underground only to resurface out of harm's way far off in the forest, where he is thought still to be living today.

Like the two culture heroes Naluwen and Moyichey—who are themselves mediators between the natural and supernatural worlds—Apunyowkunggu, aided by another pair of men (cf. Lévi-Strauss, 1975: 332–3), is a major creator of Culture as Kwoma understand it. These myths make unmistakably clear, furthermore, that Mandiikapames/Apunyowkunggu originates Culture (in the form of cooked foods, edible plants and animals, and various useful arts) in direct exchange for the gift of the services which the two men who carry him away from the forest track provide. Like 'Waley', therefore, this narrative also directly associates the origin of Culture with the exchange of 'gifts' between the mundane and supernatural worlds.

Conclusion

Sepik ceremonial men's houses constitute some of the most outstanding contemporary art-forms in Oceania, but, as with much of the painting and sculpture from this region, they have yet to be systematically documented. The purpose of this analysis has been to provide a preliminary account of the art, architecture, and mythology of Kwoma ceremonial buildings, and to explore ways in which these structures communicate information about the society that constructs them. The analysis focused on ways in which myths associated with timbers used for such architectural features as the central ridge-pole, longitudinal side-beams, and central uprights evoke ideals which men hold in relation to themselves: of creativity in human and horticultural terms, and homicidal aggressiveness in the context of warfare. I also illustrated ways in which myths associated with sculptures in one men's house ascribe a central role to exchange in the origin of culture. Limitations of space prevent this last point from being elaborated here, but the central place that myths give to exchange in the origin of culture correlates directly with, and serves as a metaphor for, the central role that inter-clan exchange relationships based on marriage play in the constitution of contemporary Kwoma society. The three themes of masculine creativity, homicidal aggression, and exchange are all interconnected in Kwoma collective representations, for killing in warfare endows homicides with horticultural creativity, and, like marriage, is conceptualized as an exchange of fertility between independent political units.[14]

Notes

Some of the ideas presented in this essay were first developed in a paper delivered at the conference 'Sepik Research Today' held in Basle, Switzerland, 19–24 Aug. 1984, under the auspices of the Wenner-Gren Foundation.

Field-work among the Kwoma was carried out between Oct. 1972 and Jan. 1974 and at various dates afterwards. For grants in support of this research I am grateful to Monash University, the La Trobe University School of Social Sciences, and the Australian Research Grants Council.

1 My spelling of village names follows that in official use. According to the orthography adopted for Kwoma here, Bangwis should be spelled 'Banggwis'.

2 The conflation in various symbolic contexts of the military enemy with wives also helps to explain why sculptures of sexually mature (i.e. married) women are

typically characterized by an overtly 'phallic', aggressive iconography. Such sculptures typically have jutting, pointed clitorises; sharply angular pubic 'triangles'; and pointed, dagger-like breasts (see Bowden, 1983a: pls. 26 and 28a). On some sculptures the clitorises are so accentuated they could even be mistaken for penises.

3 Women's face-painting, however, is usually done by men.

4 Honggwama clans average only 6 married male members each.

5 For a description of Kwoma sorcery techniques see Bowden (1987).

6 Women's houses are generally also at a lower elevation than ceremonial buildings. For an analysis of the symbolism of relative height in this context see Williamson (1979).

7 Formerly, dwelling houses were more scattered than they are today.

8 In arguing that they are 'outsiders' and occupy physically and structurally 'peripheral' positions *vis-à-vis* men in villages, I do not wish to imply that Kwoma women have low status in everyday life. On the contrary, in everyday (non-ritual) contexts men and women have broadly similar statuses. Married couples, for instance, spend the great part of their lives working co-operatively, and generally amicably, together in gardens or around their houses; spouses are expected to be good friends and companions; spouses treat each other (like all adults) with great respect and circumspection; and domestic disputes leading to assaults on women (or men) are exceedingly rare. Like their husbands, Kwoma women are immensely self-assured and will fearlessly and vociferously defend their interests if they see these as being under attack, both in private and publicly during village meetings held periodically in ceremonial buildings. Notwithstanding the broadly similar statuses of spouses in everyday contexts, wives are regarded, and are explicitly referred to by their husbands, as 'outsiders' *vis-à-vis* the natal members of the communities in which they live, including their own children. The term for 'outsider' is *akar*, which also means 'other', 'unrelated', and 'enemy'.

9 All myths have prose and song versions. Song versions are performed on ceremonial occasions and during public working bees; prose versions, which contain their own songs, are told for entertainment around domestic hearths at night.

10 Flutes are secret ritual instruments played during the yam harvest ceremonies, the sounds of which men identify as the 'voices' of the spirits that preside over the ceremonies (Bowden, 1983a; see also Forge, 1966; Tuzin, 1980).

11 *Nyembi* is also the timber from which slit-gongs are made (see Fig. 3.7). These musical instruments, consequently, are the focus of an identical range of symbolic associations.

12 Although the first men's house bearing this name is described in 'Waley' as located in the land of the dead, Kwoma say that all personages in myths, whether 'people' (*ma*) or 'ghosts' (*gamba*), are really 'spirits' (*sikiyawas*). This means that Naluwen and Moyichey, despite being represented in 'Waley' as 'humans' *vis-à-vis* the 'ghosts', are themselves (like the ghosts) spirits.

13 Some might question the utility of the 'nature–culture' opposition in the analysis of the symbolic systems of non-Western societies (e.g. Strathern, 1980). Postmodernist critiques of this and similar 'structuralist' oppositions reflect a wider uncertainty as to the analytical value of the notion of 'society' itself (Gross, 1990).

In myth and everyday discourse, however, Kwoma explicitly and implicitly oppose their own positively valued social practices (what I refer to here as 'Culture') to the different practices of other Sepik societies (of which they disapprove) and situations posited in myths in which people behave differently (often radically differently) from the way they do now—and whose behaviour by contemporary standards is often decidedly 'incorrect' (*kapasek*). It is these images of anti-culture or pre-culture that I subsume here under the rubric 'Nature'. The numerous accounts in myths of 'incorrect' social behaviour is one reason why Kwoma find these narratives humorous.

14 Whitehead's article (1986) is a stimulating discussion of the wider symbolic associations between male fertility, aggression, and exchange in New Guinea societies. But her attempt to correlate the ways in which these notions are expressed in different types of fertility cult with variations in the constitution of political groups and the relative importance of men and women in inter-group exchanges applies only partially to the Kwoma, and thus has only limited explanatory value for this society.

References

BEHRMANN, WALTER (1950–1). 'Die Versammlungshaeuser (Kulthaeuser) am Sepik in Neu-Guinea', *Die Erde*, 3–4: 305–27.

BLOCKER, H. G. (1979). *Philosophy of Art*. New York: Scribner's.

BOWDEN, ROSS (1982). 'Lévi-Strauss in the Sepik: A Kwoma Myth of the Origin of Marriage', *Oceania*, 52/4: 294–302.

—— (1983a). *Yena: Art and Ceremony in a Sepik Society* (with a preface by Rodney Needham). Pitt Rivers Museum Monograph 3. Oxford: Pitt Rivers Museum.

—— (1983b). 'Kwoma Terminology and Marriage Alliance: The "Omaha" Problem Revisited', *Man*, n.s., 18/4: 745–65.

—— (1987). 'Sorcery, Illness and Social Control in Kwoma Society', in Michele Stephen (ed.), *Sorcerer and Witch in Melanesia*. Melbourne: Melbourne Univ. Press, 183–208.

—— (1988). 'Kwoma Death Payments and Alliance Theory', *Ethnology*, 27/3: 271–90.

FORGE, ANTHONY (1966). 'Art and Environment in the Sepik', *Proceedings of the Royal Anthropological Institute for 1965*. London: Royal Anthropological Institute, 23–31.

—— (1979). 'The Problem of Meaning in Art', in Sidney M. Mead (ed.), *Exploring the Visual Art of Oceania*. Honolulu: Univ. Press of Hawaii, 278–85.

GELL, ALFRED (1975). *Metamorphosis of the Cassowaries: Umeda Society, Language and Ritual*. London School of Economics Monographs on Social Anthropology, No. 51. London: Athlone Press.

GROSS, CLAUDIA (1990). 'Anthropology and the End of "Society"', *Anthropology Today*, 6/3: 18–19.

KAUFMANN, CHRISTIAN (1979). 'Art and Artists in the Context of Kwoma Society', in Sidney M. Mead (ed.), *Exploring the Visual Art of Oceania*, Honolulu: Univ. Press of Hawaii, 310–34.

Lévi-Strauss, Claude (1975). *The Raw and the Cooked: Introduction to a Science of Mythology*, i, trans. John and Doreen Weightman. New York: Harper & Row (first published 1969).

Mead, Margaret (1972). *Blackberry Winter: My Earlier Years*. New York: William Morrow.

Meggitt, M. J. (1964). 'Male–Female Relationships in the Highlands of Australian New Guinea', in James B. Watson (ed.), *New Guinea: The Central Highlands*. Menasha, Wisc.: American Anthropological Association (Special Publication, 66/4 (pt. 2)), 204–24.

Newton, Douglas (1971). *Crocodile and Cassowary: Religious Art of the Upper Sepik River*. New York: Museum of Primitive Art.

Plato (1984). *The Last Days of Socrates*, trans. Hugh Tredennick. Harmondsworth, Middx.: Penguin.

Schuster, Meinhard (1985). 'The Men's House: Centre and Nodal Point of Art on the Middle Sepik', in Suzanne Greub (ed.), *Authority and Ornament: Art of the Sepik River, Papua New Guinea*. Basle: Tribal Art Centre, 19–26.

Strathern, Andrew, and Strathern, Marilyn (1971). *Self-Decoration in Mount Hagen*. Art and Society Series. London: Duckworth.

Strathern, Marilyn (1972). *Women in Between: Female Roles in a Male World—Mount Hagen, New Guinea*. London: Seminar Press.

—— (1980). 'No Nature, No Culture: The Hagen Case', in C. M. MacCormack and M. Strathern (eds.), *Nature, Culture and Gender*. Cambridge: Cambridge Univ. Press, 174–222.

Sutton, Peter (1988). 'Dreamings', in Peter Sutton (ed.), *Dreamings: The Art of Aboriginal Australia*. New York: Asia Society Galleries, 13–32.

Tuzin, Donald F. (1980). *The Voice of the Tambaran: Truth and Illusion in Ilahita Arapesh Religion*. Berkeley: Univ. of California Press.

Whitehead, Harriet (1986). 'The Varieties of Fertility Cultism in New Guinea', *American Ethnologist*, 13/1: 80–99; 13/2: 271–89.

Whiting, John W. M. (1941). *Becoming a Kwoma: Teaching and Learning in a New Guinea Tribe*. New Haven, Conn.: Yale Univ. Press.

Williamson, Margaret Holmes (1979). 'Who Does What to the Sago? A Kwoma Variation of Sepik River Sex-Roles', *Oceania*, 49/3: 210–20.

Wurm, S. A., and Hattori, Shiro (eds.) (1981). *Language Atlas of the Pacific Area*. Pacific Linguistics Series C, No. 66. Canberra: Australian Academy of the Human Sciences/Japan Academy.

4

Making Skins: *Malangan* and the Idiom of Kinship in Northern New Ireland

SUSANNE KÜCHLER

This essay discusses the art objects produced as gifts for final mortuary exchanges in the northern part of New Ireland. Northern New Ireland art is known under the generic name *malangan* and comprises carved and painted sculptures, as well as others woven from fibre or moulded from clay, of astonishing visual and conceptual complexity and variety of design.

Malangan sculptures exemplify one of the few flourishing art traditions in contemporary Papua New Guinea. Not only are sculptures still carved from wood for the society's mortuary ceremonies, but, collected over a period of a hundred years, they also form one of the largest collections of a single art tradition held in Western ethnographic museums. From the indigenous perspective, however, it is not the sculptures as seemingly unique and identifiable objects which are of importance, but the engraved images which serve as renewable, relocatable and memorable entities in their own right.

This essay examines *malangan* art, as we know it through museum collections, as a historical phenomenon. I argue that *malangan* art, and thus also the indigenous conception of image reproduction, is inseparable from the colonial situation in which relations of land, labour, and loyalty became institutionalized in the mortuary context. Changes in the stylistic properties of the art, such as the decreasing complexity of design and excecution, seem to demonstrate a shift in its significance, or even its cultural demise; from a different perspective, however, the development of New Ireland visual culture over the last hundred years reflects processes of social formation with an accuracy not matched by any other record.

Such an understanding of *malangan* collections requires the revision of our assumptions about similar objects elsewhere which are seemingly produced for commemorative purposes. As funerary monuments, such sculptures can be thought of as evoking memories of the past, of the deceased persons thus commemorated, and of events associated with their lives. But such a function, as a sort of *aide-mémoire*, requires that the sculpture condenses and arrests the fleeting passage of time. The accessibility of a *malangan* sculpture, however, is confined to the few hours between public display and disposal in the forest (see Küchler, 1988; Melion and Küchler, 1991).

In an important sense, an image is carved into wood to be made absent and to establish in its absence a memorized visual culture. In its subjection to forgetting and imaginary reconstitution, the art object becomes memory and is made the subject-matter of future recollections. Rendered absent through destruction, the visual culture of New Ireland thus produced social memory by fashioning a distinct practice of recollection and transmission. In colonial New Ireland, knowledge of and involvement in this practice became the crucial factor in consolidating social relationships into emerging ritual confederations.

Museum collections of *malangan* art are testimony to the political economy of memory in colonial New Ireland; collected sculptures inadvertently arrest and fix the otherwise temporary manifestations of a practice of transmission which was founded upon the forgetting and controlled recollection of images. By describing a visual culture of which there is no objective trace (or, at least, there would not be but for museum collections) this essay aims to open up the analysis of vast collections of artefacts which, like *malangan* art, were granted durability only as a result of the Western preoccupation with the objects of visual culture. I do not wish thereby to establish a dichotomy between image- and object-centred cultures, but to propose a historical perspective on object destruction with all its social and cultural ramifications.

The Art Object as Gift

New Ireland is one of the islands of the Bismarck Archipelago to the north-east of mainland New Guinea, situated between New Hanover to the north and New Britain to the south. The island is divided geographically and linguistically into three groupings, which in turn are internally subdivided into localities with distinct dialects. The northern part of one island alone encompasses seven dialects, which are spoken by about 70,000 people who live in villages along the narrow western and eastern coastlines. The interior, which rises steeply and widens towards the centre of the island, is uninhabited except for one village. This is situated along the only road between east and west, at the narrowest point of the island where it was nearly severed during its geological formation. All the other villages in the north are perched along the edge of the mountain which, together with foreign-owned plantations, constrains the expansion of settlements and gardens.

Land shortage is one of the major complaints of villagers. Where possible, gardens are planted in the mountains, often hours away from the nearest coastal settlement. For gardening, both men and women have independent ties of co-operation which stretch across several adjacent villages and even into other language areas. It is common for a married couple to have plots in several gardens of neighbouring villages and to take up residence for extended periods in places even further distant. The production of cash crops is entirely dependent on this system of extended and graded landownership, since the planting of coconut palms in the interior of the island is not feasible in most areas owing to their inaccessibility by road.

The extended system of landownership is the framework for ritual confederations which cut across both village and language boundaries and encompass a number of scattered matrilineal subclans. I call these expanding social groupings ritual confederations, because the regulation of relationships over land, labour and loyalty is virtually independent of clan identity and marriage. It is articulated rather with participation in the mortuary ceremonies which climax in the production of sculptures.

The sharing of land, which is the determining criterion of a ritual confederation, implies mutual responsibility in assisting each other in work on the land and work for the dead (*haisok ine mamat*). It is articulated with the joint memory of an image which was seen once in a sculpture with the generic name *malangan*, by which name the ceremony which accompanies its production and display is also known. The intimate relation between land and sculptured image is highlighted by the indigenous term for skin (*tak*) which applies to both, and which is a synonym for those who regard themselves as linked in this way. Those who share land on account of sharing the memory of an image call each other 'of one skin' (*namam retak*).

'Membership' (*raso*) in a ritual confederation is governed by the right to reproduce a particular image in a sculpture. This right is acquired, in the short period of time following the public display of the sculpture, through presentations of money and indigenous currency to the current owners. It is, however, never the image as a whole which is carved and handed over in such transactions, but only a variation of the design involving an alteration of shape and/or a reduction in scale and complexity. The image is thus shattered into innumerable variations in the course of its repeated reproduction for exchange, and scattered across the north of the island by the expanded, regional networks of ritual confederations.[1]

As the main item of value transacted in ceremonial exchange, the *malangan* image is comparable to the arm-shells and necklaces circulated in the Kula exchange system in the Massim of New Guinea.[2] In contrast to the artefacts circulated in the Kula, however, those exchanged in the north of New Ireland are not used to decorate the body, but objects whose representational properties allude to the body. The likeness to the human body struck by *malangan* sculptures is not merely external, it pervades the project of sculpturing as a whole. Sculpturing is a process analogous to conception, which culminates in the coming to life of the carved wood and terminates in its death and decomposition. In the Kula, the arm-shells and necklaces continue to be circulated around the islands of the Massim, undergoing cultural elaboration in spatio-temporal processes expressed in the idiom of fame.[3] With *malangan*, cultural elaboration ceases upon the dissolution of the object and the freeing of the image. In both cases, to quote Shirley Lindenbaum (1984: 351), 'media of exchange that are not bodies (women) or body products (semen) [can] undergo cultural elaboration which in turn [will] form the basis for the hierarchical positioning of those who accumulate and exchange them'.

In northern New Ireland, it is not the sculptures themselves but the named images which are the objects of exchange, secured through the mnemonic transmission of art imagery (see Küchler, 1987, 1988; Melion and Küchler, 1991). A *malangan* sculpture is thus not a unique object which might function as an *aide-mémoire* of its own exchange history, as can be said for the Kula valuables. Rather, the, sculpture is a reconstruction involving practices of recollection and transmission, and thus carries the imprint of social memory work. I was struck when visiting this culture famous for its art to find virtually no trace of it (with the rare exception of a sculpture in the local mission waiting to be bought by a Western visitor). Yet, in their absence, the images that were seen once in sculptures are in fact ever present. Detailed knowledge surrounding images is overtly restricted to elder *raso*, that is, to both female and male 'members' of *malangan*. However, knowledge about the practice of recollecting and transmitting images is culturally salient and encapsulated in an idiom that is fundamental to the indigenous cosmology. This idiom is called *wune*, a term that can be translated as 'womb', 'smoke' or 'steam', and 'water-source'. With respect to *malangan*, *wune* refers to the 'template' or framework for the composition of an image which informs every one of its innumerable reproductions. It is an idiom which implies generation and connectedness, but also differentiation, and thus provides the foundation for the formation of ritual confederations as internally ranked and yet expansive and encompassing networks.

There is a finite number of named templates known in the *malangan* culture: six templates for wooden sculptures and a further three for sculptures woven from fibre or moulded from clay. A given sculpture is interpreted in terms of the relation between the carved image and a template or framework for the selection of motifs and motif combinations. The sculptured image, however, is not a copy of the template which is, as it were, impressed upon the mind.[4] Rather, it is actively reconstructed in the light of the relationships which it is anticipated its transaction will engender. Sculptures are thus a record of the reproduction of images for transaction, and are both visually and conceptually a trace of the relationships that are established or reaffirmed in this process (see Küchler, 1988).

Museum collections in the West contain more than 5,000 *malangan* sculptures taken from prominent and easily accessible villages in the north of the island between 1870 and the present day. The collected artefacts thus represent a rich account of the culture's exchange activity. These collections document a boom in production which seems to have reached a peak at the turn of the century when three or more sculptures were produced for any single mortuary ceremony. Sculptures are still today produced for the final mortuary ceremony, with more than one ceremony likely to climax in each of the many cemeteries of a village during the year. Collections also document the distribution of images in the *malangan* region, as well as patterns of constancy and variation in the formal properties of sculptures. There is thus enormous potential in museum collections for a reconstruction of New Ireland colonial history from an indigenous perspective.

Art as Likeness

Geographical constraints have played a part in the development of the *malangan* system of image exchange. Thus, while New Ireland as a whole has been under colonial and missionary influence since 1885, the position of the harbour and town at the northernmost tip of the island exposed the population of the north more rapidly and more consequentially to the measures taken by the German colonial government. As a result of the government's programme of resettlement between 1910 and 1930, mountain villages were deserted.

Tensions over land, caused by resettlement and the alienation of large stretches of fertile coastal land to foreign-owned plantations, were intensified by the mass migration that preceded the imposition of colonial rule. The people who came to live in the newly founded villages arrived from distant locations from which they were forced to move by warfare and/or marriage by capture. When talking about the past some of the inhabitants of northern New Ireland fittingly describe it as a 'refugee camp'. Today, matrilineal clans are scattered across the north, each fragment having its own long history of migration.

Under the impact of warfare and the resulting mass migration of clans, the moiety system which used to regulate relationships concerning land, labour, and loyalty ceased to be appropriate. People still acknowledge to which moiety their own clan belongs, but claim that they have no idea to which moiety the clan with whom they have come to intermarry might belong, since this clan is from 'far away'. With their relationships to each other and to their land shrouded in uncertainty, sculpturing for the final mortuary ceremony took on a very different significance. It no longer commemorated a past encapsulated in the biography of the deceased person, as this past was no longer a shared one and no longer provided the foundation for establishing a common understanding. Instead, the sculpturing of images itself became the focus of the production of memory, thus enabling the regulation of the newly founded relationships.

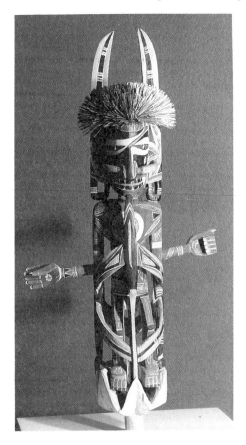

FIG. 4.1. *Malangan*; collected at
Medina, north-east coast of New
Ireland, 1931; painted wood (white,
red, black, and yellow); 56 in.
(143 cm.) high; Alfred Bühler
collection, Museum für Völkerkunde
und Schweizerisches Museum für
Völkskunde, Basle, Vb 10550.

Lamusmus 2 is a typical village situated in the Kara area on the west coast
of the island. All of its six resident clan units arrived in the area of the village
during the period of warfare, predominantly as a result of marriage by capture, but also in search of less exposed, more secure, and richer surroundings.
The original landowning clan, which is claimed to have been resident in the
area when the other clans arrived, has become extinct in this village, though
related subclans remain in adjacent villages. Three of the six currently resident
clans, which once intermarried with the now extinct landowning clan, consider
themselves to be jointly owning the land. They articulate their relationship by
performing a *malangan* dance called Langmanu at each others' mortuary
ceremonies. In order to renew their entitlement to the land in every generation, each of the three clans has to repurchase rights over Langmanu in the
exchanges which accompany the performance. New clans, which have joined
the village since its foundation during the period of resettlement, have acquired restricted land rights by supporting one of the three clans in their

ceremonial transactions, and by acquiring rights over versions of the dance which are reduced in complexity or require fewer dancers.[5]

There are three possible translations of the term *malangan*: 'likeness', 'heat', and 'notation'.[6] Each of these refers to a particular aspect of sculpturing, which in turn is inseparable from specific historical conditions.[7] The meaning 'likeness' can be related most clearly to the formal properties of the sculptures. It concerns first of all the range of materials used for sculpturing. The three materials—wood, fibre, and clay—are taken from different parts of the environment respectively associated with the social, the ancestral, and the spirit realms. The wooden *malangan* objects are best known, because it is these richly carved and painted figures that have reached Western museums in large numbers (see e.g. Fig. 4.1). The wood (*Alstonia scholaris*) is taken from the garden area separating the village from the mountains in the interior of the island. This area is called 'the place of the skin' (*laten*). The garden area is always also former or prospective settlement land, and is thus turned temporarily into a house-site which is called 'the place of the womb' (*larune*). The inversion of inside and outside associated with the land from which the wood is taken will emerge as significant for understanding the appearance or 'skin' (*tak*) of the carvings which I discuss below.

Only rarely seen in Western collections are sculptures woven from fibre. These can take a round, disc-shaped form or a figurative one.[8] The material is collected from the interior of the island known as 'the place of the ancestors' (*labung*). Unlike wood, which is carved over several weeks or even months by a professional who is paid for his work in pork and money, the fibre is woven by all the resident men of the matriclan of the deceased person over a period of about one week. The weaving of sculptures, particularly of the round *marwara*, completes the funerary work for deceased women, particularly for those who died unmarried or widowed, or who had severed their ties with their husband's clan, as well as for adolescents and children. This is in contrast to the carved sculptures which are produced to complete the funerary work of those women and men who worked, usually as a result of marriage, with members of at least one other clan on land which thus was also jointly owned.

Differences between the sculptures carved from wood and those woven from fibre can be traced even further. While it is expected and desired that rights over the reproduction of a carved image will be acquired by different clans resident in other settlements, in other villages, and even in other language areas, the image woven into a *malangan* is the unique property of a localized subclan. The woven image can only be transferred between different places so long as it remains within the matriclan. Such a transfer of ownership is usually caused by the permanent shift of residence of a woman on marriage.

The image moulded into clay stands midway between the other two types of *malangan* sculpture. The clay is taken from places associated with spirit beings called *rulrul*, which are believed to cause the death of humans by snatching their skins and to trick humans by appearing in disguise. *Rulrul* are neither dead nor alive, and hover on the edge of the sensible realm. These places, also known as *masalai*, are usually marked by a spring, or deep water-hole, and by gigantic trees which stand out from the otherwise limited undergrowth of the secondary forest. Ceremonial gardens are planted in these spots, as the earth is deemed to be more fertile there. This potent earth is moulded most commonly into the shape of a snake, which, like the spirit beings, is known to shed and renew its skin. While the body of the sculpture is made from clay, the head is carved.[9] The clay sculpture is produced by all the members of a settlement when a death suddenly occurs while preparations are under way for the final days of a *malangan* ceremony. Such a sudden death is usually attributed to the snatching of the skin by the spirit beings, or to sorcery.

Malangan as likeness thus captures the matrix of social differentiation as a process that originates in and through death, and through forgetting. Before returning to this point when discussing the second possible translation of *malangan*, that is, as 'heat', a few words are required on how sculptures, especially carved ones, represent 'likeness', not as a static state as found in the appearance of a person but as a process.

The mimetic function of carved sculptures is evident at a superficial level in their anthropomorphic character. Their production for funerary purposes has led some anthropologists to search for traces of *memento mori* in their formal properties. However, the shape of the face is standardized and gender is disguised in all *malangan* sculptures, and one sculpture can complete the work for several deceased persons at once. It has been assumed that the image carved into the wood functions like a seal or signature of the social group of which the deceased was a part.[10] This is, however, a misguided view. The image is reproduced in the light of anticipated, rather than past, social relationships; the flexible and dynamic character of group identity has no use for a fixed signature. The assumption that likeness resides in the sculpture's function as a sort of *memento mori* is, however, doubly misleading, as it results in the neglect of the most fundamental formal property of carved *malangan* sculptures—the overlaying of carved planes with painted patterns (see Fig. 4.1).

The key concept for understanding the sculptured image as 'likeness' is a process which can be described as a movement from inside to out. Visually, this process is discernible in the enveloping of the carved planes of the sculpture in a painted pattern. The carved planes refer to the exchange history of the sculptured image, or its 'outer' or 'public' identity, whereas the painted pattern signifies the present ownership of the image, or its 'inner' identity. Carved planes and painted patterns together constitute what is called the 'skin' (*tak*) of the sculpture. The conceptual inversion of inner and outer creates the visual impression of a textured surface or map that negates the three-dimensionality of carving.

Metaphorically, the visual inseparability of painting and carving, or of 'skin' as both container and envelope, alludes to the practice of transforming house-sites (or the place of the womb) into garden land (or the place of the skin). This transformation is instigated by the death of a person, and culminates in the making of an ancestor through *malangan*. The making of ancestors mirrors the process of merging the categories of inside and outside in both carving and land use. The transition from deceased person to ancestor is effected by the representation of an 'inner', remembered name in the form of a sculptured, externalized image and the transference of this name to a child or adolescent.[11] The name of the *malangan* image is given to a child that is 'baptized' during the ceremony. In this way, all personal names are names of *malangan* images. As a result, the distinction between 'ancestors' and 'the living' is effaced, in the same way that there is no distinction between the 'inside' and the 'outside' of a sculpture, or even of a person.[12]

There are further ways in which the carved *malangan* image constitutes a likeness. When first surveying the extensive museum collections of *malangan* sculptures, I was struck by the seemingly unlimited inventiveness exhibited in the different ways of composing motifs (of which there are actually only about twenty-seven) into ever different and 'new' combinations. Beneath this confusing richness of design, however, is a range of formal properties which are consistent and easily recognizable in sculptures regardless of where and when they were produced and collected.[13]

All figurative, carved sculptures, whether they are parts of a vertical or horizontal carving, have to exhibit a definite position which emphasizes the neck, the hands, and the legs (see Fig. 4.1). The position is simply that of a *malangan* dancer in arrested motion. The neck has to be straight so that the eyes look straight ahead, the hands in front or extended with the arms away from the body, while the legs have to be bent as far as possible while still permitting some movement. One could perhaps account for this feature of 'arrested movement', which impresses itself on anyone trying to perform a *malangan* dance, with reference to the conception of temporality underlying the periodically objectified *malangan* image.

The parts of the body which are emphasized in this way in both sculpture and dancer have, however, another quality which emerges when investigating their linguistic structure. All parts of the body, as well as all relationship terms, are divided into two types: terms ending in *ak* and those ending in *ang*. Skin (*tak*), neck (*wuak*), eye (*merak*), and hand (*mak*), as well as affinal relationship terms, are of one type, whereas all other body parts such as legs (*kining*) and all relationships, including the paternal one, within the matriclan are of the other type. Body parts of the latter type are thought to depend for their maturation on the observation of food taboos by the parents and those standing in *ang* relationships to the child. Body parts ending in *ak*, in contrast, are manipulated externally to ensure maturation, such as in the 'burning' of the skin of the new-born infant over the fire, or are the subject of taught discipline, such as the lowering or averting of the eyes in the presence of an elder or affinal relation and the avoidance of touch, and its mediation through exchange, among affines.[14]

Thus, in a complex way, the carved sculpture strikes a likeness with the conception of the person as composed of opposed and yet inseparable principles of communication and nurture. A full discussion of the metaphoric relation between sculpture and person would go beyond the scope of this essay. However, this relation has implications for an understanding of the production of the sculpture as a container of life force, with all the implications that has for the durability and appearance of the carving.

Making Skin

The carving of wooden *malangan* is called 'the making of skin' (*tetak*). It takes up to three months and the process is divided into twelve stages, each marked by payments to the carver (*retak*). The carver is a man who is usually of an age where he might have adult children, and who is thus in the right position of seniority to claim knowledge over *malangan*. He has inherited his skill, which is passed on to him with the secret knowledge of a magical potion of leaves which, when cooked and eaten, is thought to induce a vision of the image to be carved. Prior to dreaming, the carver is told in detail about the image by the eldest person of the clan responsible for the production of the sculpture. What he is told encompasses not only the image as it is remembered, sometimes from as many as twenty years ago when it was last seen in a sculpture, but also certain changes in shape and design which anticipate the forthcoming transaction of the image. The carver is well equipped to interpret what he is told verbally, since he will have joined the men in the carver's hut since his early childhood. Nevertheless, the dreaming during the night prior to the carving is held to be essential for the success of the work.

The significance of dreaming can be understood in relation to the recalling of the image which has not been seen, and has been effectively forgotten, for many years. The image is not just known and remembered as one would remember other aspects of knowledge, that is, with seeming effortlessness, but encapsulates, and is inseparable from, the practice of memory work with its component of active construction.[15] The carver is the mediator between the image that was handed over to forgetting and its reconstruction as memory in the process of its representation.[16]

However, carving is not just undertaken for the purpose of re-presenting a 'forgotten' image so that it can become shared memory. The image is merely the vehicle of something that is described as the seat of thought and creativity during life, and that becomes raw energy (*noman*) after death. We might call this potency 'vital substance' or 'life force'. Death is not thought of as the collapse and vanishing of life force, but the beginning of a long process of renewal which is initiated with bodily decomposition. As it is gradually freed from its earthly container, the life force grows in strength and becomes energy in the form of heat. Carving aims at recapturing this energy by channelling it into the image with its capacity for infinite renewal.

Once carved and painted in the funerary enclosure and transferred on to the grave during the last night of the four-day-long climax to the *malangan* ceremony, the sculpture is considered to be alive. It is 'hot' (*malang*) like a fire after it has ceased to flame. Heat is thus the second possible translation of the term *malangan*, and refers to the process of carving. Even today, when carvers use iron tools, heat is thought to be essential for the piercing of the many incisions which characterize carved *malangan* sculptures. Heat is also used for other practices analogous to 'the making of skin' in carving: a new-born infant is given a name by its paternal grandfather as he holds it over the heat of a fire, and fire is used for the clearing of the forest prior to planting a garden.

As the final stage in the funerary cycle, the carving of sculptures stands in a necessary relation to the funerary work as a whole. As a result, it is capable of synthesizing disparate aspects of cultural reproduction through the concept of 'skin': as a replacement for the body and as a container of life force, the sculpture is not just a reminder of a life once lived but is itself alive; as a vessel for the 'soul' or life force, the sculpture is marked by the relationships of the mourners; and as a wood carving, the sculpture situates such relationships *vis-à-vis* the land from which the tree-trunk was taken.

'The work for the dead' (*haisok ine mamat*), as the ceremonies following the burial of a deceased person are known, follows the physical decomposition of the corpse by eradicating the traces left on the land by the deceased person. During the first year after the burial, all ripening garden produce and produce harvested from trees or palms planted in the settlement of the deceased is taken to the funerary enclosure adjacent to the cemetery in which the deceased was left to rest before burial, and in which some years later a sculpture will be carved. The produce is eaten by the inhabitants of the village who have at least one garden which they plant together.

All the produce of the deceased's labour is consumed in this way as it ripens. About two years after the burial, when a pig marked during the funerary ceremony has grown sufficiently to be slaughtered, the final ceremony of this first sequence of rituals is performed. The ceremony, called *a gom*, is focused on the house of the deceased referred to by a term translatable as 'the place of the womb' (*larune*). It is a two-day event in which the clanspeople and affines of the deceased, who live in adjacent villages which rely on each other's resources, participate. The occasion is marked by ex-changes of cooked taro between the mourning clan and the deceased's affines, exchanges which invert the exchanges of raw taro between these same groups during the deceased's marriage ceremony. This dissolution of the ties be-tween these clans which were linked through the deceased is dramatized by the destruction of the house which was the product of the relationship.

The clan emerges as a separate entity most distinctly during the first major ceremony following the burning of the house. This three-day ceremony is called *a gisong* and is regarded as marking the completion of the decom-position of the body in the grave and the freeing of life force from its bodily container. On the last day of the ceremony, mourners of the same clan as the deceased gather at a place of commemorative significance. From there they walk back to the settlement of the deceased along pathways used by the deceased on his or her way to and from the gardens. While singing *malangan* songs, several men carrying axes rush along on both sides of the group and cut down any palm or other type of tree planted by the deceased person. *Laten* or 'the place of the skin', as the worked land is called, is rid finally of the last traces of the deceased person's productive life. Like the life force freed from the body, the land has been freed from a pattern of habitual usage, and can thus be reallocated.

The reappropriation of land is a matter of great concern, since no resident clan in the emerging villages can claim to have a territory of its own. The perceived shortage of land further supports the need to establish shared land-rights and to differentiate degrees of co-ownership. Thus, it is not just the freed life force which is incised into the wood, constituting the simple com-memorative function of the object, but also a statement about a new relation-ship involving a particular form of shared land-rights.

The clans competing over stakes in the land assert their position during a ceremony immediately following the burial of the deceased. Money and shell currency pass to and fro between the deceased's matrilineal clan and his or her affines, the amounts given deciding which of the two groups will be responsible for organizing the final *malangan* ceremony. Those bearing the responsibility are in an advantageous position, as they effectively control the reallocation of land. The other group is expected to seek to acquire rights over the carved image and thus also rights over the land.

Thus, there are a number of things already known before the beginning of carving. It is known who wants to establish a claim to control over the land, who will seek to have the right also to cultivate it, and also to what degree each would like to use it. There are, in fact, several degrees of land-ownership: involving, for example, the right to start one's own garden and to harvest coconut palms, the right to have a plot in a garden started by somebody else, and the right to harvest fruit-bearing trees. The named image that is carved into the wood thus not only recalls the identity of the deceased person *vis-à-vis* his or her clan, but also anticipates a future relationship to the land which defines a clan's political identity.

'The making of skin' is a process encompassing three stages which are analogous, but in an inverted sequence, to the process of the decomposition of the skin after burial. The first stage is the carving proper, the second the exhibition of the sculpture on the grave, and the third, almost unnoticed, the rotting of the wood after the spectacle of the 'death' of the enlivened sculpture on the grave. What is called the 'killing' (*lukfumari*) of the sculpture takes place seconds after its revelation to the assembled public who rush forward, throwing money and shell currency at its base. The money and shells are carried to the clan responsible for the carving, and this effects, by the clan's acceptance of the payments, the transference of the engraved image to the major bidding group. The kind of image received in this way indicates both possibilities for and restrictions on its future reproduction and, by implication, possibilities for and restrictions on the use of the lands. The use of land is authorized by the image that has become memory, before it is handed over again to forgetting.

The Fragmentation of the Image and the Sharing of Land

The carved image is thus not merely a signature of the identity of a clan. This would be the case if carving were interpreted as the rechannelling of life force only, and not also as a means of reallocating land among co-resident clans. Visually and conceptually, sculptures made as *aide-mémoires* of a person or clan would differ radically from *malangan* as evidenced in museum collections. On the one hand, such objects would embody identity in the form of an image which would appear as original and singular in relation to other images carved into wood. On the other hand, any change that occurred in the clan signature over time would be either the accidental result of a process of transmission or indicative of changes in the conception of clan identity. Neither can be said to characterize *malangan* sculptures.[17]

Every image is remembered by its relation to a named template, and is recognized by a central motif such as the 'eye of the fire' (*mataling*). This motif can be represented either as an encircled raised and dotted area in whose centre is an iris-like suction pod, or as an empty circle. This image can appear in three dimensions: as tall vertical shape, as horizontal shape, or as figurative shape. Of these, only the horizontal and figurative shapes (compare Figs. 4.2, 4.3, and 4.4) are still produced.

The different shapes are the products of the reproduction of an image for a transaction called *sorolis*. This transaction establishes a relation between two villages which have no present relationships established through marriage, but which do have a remembered relationship from the time of warfare as a result of the capture of a woman from one village by another. *Sorolis* may be carried out if the clan connected in this way to both villages requires an image for reproduction in a *malangan* sculpture, or if it simply wants to use the occasion of its taking responsibility for the carving of a sculpture to re-establish land-rights in the other village. The clan of the partner village brings its image to the clan organizing the ceremony. It is expected to hand over complete rights in the reproduction of the image, including knowledge about the type of fence surrounding the funerary enclosure at the time of a *malangan* ceremony, and about the house in which the sculpture is displayed, as well as dances and songs associated with the image, and certain formalized practices surrounding the distribution of food at the ceremony. To avoid the partner clan becoming unable to reproduce the image themselves in the future, but also to highlight the relationship created by the anticipated transference of the carved image, the image is reproduced as a detail projected into a different dimension—either from the vertical into the horizontal, or from the horizontal into the figurative. The sharing of an image in this way entitles members of the clan from either village to take up residence in the other village, but also implies a responsibility to assist the clan in the other village in all matters of the work for the dead.

The creation of variations of an image is the result of its recall for an anticipated transaction between settlements in the same or adjacent villages which have plots in each other's gardens. This mode of transference is called *aradem*. The transmission of an image in this way implies that it has to be reproduced exactly as remembered in order to be received, unless the settlement from which it was received goes out of existence due to failure to give birth to daughters, or the permanent departure of its remaining residents to another village. The image can also be recalled for reproduction with a reduced number of motifs if it is anticipated that it will be acquired by an in-marrying clan whose permanent residence is in another village. The reduction of motifs implies an even more restricted form of a share in the image and thus also in the land; often the image cannot be broken down any further and can thus only be reproduced as received, while the land to which rights are passed on in this way may not be worked upon but merely harvested.

Conclusion

As a result of the boom in the production of sculptures around the turn of the century, each settlement within a village owns variations of at least one image and often of two or more. Accusations of breaches of ownership rights are common in village court sessions. The likelihood that an image will be reproduced in contestable ways has increased as a result of a temporary ban on the performance of *malangan* ceremonies during the Second World War,

FIG. 4.2. *Malangan*; collected at Lessu, north-east coast of New Ireland, 1931; painted wood (black, white, red, and yellow); 83 in. (212 cm.) long; Alfred Bühler collection, Museum für Völkerkunde und Schweizerisches Museum für Völkskunde, Basle, Vb 10584.

FIG. 4.3. *Malangan*; collected at Fatmilak, north-east coast of New Ireland, 1931; painted wood (black, white, red, blue, and yellow); 85 in. (217 cm.) long; Alfred Bühler collection, Museum für Völkerkunde und Schweizerisches Museum für Völkskunde, Basle, Vb 10583.

as well as before it when the mission imposed a ban upon the carving of sculptures. It is reported that many elders died without the images to which they had rights having been carved, thus preventing the now senior generation from seeing them. Not having seen images which are still remembered by name leads many people to attempt either to acquire an image from another village or to invent a new one through dreaming.

Museum collections document the fact that, with the increasing reproduction of images for the regulation of land-rights, sculptures became less and less complex. Sculptures collected this century tend to be predominantly of the figurative kind, with fewer motifs than figurative sculptures collected at the close of the nineteenth century. This simplification is, however, not an indication of the 'death' of the tradition; rather, it is a consequence of the fragmentation of social relationships defined by the sharing of land, which is itself at least partly the result of the production of images for exchange.

Museum collections also document the degree to which sculptures produced today are far less incised. Sculptures collected before the turn of the century tend to be so heavily incised that they appear to have been carved to

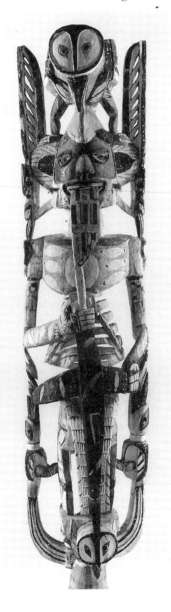

FIG. 4.4. *Malangan*; collected at Beilifu, south-west coast of New Ireland, 1931; painted wood (white, red, and black); $80\frac{1}{2}$ in. (205 cm.) high; Alfred Bühler collection, Museum für Völkerkunde und Schweizerisches Museum für Völkskunde, Basle, Vb 10576.

the point of fracture (Fig. 4.4). One obvious reason for the bulkier appearance of sculptures collected more recently is the time required for carving. With the imposition of colonial rule and the consequent introduction of a head tax and forced labour in the first decade of this century, the time set aside for feasting shrunk drastically. It has continued to shrink up to the present when every passing day seems to bring another kind of responsibility—towards the village, the provincial government, or the church. Another less obvious reason for the creation of sculptures that are less incised is the shift in emphasis from the rechannelling of life force to the regulation of land, labour, and loyalty. With the cessation of warfare, the increase in the birth rate and the decrease in the mortality rate around the turn of the century, the concern over reproduction focused on other pressing problems. Between 1910 and 1930 many new villages, with inhabitants from all parts of the island who had no common history except that of migration, were founded. Newcomers continue to arrive to the present day, partly because of the very possibility of changing residence frequently during adult life created by the transference of *malangan* images.

There is thus an inextricable and dynamic relation between social processes and the transformation of images carved into *malangan* sculptures. *Malangan* art could be a rare example of a gift-object with representational properties; yet how many other artefacts might have been categorized wrongly as 'ancestor sculptures' and their supposed purely commemorative function and symbolic status merely assumed?

Notes

The research in northern New Ireland on which this essay draws was carried out between Feb. 1982 and Feb. 1984. It was funded by the Volkswagenwerk Research Foundation, Germany.

1 For more detailed discussions of the exchange of *malangan* images, see Küchler (1987; 1988).
2 For the Kula, see above, p. 62, n. 2.
3 See Munn (1986). For a discussion of the classification of Kula arm-shells in relation to the duration of their circulation, see Campbell (1983).
4 Compare Scoditti's recent description (1990) of the production of Kula canoe-prows, in which the master carver's apprentice copies from existing models and from a template impressed upon his mind during initiation.
5 *Langmanu* is a term that can be translated as 'like a bird'. It designates a performance by 4–12 men. The dancers carry carved hornbill beaks (*cocomo*) between their teeth and wear feather head-dresses. The dance is seen as complementary to *malangan* sculptures.
6 I am referring here specifically to the meanings of the term in the Kara language; however, the range of meanings in other northern New Ireland languages is the same.
7 Popular memory suggests the existence of an uncarved sculpture in pre-colonial northern New Ireland, an uprooted tree called Kabal. A number of origin myths connect the creation of sculptures of the *malangan* type with the ravages of warfare.
8 The round sculpture is known as *warwara*, and the figurative sculptures woven

from fibre as *marandang* and *tetegap* (Powdermaker, 1933: 211; Lewis, 1969: 99–110).

9 The carved head is wrapped in leaves and stored in the roof of a house to be used again some time in the future.

10 See esp. Powdermaker (1933), Lewis (1969), Wilkinson (1978), Gunn (1987).

11 A person is known by a number of names which increases with age and the expanding range of affinal relationships. All these names, particularly the *malangan* name with which the deceased person was 'baptized' during childhood, are transferred around the time of death to new-born members of the matriclan and the extended ritual confederation. The name of the *malangan* image carved into a sculpture does not have to bear any relation to the *malangan* name of the deceased.

12 As elsewere in New Guinea, the condition of the skin, described negatively in terms of dullness or flakiness, and positively in terms of lustre and lightness, reflects upon a person's health and agility (cf. O'Hanlon, 1989).

13 There is, however, a recognized method for producing sculptures for sale to Western collectors which diverges from these principles.

14 Children are trained from their first day of walking to carry items such as food, tobacco, and areca nut from one affine to the other, for affines are not allowed to address each other directly or to come into any direct contact with each other.

15 See also Bartlett (1932), Casey (1987), Küchler (1987, 1988), and Melion and Küchler (1991).

16 See Melion and Küchler (1991) for a discussion of the carver as mediator.

17 See Gunn (1987) and Küchler (1985) for discussions of transference of ownership of *malangan* images.

References

BARTLETT, F. C. (1932). *Remembering: A Study in Experimental and Social Psychology.* Cambridge: Cambridge Univ. Press.

CAMPBELL, SHIRLEY F. (1983). 'Attaining Rank: A Classification of Kula Shell Valuables', in Jerry W. Leach and Edmund Leach (eds.), *The Kula: New Perspectives on Massim Exchange.* Cambridge: Cambridge Univ. Press, 229–48.

CASEY, EDWARD (1987). *Remembering: A Phenomenological Study.* Bloomington: Indiana Univ. Press.

GUNN, MICHAEL (1987). 'The Transfer of Malagan Ownership on Tabar', in Louise Lincoln (ed.), *Assemblage of Spirits: Idea and Image in New Ireland.* New York: George Braziller in association with The Minneapolis Institute of Arts, 74–83.

KÜCHLER, SUSANNE (1985). 'Malangan: Exchange and Regional Integration in Northern New Ireland, Papua New Guinea'. Ph.D. thesis, London School of Economics.

—— (1987). 'Malangan: Art and Memory in a Melanesian Society', *Man*, n.s., 22/2: 238–55.

—— (1988). 'Malangan: Objects, Sacrifice and the Production of Memory', *American Ethnologist*, 15/4: 625–37.

LEWIS, P. (1969). *The Social Context of Art in Northern New Ireland.* Fieldiana: Anthropology, 58. Chicago: Field Museum of Natural History.

LINDENBAUM, SHIRLEY (1984). 'Variation on a Sociosexual Theme in Melanesia', in Gilbert H. Herdt (ed.), *Ritualized Homosexuality in Melanesia*. Berkeley: Univ. of California Press, 337–61.

MELION, WALTER, and KÜCHLER, SUSANNE (1991). 'Introduction: Memory, Cognition, and Image-Production', in Susanne Küchler and Walter Melion (eds.), *Images of Memory: On Remembering and Representation*, Washington, DC: Smithsonian Institution Press, 1–46.

MUNN, NANCY W. (1986). *The Fame Of Gawa: A Symbolic Study of Value Transformation in a Massim (Papua New Guinea) Society*. Cambridge: Cambridge Univ. Press.

O'HANLON, MICHAEL (1989). *Reading the Skin: Adornment, Display and Society among the Wahgi*. London: British Museum.

POWDERMAKER, HORTENSE (1933). *Life in Lesu: The Study of a Melanesian Society in New Ireland* (with a foreword by Clark Wissler). London: William & Norgate.

SCODITTI, GIANCARLO M. G. (1990). *Kitawa: A Linguistic and Aesthetic Analysis of Visual Art in Melanesia*. Approaches to Semiotics 83. New York: Mouton de Gruyter.

WAGNER, ROY (1986). *Asiwinarong: Ethos, Image, and Social Power among the Usen Barok of New Ireland*. Princeton, NJ: Princeton Univ. Press.

WILKINSON, G. N. (1978). 'Carving a Social Message: The Malangans of Tabar', in Michael Greenhalgh and Vincent Megaw (eds.), *Art in Society: Studies in Style, Culture and Aesthetics*. London: Duckworth, 227–41.

5

Representing the Spirits: The Masks of the Alaskan Inuit

JARICH OOSTEN

Introduction

The word 'person' is derived from the Latin *persona*, 'mask'. In modern English the word 'person' usually refers to an individual being. 'Mask' and 'person' have become opposed. The mask is thought to hide a person, not to reveal him. Yet the relation between a mask and the person who wears it is usually more complex. A mask may hide someone by providing him with a new identity, but it may also represent someone's true identity. Thus the mask can reveal what the face hides, and it can hide what the face reveals. The use of masks in play and ritual usually provides an insight into the relations between different perspectives on human identity.

In the art of the Alaskan Inuit[1] masks assume a prominent place. The relations between the mask, its wearer, the being that is represented in the mask, the participants in play and ritual, and the spectators are elaborated in a variety of ways. In this essay I will examine the significance and use of these masks in traditional Inuit religion and society. I begin with a general outline of traditional society and religion as it existed in the eighteenth, the nineteenth, and, in the north of Alaska, the first half of the twentieth century.

Traditional Inuit Society

Inuit society consisted of local villages which might be organized in rather informal groupings for the celebration of religious festivals, or in temporary alliances in the case of warfare. Considerable variation in settlement patterns existed. Most Inuit led a nomadic existence. In winter, they lived in villages that might comprise forty to fifty people, or a few hundred in a large settlement. In summer, the village population usually dispersed in small family groups, spreading over the land for summer hunting. Kinship and various forms of partnership were the main factors determining the composition of a village. Kinship organization provided the framework for integrating non-related people through adoption or namesake relations into the family. Trade partnerships and dance partnerships also served to create relations of mutual obligations that were constitutive in the formation of local settlements.

Differences in status existed, depending on qualities as a hunter, number of sons, social abilities, and so on. In the north of Alaska, the *umealik*, the owner of a boat used for whaling, was often an accepted leader. He had no formal authority, usually recruiting his crew from his kinsmen and various partners. As a rule, Inuit society was not a ranking society. In some parts of South Alaska the situation was different. Thus, on Kodiak Island the institution of slavery existed; slaves were mainly recruited in warfare. Here, chieftainship was usually hereditary.

The question to what extent larger political units than local villages played a part in Inuit society has been much debated (cf. Fienup-Riordan, 1983). The first explorers and ethnographers gave varying accounts of the nature and organization of Inuit groupings. Usually they assumed the existence of tribes. Generally, group stability does not seem to have been very high (Pratt, 1984: 58). The names of the tribes are usually local ones referring to a particular area. When a group of Inuit moved to another area, they would usually be named after their new location.

Yet there was considerable cultural uniformity within particular areas, while different cultural areas exhibited significant cultural variation. The Inuit in a particular area were very much aware of these regional variations, and con-trasted their own traditions with those of other Inuit.

General descriptions of Inuit religion have been given by Lantis (1950) and Hultkrantz (1962). No comprehensive study of the religion of the Alaskan Inuit has yet been made, although Lantis's *Alaskan Eskimo Ceremonialism* (1966; originally published in 1947) was an important step in that direction.

I will confine myself here to an outline of the basic principles that deter-mined the organization of Inuit religion as it existed in its many variations among the Alaskan Inuit.

A Universe of Souls

In Inuit culture, all beings were thought to be endowed with a spiritual nature. A clear distinction between spirits as autonomous beings and souls as aspects of persons and objects does not apply to Inuit religion. Thus the concept *inua* (or *yua*), 'its person', refers to independent spirits as well as to a particular type of soul. The word is derived from the root *inu-*, 'human life', and is best translated as 'its human being' or 'its person' (cf. *inuk/yuk*, 'person', 'human being'). All animals had a human soul and were therefore potentially able to

PL. I. Trobriand canoe-prow. (*See also Fig. 2.1.*)

PL. II. Ceiling paintings, men's house Waypanal, Bangwis, New Guinea. (*See also Fig. 3.4.*)

PL. III. Slit-gong, men's house Wambon, Washkuk, New Guinea. (*See also Fig. 3.7.*)

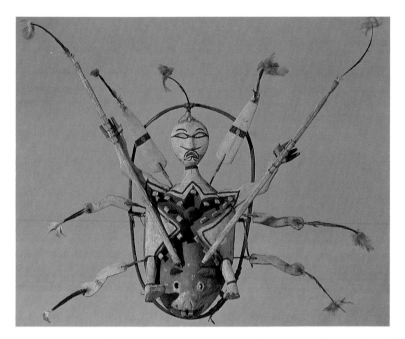

PL. IV. Inuit mask depicting a shaman's spirit astride a beaver. (*See also Fig. 5.3.*)

PL. V. Inuit two-face mask. (*See also Fig. 5.6.*)

PL. VI. Old Mick Tjakamara, *Children's Water Dreaming with Possum.* (*See also Fig. 6.3.*)

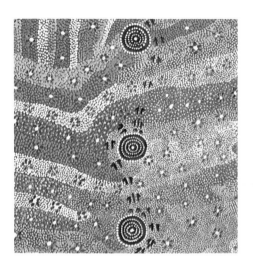

PL. VII. Charlie Eagle Tjapaltjari, *Wallaby Dreaming in the Sandhills*. (*See also Fig. 6.5.*)

PL. VIII. A Lamalera woman displaying a *patolu* cloth. (*See also Fig. 7.5.*)

PL. IX. Central panel of a Lamalera three-panel bridewealth cloth. (*See also Fig. 7.6.*)

PL. X. Circumcision ceremony at Yirrkala: outlining a design. (*See also Fig. 8.2.*)

PL. XI. Circumcision ceremony at Yirrkala: painting designs. (*See also Fig. 8.3.*)

PL. XII. Welwi Warnambi, *Dhuwa Moiety Wild-Honey Painting*. (*See also Fig. 8.6.*)

PL. XIII. Huichol prayer mats. (*See also Fig. 9.2.*)

PL. XIV. Huichol shoulder-bags. (*See also Fig. 9.4.*)

PL. XV. Huichol yarn painting. (*See also Fig. 9.6.*)

appear as human beings. In Inuit mythology we find many tales of Inuit visiting villages where animals lived in human appearance.

Hultkrantz (1953) attributes soul dualism, the contrast between a free soul and a life soul, to Inuit religion. Many ethnographers mention the belief in the existence of two or more souls. Rainey (quoted in Hultkrantz, 1953: 60) distinguishes between the *inyusaq* and *ilitkosaq* and Gubser (1965: 213) refers to soul dualism among the Nunamiut: *inua* and *taganinga*. Nelson (1983: 422) distinguishes between different types of soul:

My inquiries among the people developed the fact that they believe in the existence of two or three distinct forms of the spiritual essence or soul. The *ta-ghun-u-gak* or invisible shade, is formed exactly in the shape of the body, is sentient, and destined for a future life. Another is the *po-klihm ta-ghun-u-ga*, which has a form exactly like that of the body and is the life giving warmth. It is without sense and takes flight into the air when a person dies.

He also mentions a third kind of soul, a shade 'which is supposed to remain with the body and to possess evil powers', but he was unable to obtain more information about it. Nelson is not always clear and consistent in his presentation of the conceptions of the soul. Elsewhere (ibid. 394) he distinguishes between *yua* and *tunghat* in his description of Inuit masks: 'These may be *yu-a*, which are the spirits of the elements, of places, and of inanimate things in general; the *tunghat*, or wandering genii, or the shades of animals.' He also mentions the *inua*, which represents the power of an animal to transform itself into a human being: 'It is the thinking part of the animal and at death becomes its shade' (ibid.).

Ray has correctly pointed out that the *yua* and the *inua* are terminologically equivalent in, respectively, *yupik* and *inupik*. The words refer not only to conceptions of the souls, but also to masks. Therefore we may infer that masks generally represented the 'human person' or 'owner' of an animal or object. Ray thinks that the *inua* did not represent the individual animal but 'the vital force representing a chain or continuum of all the individual spirits of that genus which had lived, were living, or were to live' (Ray, 1967: 10). It seems more probable that a mask did not represent a particular animal, nor the vital force of its genus, but an animal as prototype of its genus. In the mask an unspecified animal is completely represented, that is to say, with its *inua* or its human being and appearance (Oosten, 1976: 33).

When considering the ethnographic data provided by Nelson, it seems most probable that the Inuit of the Bering Strait still preserved the well-known soul dualism of 'life soul' and 'free soul' that also existed among the Central Inuit in the concepts *inua* and *tarneq* (or derivations of these terms). The contrasts between *po-klihm ta-ghun-u-ga* and *ta-ghun-u-gak*, and between *yua* and *tunghat* both conform to this pattern.

The notion that men and animals share the same human nature is obviously of great significance in a hunting culture where men kill animals in order to survive. The unity of men and animals is emphasized in diachronic as well as in synchronic perspective. Nelson (1983: 394) states that among the Inuit of the Bering Strait

It is also believed that in early days all animate beings had a dual existence, becoming at will either like men or the animal forms they now wear. In those early days there were but few people; if an animal wished to assume its human form, the forearm, wing, or other limb was raised and pushed up the muzzle or beak as if it were a mask, and the creature became manlike in form and features.

Thus the distinction between men and animals did not exist in the mythical past in the way it does now. Yet the masks expressed the ancient unity of men and animals. In the context of ritual, the wearer of the mask represented the animal, and when he opened the mask his face represented the *inua* of the animal. The fundamental unity that existed in the mythical past was momentarily restored. Moreover, many tales relate how particular species of animals originated from human beings.[2] From a synchronic perspective we see that animals still possessed this essentially human nature. Many tales relate visits to and marriages with animals in human appearance (ibid. 516).

Objects, places, and cosmic phenomena could also have an *inua*. Many Inuit tales explain their human origin. There is, for example, the famous tale of sun and moon, originally a brother and a sister who had an incestuous relationship (ibid. 481–2). Thus the *inua* concept expressed the fundamental human nature of the universe. Sun and moon, animals, plants, and so on all had the same spiritual nature as the Inuit. As a consequence, animals were not just inferior beings to be killed at will by human hunters. They were spiritual beings, equal to man and to be treated with due respect. When game was killed, ritual injunctions had to be observed. The killed animal had to be given water to quench its thirst. The killing of the great sea mammals especially was connected with much ceremonial. The relationship between the Inuit and their game was a central issue in tales and rituals. Its significance was expressed in a complex code of contrasts (male/female, nature/culture, land/sea, etc.) that played a crucial part in traditional Inuit religion.

The second concept of the soul represented the essence of a being. It is not quite clear to what extent the two concepts were always distinguished. Sometimes they appear to have merged as two aspects of a particular type of soul. Here we will discuss them as two distinct conceptions, since they expressed different notions about human nature. The essence of a being, often thought to be its shade, played an important part in shamanistic treatment. Loss of this soul could be caused by ritual transgressions, but also by sorcery or witchcraft.

Loss resulted in sickness and, if a shaman did not return the soul to the body of the patient, in death.

The soul of the deceased survived its owner. It had to be treated with due respect, for otherwise it might turn against those who had offended it. An animal also had a soul that survived its owner. It was usually located in a central organ such as the liver, the kidneys, or the bladder. The shades of the dead were thought to linger for some time with their bodies before they departed to their destination in the land of the dead. During this period, ritual injunctions had to be observed. The same principle applied to the souls of the game that were killed.

Usually a land of the dead was thought to exist somewhere under the earth or sea. Sometimes another realm of the dead was located in the sky. A principle of reincarnation also existed. The deceased might reincarnate in a human being or in an animal. But if ritual injunctions were transgressed, the soul of the deceased might turn into an evil spirit.

A third concept, not quite a concept of the soul but closely related to it, is that of the name. Names connected namesakes, and namesakes shared the same spiritual nature. At the great feasts of the dead, namesakes of the deceased received presents from the relatives of the deceased. This custom suggests ritual identification between the living and the dead namesakes. This notion was also expressed in the name-giving procedure. At Norton Sound, a long list of names was recited at the birth of a child. The name that was mentioned at the moment the child stopped crying was given to the new-born baby. A shaman told Nelson how he had been to the land of the shades and was then reborn as a small child (Nelson, 1983: 433). Thus the name identified the person, and the notion of reincarnation connected animals and human beings in a great cycle of life and death. This notion was not systematized, however, and different concepts of the fate of the soul after death did not exclude each other. The souls of the ancestors might reside in the realm of death but at the same time they were thought to support their descendants and to live on in their namesakes. The *tunghät* or spirits were often souls of the dead, and they often functioned as helping spirits of the shamans.

The world of the spirits was not a closed universe. The number of spirits was virtually unlimited. Any Inuk could meet a spirit that had never manifested itself to human beings before. Spirit-people like dwarfs and giants played a prominent part in Inuit folklore. Individual spirits like the ten-legged polar bear or the giant thunderbird were often depicted in drawings and ornaments. The great spirits of sky, sea, and moon played a less prominent part among the Alaskan Inuit than among the Central Inuit. The spirit of the moon usually represented male virtues (hunting, male fertility). Though he played an important part in mythology, he was seldom represented in masks. I discuss his significance below.

The Practice of Inuit Religion

Although all Inuit could have encounters with spirits, the shamans were considered to be the religious specialists *par excellence*. They could perceive the true nature of animate and inanimate beings. They could see the *inua* of an animal and other spirits that were invisible to ordinary people. The shaman (*angatkoq, tunghalik*) was a mediator between spirits and men. He performed many different functions in Inuit society, such as treating the sick, procuring game in times of scarcity, divination, and influencing the weather. He had acquired an intimate knowledge and experience of the spirit-world. He controlled helping spirits who assisted him in his practices. Shamanistic seances were organized for different purposes: to obtain game from the moon spirit, to influence the weather, to treat the sick, and so on (Nelson, 1983: 427–34). Several shamans could perform in a seance at the same time. Shamans often competed with each other, cutting themselves with knives, diving under the ice, disappearing under the ground, and so on. These tricks were appreciated and applauded by other Inuit who probably knew very well how the shaman performed them, and appreciated his techniques and dexterity. Mythical tales relate impressive stories about the magical prowess of shamans of the past. These tales added prestige to the shamanistic complex. Shamanistic activities were interwoven with everyday life, and particularly in winter they might occur almost daily.[3]

The Alaskan Inuit celebrated many great feasts.[4] They usually took place in the *qasgiq*, the men's house which was the ceremonial centre of the village. Although women participated in the great feasts, the *qasgiq* was predominantly a male domain. It was usually a large, semi-subterranean construction. Here the men took their sweat-baths and performed ceremonies.

Petugtaq ('something tied on'), celebrated in the autumn, was a feast where men made replicas of the gifts they wanted from the women. The women made their choice from those replicas. Ideally they did not know for which man they were preparing a gift. The men often returned gifts to their female exchange partners. A partnership between cross-cousins appears to have been favoured, and sexual relations may occasionally have been part of the ritual (see Morrow, 1984: 116–18; Nelson, 1983: 360).

The bladder festival was the most famous hunting feast. Nelson and Lantis give extensive description of its celebration in St Michael and Nunivak Island. It lasted for several days of singing and dancing, and culminated in the return of the bladders of the seals to the sea so that the seals could reincarnate and be caught again (Lantis, 1966: 55–60). Preparations were complex (ritual bathing, usually in urine, painting of dishes, and so on). Masks were not used in the bladder festival, although animals were imitated in dance (Nelson, 1983: 379–93).

The great feast of the dead was celebrated among many Inuit groups.

Nelson was told that this feast was a male affair. Many people were invited from other groups. Frequent singing and dancing in honour of the dead constituted an important part of the feast. The organizers gave many gifts to the visitors, particularly to the namesakes of the deceased. The feast usually lasted for five days (ibid. 363–79).

At the messenger feast, one village served as host to other villages. Gifts were exchanged, and singing and dancing ensured good hunting. At this feast the dancers wore masks on several occasions. The messenger feast is often confounded with the inviting-in feast as described by Hawkes (1973), in which guests from other villages also participated. Masks were also used during this feast, which lasted for several days (Morrow, 1984: 131–5).[5]

According to Lantis (1966: 52–3), all the great winter ceremonials could be brought into one system, from which, however, she excluded the great feast of the dead:

> The hunting complex is characterised by the following features: 1) elaboration of the paraphernalia used in the ceremony, such as mechanical contrivances rigged up to be moved by strings, 2) use of ceremonial paddles, 3) mimic portrayals of hunting scenes and of animal behavior, often with the use of masks, 4) the concept of honoring the animals, doing as the animal spirits have instructed in some great mythical encounter between them and a human hero, 5) an exchange of real goods.

Although I do not think that all these elements were essential (in fact, features 1 and 2 did not always occur, and masks were not used in all feasts), Lantis is right in concluding that all the great feasts were closely connected. But I do think we have to include the feast of the dead in the great ceremonial complex. It referred to the great cycle of life and death, which was constituted by the Inuit who died and lived on in their namesakes and the animals which were killed and would be born again. This cycle was expressed in rituals of exchange between men and women, animals and men, and the living and the dead.

The life of the Inuit was structured by many ritual events of an initiatory nature. The name-giving ceremony identified the soul of a new-born child and determined its relation to its namesakes. The first catches of a boy and the first menstruation of a girl constituted their transition to manhood and womanhood. Ritual injunctions marked these occasions. Daily life was punctuated with ritual injunctions. Menstruation and giving birth were thought to make women unclean. In that condition they had to be separated from the hunters and their game, and to abstain from fresh meat. When a person died, the relatives of the deceased had to observe ritual injunctions. The period of mourning was ended by a ritual of purification (ibid. 20).

Hunting was very much a ritual affair. The preparation for the hunt, the killing of the game, and the preparation of the meat and skin were all subject to ritual injunctions. Preparation for hunting was often marked by fasting and abstinence from sexual intercourse. Once an animal was killed, its thirst had to be quenched, its bones were never to be gnawed by dogs, and so on. The launching of boats, the first catches of the season, and the end of the hunting season were marked by ritual celebrations. Ritual injunctions organized the separation of land-game from sea-game, men from women, life from death.

Men as well as women wore many kinds of amulets and charms to ensure good hunting and fertility. These objects were often handed down from one generation to the next. Daily life, therefore, implied a continuous application of ritual practices and rules. Much emphasis has been put on shamanistic activities, but all Inuit were continuously involved in religious practices. Only in those cases—such as sickness, scarcity of game, bad weather—where direct communication with the spirit-world was required was the intervention of a shaman necessary. Shamanism does not appear to have been a central issue in the great feasts. The main protagonists in the feasts of the dead were the relatives and the namesakes of the deceased. In the bladder feast the hunters played the central part. In other feasts like the messenger feast and the inviting-in feast the organizers of the feasts and their guests seem to have been the main protagonists.

The great religious feasts had important social functions for the distribution of goods and the development of status and prestige, as well as religious functions such as the assurance of, for example, good hunting and fertility (Sonne, 1978). Finally, they served to honour the spirits and to maintain the cosmic cycling of souls. The celebration of the great feasts may have varied considerably, depending on regional differences as well as on personal preferences of those who organized the feasts.

The flexibility and variety in the practice of Inuit religion was considerable. Yet there is consistency in the way fundamental contrasts such as male/female, life/death, Inuit/game operated in the practice of Inuit religion.

Inuit Masks

Masks are one of the most striking features of Inuit art. The tradition of making masks is very old in Inuit societies. Many burial masks have been found in prehistoric sites (see Fig. 5.1). They were usually placed beside the body. Masks had an important place in the traditional culture of the Alaskan Inuit, particularly south of Norton Sound. Here the cycle of the great feasts was also most elaborate. Boas (1901: 369–70; 1907: 564) attributed great importance to the influence of the Indian cultures of the north-west coast on Inuit culture. This raised the problem of the extent to which Inuit masks were influenced by Indian culture. The notion that Inuit masks were borrowed from Indian cultures was contested early on by Thalbitzer (1914: 640), and today such a view is no longer held. Inuit masks and north-west-coast Indian masks are stylistically quite different (Lantis, 1966: 90 ff.; Ray, 1967: 81 ff.). Inuit styles influenced Indian styles as well as Indian styles Inuit styles (Collins *et al.*, 1977: 177).

Many masks were collected in the nineteenth and early twentieth centuries, particularly in the Lower Yukon and Kuskokwim areas and south-west Alaska (Kodiak Island, Prince William Sound). We are best informed about their use and significance in the Lower Yukon and Kuskokwim area. It is not quite clear to what extent the collection of masks influenced the production of masks. In 1892 Murdoch (1988: 368–9) already speaks of 'commercial masks', and notes that the only female masks he found were new, and made for sale. The collectors may not only have stimulated the production of new masks, they may also have influenced the development of Inuit art as it adapted to the taste of the collectors.

Masks were usually carved from spruce and painted in various colours. There are great stylistic differences between masks from different areas, and their use and significance may also have varied considerably. Most masks were made for dancing. Feathers, ornaments, and so on were usually attached to hoops around a mask, so that it would move and sway when its wearer danced (see Figs. 5.2 and 5.3). Different types of mask existed: burial masks, forehead-masks (Fig. 5.2), finger-masks, masks attached to dance-staffs, and so on. Finger-masks were used by women. Ivanov (1930) has demonstrated that the elaborate hunting hats of the Aleuts and Inuit were derived from animal masks.

Generally our information on the use and significance of masks is scarce and contradictory. More than a hundred years ago Dall (1884: 133) wrote in his discussion of the masks from Norton Sound: 'It is to be hoped that when Mr Nelson has recovered his health he will unravel for ethnologists the mysterious web of fact and fancy which veils to us the relations and uses of Inuit masks.' Nelson published his excellent monograph on the Inuit of Bering Strait in 1899, but he did not solve the problems of Inuit masks.

Since the Second World War considerable progress has been made in the study of the use and significance of Inuit masks. Here, I would like to mention Himmelheber's excellent study of Inuit art on Nunivak Island (1953), Lot-Falck's examination of the Inuit masks in the Pinart collection (1957), Ray's study of Inuit masks (1967), and Black's important work on Aleut art (1982).

The Use of Masks

According to Dall (1884: 122) the use of masks was 'shamanic, pantomimic, and ceremonial; and in some exceptional cases mortuary'. It may have varied considerably in different areas. Zagoskin (1967: 119) reports that the Inuit along the coast did not use masks or visors in their public or private

FIG. 5.1. Burial mask from Ipiutak (prehistoric site near Point Hope); *c.* AD 350; walrus tusk with jet inlay; *c.*5 in. (13.0 cm.); American Museum of Natural History, New York, 60.1-7713 (courtesy Department Library Services, neg. no. 2A 13707A). These small burial masks were common in Ipiutak culture (Dumond, 1987: 116; Collins *et al.*, 1977: 22; Haberland, 1977: 21). Their significance is not known.

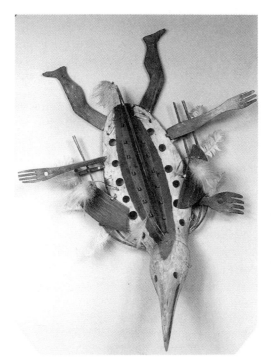

FIG. 5.2. Loon forehead-mask from St Michael, Norton Sound; collected by the Rev. Sheldon Jackson in 1892; wood, with white, black, and red pigment, seagull feathers, baleen strips with eagle down, willow bands, skin and woven fibre lashings and straps; $31\frac{1}{2}$ in. (80.0 cm.) long; Sheldon Jackson Museum, State of Alaska II.G.11.
The bird's 'spirit face' is hidden inside the movable outer head at the base of the neck. The double nature of the mask is expressed in its bird head and its human hands and legs.

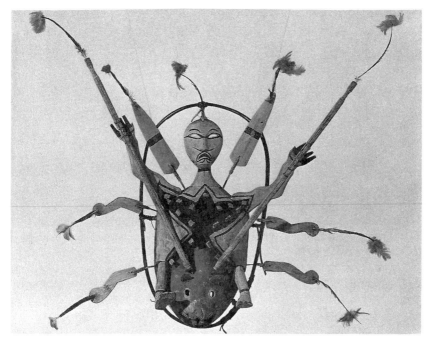

FIG. 5.3. Mask: shaman's spirit astride a beaver (?); from the lower Kuskokwim River; inscribed with the date 'September 1881'; wood, with white, red, green, and black pigment, jaeger feathers, willow bands, gut fibre lashings, and twine; 35 in. (88.9 cm.) long; Department of America, Hamburgisches Museum für Völkerkunde, 36.52.1. The mask represents an anthropomorphic being riding a beaver. The human body is open and its insides can be seen. This feature is quite common in the depiction of spirits in Inuit art. According to Haberland (1977: 38), it represents a helping spirit. He assumes the mask was used by shamans to turn themselves into helping spirits. See also Pl. IV.

ceremonies, but daubed their faces with graphite or charcoal at religious ceremonies. Along the Yukon and Kuskokwim Rivers, people performed dances which were 'actually the communication in mime of how the spirits have appeared to the shamans on certain occasions in their private lives, and as the spirit appears in the shape of an animal, a bird, or a man, or some other fantastic form, the shaman presents this with a mask together with a dance' (ibid. 226).

Zagoskin describes several masked dances. The idea that masks referred to unusual events, particularly meetings with spirits, is corroborated by later research. Nelson collected a mask of a crane: 'This mask was said to represent the inua of the crane. The maker was a shaman who claimed that once, when he was alone upon the tundra, he saw a sand-hill crane standing at a distance looking at him; as he approached, the feathers of the bird's breast parted, revealing the face of the bird's inua' (Nelson, 1983: 402). Meetings with spirits were also represented in carvings and paintings. Himmelheber gives several examples of stories which explained the origin of a mask, a carving or other artefact. He states (1953: 13) that masks were only used in the inviting-in feast and had to be burnt immediately after it. The only exceptions were the Ichzit forehead-masks, which were used at the great feast of the dead (ibid. 49). Apparently masks were often stored in the *qasgiq*. Sometimes they may have been thrown away and only recovered later for the benefit of Alaskan collectors (Dall, 1884: 125).

Shamans often had masks made by specialist carvers. As a rule, the masks referred to particular events or encounters with the spirits, and the carvers had to follow the instructions of the shamans. Usually shamans did not use the masks in their seances. Instead they were worn by dancers in performances that portrayed the shamans' great deeds (Himmelheber, 1953: 56–7). Himmelheber's information concerning the use of masks is corroborated by Morrow, who states that Mather's informations connected only the inviting-in feast to the use of masks (Morrow, 1984: 137).

Lantis (1966) and Ray (1967) have other views on the use of masks in ritual. Lantis (1966: 90) distinguishes between secular and religious masks: 'The latter were made by shamans or at his directions and were supposed to represent spirits he had seen in his visions.... Numerous animal-face and human-face masks worn by laymen might be carved by anyone.' Religious masks were used for religious purposes: 'Shamans wore masks in their public performances, although not normally while curing. Among the Aleuts and St Michael Eskimos, the shaman definitely wore a mask when communing with the spirits for the purpose of divining the future' (ibid. 91).

Lantis states that masks were worn in what appear to be secret society performances on Kodiak Island and in the Aleutians. She asserts that masks were used in some feasts, particularly in the messenger feast, where their use was essential. According to Lantis, they may have been used in the bladder feast, but their use there was not essential and may have been a later development (ibid. 91–2). Ray attributes an important role to the shaman as instructor of the carver of the mask. She acknowledges that masks were used much more in feasts than in shamanistic seances, but states that they were used for all occasions except outdoor dancing and memorial feasts for the dead (Ray, 1967: 34). Ray connects masks particularly to the messenger feast.

The ethnographic data are inconclusive. Masks were undoubtedly used in the inviting-in feast, and possibly in the messenger feast. They do not appear to have played a significant part in the great feasts of the dead or the bladder feast. They may have been used in shamanistic seances on Kodiak Island and in the Aleutians, but as a rule the shamans did not wear masks. Apparently masks played an important part in feasts where the significance of maintaining social relations with other communities was emphasized (inviting-in feast, messenger feast), while their role in feasts that emphasized relations with deceased ancestors and game was minimal (feasts of the dead, bladder feast).

Masks were not usually instrumental in establishing relations with spirits. They served to represent meetings with spirits, and expressed the human nature of animals and spirits: their *inua*. Masks were sometimes intended to be funny and to provoke laughter, but a clear distinction between secular masks and religious masks does not appear to have existed.

Hawkes (1973) gives a description of the celebration of an inviting-in feast at St Michael in 1911. A young missionary attempted to prevent the feast, but Hawkes's intervention with the military commander prevailed, and the feast was duly celebrated. On the third day the military commander was also invited, and the Unalit chief made a speech explaining the purpose of the dances. He stated (ibid. 3) that

they did not dance for pleasure alone, but to attract the game, so that their families might be fed. If they did not dance, the spirits (inua) who attended the feast would be angry, and the animals would stay away. The shades of their ancestors would go hungry, since there would be no one to feed them at the festivals. Their own names would be forgotten if no namesake could sing their praises in the dance. There was nothing bad about their dances; which made their hearts good toward each other, and tribe friendly with tribe. If the dances were stopped, the ties between them would be broken, and the Eskimo would cease to be 'strong'.

Thus the dances served to maintain the ties between Inuit and game, between Inuit and ancestors, and between different Inuit groups. The feast comprised many different dances. Masks were worn on several occasions. The first day they served to arouse the guests to laughter. These dances are described by Hawkes as comic dances and the masks which were used as comic masks. On the first day of the feast an old man wore an Indian mask and succeeded by his funny behaviour in making the guests laugh. The next day they had to pay for their defeat with gifts. On several occasions masks were used to represent game that was hunted. According to Hawkes (ibid. 12), the Inuit believed that they were possessed by the animal they depicted when dancing. At the end of the feast the shaman donned an *inua* mask. He daubed soot from the wall of the feast-house on his breast. This was supposed to put him in rapport with the spirit-guests. He lay in trance for a while, and finally informed the hunters that the *inua* had been pleased with the dances and promised their further protection for a successful season (ibid. 12–16). So in this feast masks were used for various purposes. They should have been destroyed after the feast, but in return for some gifts they were handed over to Hawkes to thank him for saving the feast.

The Significance of Masks

Unfortunately the first collectors usually acquired little or no information about the masks they obtained. Their attitude towards masks was often rather negative. Thus Lisiansky (1814: 210) notes: 'Their festivals consist chiefly of

FIG. 5.4. Human mask from
Chugach (Prince William Sound);
presumably collected by the Rev.
Sheldon Jackson at the end of the
nineteenth century; wood, with white,
black, and red pigment; $14\frac{1}{8}$ in.
(36.0 cm.) high; Sheldon Jackson
Museum, State of Alaska, II.CC.2.
There is also an impressive collection
of masks from Prince William Sound
and Kodiak Island in the Museum of
Boulogne, France. Most such masks
are anthropomorphic. Asymmetry is
less marked than in many of the masks
from the Kuskokwim and Yukon area,
but it still plays an important part
(Lot-Falck, 1957).

FIG. 5.5. Half-man, half-animal
mask from King Island; collected by
Wallace Barstow, provenance and date
unknown; wood, with black paint; $8\frac{3}{4}$ in.
(22.2 cm.) high; Hearst Museum of
Anthropology, The University of
California at Berkeley, 2-16645.
According to Ray (1967: 198–9), it is
an old King Island product,
representing Yeyehuk, the female
version of the half-man, half-animal, a
familiar figure in Inuit mythology.

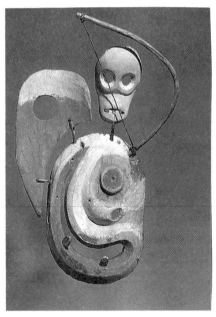

FIG. 5.6. Mask; probably from the Lower Yukon; collected by the Alaska Commercial Company, date unknown; wood, with white, grey-green, and reddish-brown paint, seal thong, baleen, and split root; 16 in. (40.3 cm.) high; Hearst Museum of Anthropology, The University of California at Berkeley, 2-5854. Two faces are represented. The principle of asymmetry is a marked feature of the lower face, but not of the upper face. According to Ray (1967: 172), it may represent the half-man, half-animal. See also Pl. V.

FIG. 5.7. Bird mask from St Michael or Pastolik; donated by the Alaska Commercial Company, probably collected *c*.1880; wood, with white and red pigment and seal-gut lashing; Hearst Museum of Anthropology, The University of California at Berkeley, 2-4597. The bird's bill is fixed and cannot close over the face. The mask clearly reveals the human spirit of the mask. Ray (1967: 174–5) provides a description of the mask.

FIG. 5.8. Whale's-tail design mask; probably from Point Hope and presumably collected by the Rev. Sheldon Jackson in the late nineteenth century; wood, with traces of fibre cord and fragments of nails; $11\frac{1}{8}$ in. (28.3 cm.) high; Sheldon Jackson Museum, State of Alaska, II.K.82. Although the animal aspect of the mask is less conspicuous, it clearly combines human and whale features. Generally, Point Hope masks are less elaborate and asymmetrical than masks from the Lower Yukon and Kuskokwim areas.

dancing, which differs but little from that of other savage nations, except that masks of the most hideous figures are worn. I was present at some of these festivals, but found nothing pleasant or amusing in them.'

Other researchers showed more interest. Generally, however, the significance of the masks was not adequately recorded and in most cases their significance is lost, not only to the anthropologists but also to the participants. Ray confronted some of her informants in St Michael with traditional masks. Usually they could not interpret them with any precision (Ray, 1967: 171 ff.). The interpretation of many features of Inuit masks is problematic. Himmelheber (1953: 58) informs us that on Nunivak Island the inner hoop around a mask represents this world, while the outer hoop represents the world above. We do not know to what extent a similar symbolism existed elsewhere. Masks were usually painted, but it is not clear to what extent an elaborate symbolism of colours existed.

Masks may be symmetrical (see Fig. 5.4), but many are asymmetrical. Asymmetry can be expressed in a slight difference between the right half and the left half of a mask (Fig. 5.5), in a completely distorted face (Fig. 5.6), in two apparently independent halves which constitute the mask as a whole, and so on. The reasons for this asymmetry may be explained by the nature of the masks themselves. When they represent animals, two distinct aspects of this being have to be represented: its animal nature and its human nature, or its body and its human spirit. Figs. 5.7 and 5.8 are examples of masks where this duality is clearly expressed. Many masks depict an animal as well as its *inua*. The duality of animal and human spirit may also be expressed in the relation between the mask and the man who is wearing it. The mask represents the animal while its human spirit is represented by the man who is wearing it. He can reveal himself, not as a person, but as a spirit, by opening the mask. Thus the animal, the spirit, the wearer of the mask, and the spectators are all involved in a process of representation and communication. Asymmetry can also be expressed in other ways. A mask may have a male side and a female side. A mask may consist of two halves, which are worn by different performers. The mask thus appears to express a notion of encompassment. Contrasting principles are encompassed in the mask: male and female, man and animal, etc.

In an admirable essay, Lot-Falck (1957) has tried to assess the significance of Aleut and Inuit masks in the Pinart collection in Boulogne. She pays much attention to the problem of asymmetry. Asymmetry is often confined to one particular part or feature of the mask such as the mouth or the eyes. Often one of the eyes is open while the other is closed. The mouth may be open or closed, round or wide, and often it is heavily distorted and exaggerated on one side of the face. This basic asymmetry has not yet been explained satisfactorily.

Lot-Falck analyses the significance of the different forms of the mouth on varying types of mask. The rounded mouth is taken to signify the emission of sound (outward-directed function of the mouth), while the wide mouth is taken to indicate bestiality and to refer to immoderate consumption of food (inward-directed function of the mouth) (ibid. 16). Her interpretation of the significance of different types of mouth does not, however, provide an explanation for the asymmetry of the mouth that can be found in many Inuit masks. She also attempts to explain asymmetry of the eyes with reference to certain beliefs of the Chuckchee. When the master of the reindeer closes one eye, he reduces the supply of reindeer. When he closes both eyes he withholds them completely. The closed eye of a spirit might therefore express a threat (ibid. 14). Although her interpretation of the significance of the closed eye is interesting, it is doubtful whether the significance of a particular feature in Chuckchee symbolism can be extended to Inuit culture as a whole.

Lévi-Strauss argues that if the plastic form of a mask remains the same among two different groups, its semantic functions will be inverted (Lévi-Strauss, 1975: ii. 29). The validity of this formula is problematic. Chuckchee and Inuit are usually considered as two different cultures, but interaction between them was always intensive, and the boundaries between the Siberian Yuit and the Chuckchee are often unclear. Therefore it is difficult to apply Lévi-Strauss's argument here. When should we consider two groups as different? Perhaps we should invert Lévi-Strauss' formula: if the plastic form of a mask remains the same among two groups while its function is inverted, the two groups should be considered as distinct cultures.

Fortunately, we do not have to have recourse to Chuckchee culture, since Inuit culture itself provides a rich symbolism connecting the categories of seeing and eating in the relations between men, animals, and the shades of the dead. Clear sight is associated with hunting outside the house. The hunter should perceive the game before it perceives him. He should be able to come close enough to kill it. Thus the hunter seems to be superior to the game with regard to eyesight. At the same time it is thought that the game gives itself willingly to the hunter. Here a distinction between the animal and its *inua* seems to operate. While the animal should not see the hunter, its *inua* sees him and decides whether the hunter behaves correctly and observes all ritual injunctions. If that is the case, the *inua* decides that the hunter will be successful.

The code of seeing and not seeing also pertains to the part of women in the hunting cycle. Women who are menstruating or who have just borne a child should remain inside the house, and when they have to go outside they should not be seen by the game. The wife of the hunter should remain passive; by not being seen she entices the game to be caught by her husband. Thus men and women play different but indispensable parts in the hunting process. Men are marked by their capacity to kill, women by their capacity to bring forth life.

The domains of fertility and hunting are strictly separated by ritual injunctions, and yet they are symbolically connected: the act of killing is a metaphor for the act of copulation. By killing animals the hunters maintain the cycle of life and death and allow the souls of the game to be reincarnated. Ritual injunctions maintain the correct relations between different categories. Transgressions of ritual injunctions result in inversions of relations, as can be illustrated by two versions of the myth of the origin of sun and moon as recorded by Nelson.

According to the St Michael version of the tale, sun and moon were originally an incestuous brother and sister. The sister wanted to evade her brother and floated away in the sky. She became the moon. The boy became the sun and has pursued her ever since. Sometimes he overtakes and embraces her, thus causing an eclipse of the moon. After they had gone their father became gloomy and spread disease and death among mankind. He became a cannibal, and he was finally bound by shamans. He can still cause disease. Nowadays, to prevent them from becoming evil spirits the dead are tied hand and foot in the position in which the father was bound in the grave box (Nelson, 1983: 481).

The Lower Yukon version relates how four brothers and a sister once lived together. The sister was very fond of the youngest brother, who was very lazy, while the other brothers were good hunters. One night the sister found the youngest brother beside her in her bed. The next day she served food to the three eldest brothers, but she gave none to the youngest. Then she cut off one of her breasts and offered it to him with some deer fat and berries, saying: 'You wanted me last night, so I have given you my breast. If you desire me, eat it.' Then she went out and climbed a ladder to the sky. The youngest brother followed her, but she floated away and became the sun. The youngest brother became the moon. He pursues her all the time, but never overtakes her. The moon gradually wanes until it disappears completely. Then the sun feeds him from the dish in which the girl had placed her breast. Thus the process of waxing and waning is explained (Nelson, 1983: 482).

In the first myth the moon is female, in the second male. Thus the gender of the moon varies, although the moon spirit is usually considered to be male. Both tales deal with the problem of incest in relation to the problem of eating the wrong food. The father eats people, the son eats the breast of his sister. Both take human food instead of animal food. The father is bound, and thus reduced to immobility, while mobility is the mark of the hunter. The dead might become hunters of men if they were not properly bound. When they were bound in the right way they could probably reincarnate as human beings or as game which was eaten by human beings. The brother is fed by a woman, while usually the men provide food for the women. In the first myth it is the father who is mistaken about food, not the brother and the sister. The latter have intercourse at the eclipse of the moon. In the second myth, they substitute an exchange of food for sexual intercourse; the moon never overtakes the sun, and can have no intercourse with her. The moon spirit was usually thought to be a great hunter and spender of fertility. In the myth, his relation with the sister is sterile, and he depends for his food on a woman. Sun and moon are caught in a never-ending cycle of pursuit. Thus ritual transgressions, notably the incest between a brother and a sister, turn human beings into food and spirits into eaters of human flesh.

The moon spirit has an incestuous relationship with his sister in the dark. In the versions of similar myths among the Central Inuit, the moon spirit was originally a blind boy confined within the igloo of his (grand)mother. After being immersed in a lake, he turned into a great hunter with clear sight (Oosten, 1976: 49–61).[7] In a variant of the Sedna tale recorded by Boas, the father of Sedna pierced one of her eyes (Boas, 1964: 177) and killed her. She was the mother and the mistress of the animals and she withheld them whenever she was angry. The association between seeing and hunting on one side and not seeing and female fertility on the other is particularly marked in these myths among the Inuit of north-east Canada.

In a mask, an animal and its *inua* are usually represented while a human being may wear the mask. Relations between these categories are marked in terms of the symbolism of seeing and eating. The contrasts between seeing and not seeing, between being seen and not being seen, between eating and not eating, between eating and being eaten, may be reflected in the asymmetry in the eyes and the mouths of the masks.

Men, women, game, and ancestors all contribute to the maintenance of the cycle of life and death. The separation of these categories by the observation of ritual injunctions is essential to the survival of society. But in wearing the masks structural boundaries can be transcended and contrasts encompassed. Animal, man, and spirit merge into one being.

It may be significant that masks did not play an important part in the feast of the dead and the bladder feast. These feasts deal with the interaction between Inuit, animals, and ancestors within a society. The separation of distinct categories should be preserved. In the inviting-in feast and the messenger feast, however, a society faces other societies. Here the *inuat* are worn, representing the ties between Inuit, spirits, ancestors, and game, and unifying them in the performance of the dances.

Conclusion

In Inuit religion all beings had a spiritual nature. Masks represented not only the outward appearance of a being but also its spiritual nature. The Inuit, their ancestors, and their game were part of a great cosmic cycle in which different categories were contrasted in terms of life and death, animal and human, male and female. When the Inuit wore masks, contrasting categories were united. The categories of men, animals, and spirits merged by represent-ing the *inuat*. Thus the ritual use of masks enabled the Inuit to encompass contrasts that structured their daily life. In the speech of the Unalit chief quoted by Hawkes, it was clearly emphasized that the performance of the inviting-in feast, with its dances, songs, and masks, was essential to the maintenance of the great cosmic cycle involving spirits, game, and Inuit.

Notes

1 The Inuit (singular Inuk) are commonly referred to as the Eskimo. The word 'Eskimo' is usually thought to be derived from an Athabaskan word meaning 'eaters of raw meat'. This etymology is contested (Goddard, 1984: 5–7). The Inuit themselves consider the word to be a pejorative. The Circumpolar Conference in Barrow in 1977 officially adopted 'Inuit' as a designation for all people who were traditionally referred to as Eskimos. Therefore I will use the term Inuit, although other terms like Yuit and Inupiaq are used by the people themselves.
2 See e.g. the tale of the owl-girl as recorded by Nelson (1983: 499), and the tale of the origin of caribou recorded by Rasmussen (Ostermann, 1952: 17).

3 For descriptions of shamanistic activities in Inuit society see e.g. Nelson (1983: 427–34) and Spencer (1977: 315–27).
4 Lantis (1966) provides an excellent survey of Inuit feasts. Her data can be supplemented by the results of Mathers's research in the Yupik area, where the great feasts were extensively celebrated (see Morrow, 1984).
5 Apart from these great feasts, smaller festivals were also held during the winter; see e.g. the doll feast described by Nelson (1983: 379).
6 See Fienup-Riordan's excellent study (1983) of the cosmic and ritual cycles in Inuit religion.
7 For a discussion of sun and moon see Lévi-Strauss (1978: 195) and Oosten (1983).

References

BLACK, L. (1982). *Aleut Art: Unamgam Aguqaadangin, Unangan of the Aleutian Archipelago.* Anchorage: Aleutian/Pribilof Islands Association.
BOAS, FRANZ (1901). *The Eskimo of Baffin Land and Hudson Bay.* Bulletin of the American Museum of Natural History, 15/1. New York: American Museum of Natural History.
—— (1907). *Second Report on the Eskimo of Baffin Land and Hudson Bay.* Bulletin of the American Museum of Natural History, 15/2. New York: American Museum of Natural History.
—— (1964). *The Central Eskimo.* Lincoln: Univ. of Nebraska Press (first published 1888).
COLLINS, H. B., DE LAGUNA, F., CARPENTER, E., and STONE, P. (1977). *The Far North: 2000 Years of American Eskimo and Indian Art.* Bloomington: Indiana Univ. Press.
DALL, W. H. (1884). 'On Masks, Labrets, and Certain Aboriginal Customs, with An Inquiry into the Bearing of their Geographical Distribution', in *Third Annual Report of the Bureau of Ethnology, 1881–82.* Washington, DC: Govt. Printing Office, 67–203.
DUMOND, DON E. (1977). *The Eskimos and Aleuts.* London: Thames & Hudson.
FIENUP-RIORDAN, A. (1983). *The Nelson Island Eskimo: Social Structure and Ritual Distribution.* Anchorage: Alaska Pacific Univ. Press.
GODDARD, YVES (1984). 'Synonymy', in David Damas (ed.), *Handbook of North American Indians*, v: *Arctic.* Washington, DC: Smithsonian Institution, 5–7.
GUBSER, NICHOLAS J. (1965). *The Nunamiut Eskimos: Hunters of Caribou.* New Haven, Conn.: Yale Univ. Press.
HABERLAND, W. (1977). *Nordamerika: Indianer, Eskimo, WestIndien.* Baden-Baden: Holle.
HAWKES, E. W. (1973). *The 'Inviting-In' Feast of the Alaskan Eskimo.* Ottawa: National Museum of Man (first published 1913).
HIMMELHEBER, H. (1953). *Eskimokünstler*, 2nd edn. Eisenach: Roth.
HULTKRANTZ, A. (1953). *Conceptions of the Soul among the North American Indians.* Stockholm: Ethnographical Museum of Sweden.
—— (1962). 'Die Religion der Amerikanischen Arktis', in I. Paulson *et al.* (eds.), *Die Religionen Nordeurasiens und der Amerikanischen Arktis.* Stuttgart: Kohlhammer, 359–415.

IVANOV, S. V. (1930). 'Aleut Hunting Headgear and its Ornamentation', *Proceedings of the Twenty-Third International Congress of Americanists (Held at New York, Sept. 17–22, 1928)*. New York: International Congress of Americanists, 477–504.

LANTIS, M. (1950). 'The Religion of the Eskimos', in Vergilius Ferm (ed.), *Forgotten Religions*, v. New York: Philosophical Library, 309–90.

—— (1966). *Alaskan Eskimo Ceremonialism.* Monographs of the American Ethnological Society 2. Seattle: Univ. of Washington Press.

LÉVI-STRAUSS, C. (1975). *La Voie des masques.* 2 vols. Geneva: Skira.

—— (1978). *The Origin of Table-Manners: Introduction to a Science of Mythology*, iii, trans. John and Doreen Weightman. New York: Harper & Row.

LISIANSKY, UREY (1814). *A Voyage Round the World in the Years 1803, 4, 5, 6, ... etc.* London: John Booth.

LOT-FALCK, EVELINE (1957). 'Les Masques eskimo et aléoutes de la collection Pinart', *Journal de la Société des Américanistes*, n.s., 46: 5–43.

MORROW, PHYLLIS (1984). 'It is Time for Drumming: A Summary of Recent Research on Yup'ik Ceremonialism', *Inuit Studies*, 8 (supplementary issue: 'The Central Yupik Eskimos'), 113–40.

MURDOCH, JOHN (1988). *Ethnological Results of the Point Barrow Expedition.* Washington, DC: Smithsonian Institution (first published 1892).

NELSON, E. W. (1983). *The Eskimo About Bering Strait.* Washington, DC: Smithsonian Institution (first published 1899).

OOSTEN, J. G. (1976). *The Theoretical Structure of the Religion of the Netsilik and Iglulik.* Meppel: Krips.

—— (1983). 'The Incest of Sun and Moon: An Examination of the Symbolism of Time and Space in Two Iglulik Myths', *Inuit Studies*, 7/1: 143–51.

OSTERMANN, H. (1952). *The Alaskan Eskimos as Described in the Posthumous Notes of Dr Knud Rasmussen.* Copenhagen: Gyldendalske Boghandel/Nordisk Forlag.

PRATT, KENNETH L. (1984). 'Classification of Eskimo Groupings in the Yukon–Kuskokwim Region: A Critical Analysis', *Inuit Studies*, 8 (supplementary issue: 'The Central Yupik Eskimos'), 45–61.

RAY, D. J. (1967). *Eskimo Masks: Art and Ceremony.* Seattle: Univ. of Washington Press.

SONNE, B. (1978). 'Ritual Bonds between the Living and the Dead in Yukon Eskimo Society', *Temenos*, 14, 127–83.

SPENCER, ROBERT F. (1977). *The North Alaskan Eskimo: A Study in Ecology and Society.* New York: Dover.

THALBITZER, WILLIAM (1914). 'Ethnographical Collections from East Greenland (Angmagsalik and Nualik)', in William Thalbitzer (ed.), *The Ammaassalik Eskimo: Contributions to the Ethnology of the East Greenland Natives.* Meddelelser om Grønland 34. Copenhagen: Reitzel, 319–755.

ZAGOSKIN, L. P. (1967). *Lieutenant Zagoskin's Travels in Russian America 1842–1844: The First Ethnographic and Geographic Investigations in the Yukon and Kuskokwim Valleys of Alaska*, ed. Henry M. Michael. Arctic Institute of North America, Anthropology from the North: Translations from Russian Sources, No. 7. Toronto: Univ. of Toronto Press.

PART III

Traditions and Innovations

6

Traditional and Contemporary Art of Aboriginal Australia: Two Case Studies

R OBERT L AYTON

In his introduction to the book *Ethnic and Tourist Arts*, Nelson Graburn addresses himself to the contemporary role of the arts among the communities of the 'Fourth World', whom he defines as 'peoples without countries of their own . . . usually in the minority and without the power to direct the course of their collective lives' (1976*b*: 1). Such peoples, he claims, rarely now produce arts for their own consumption, according to canons of taste unaffected by the dominant world; although he accepts that the Aboriginal community of Yirrkala in northern Australia is an exception (see Williams, 1976: 282). Rather, they produce arts primarily for sale to another culture. Graburn rightly argues that the 'inwardly directed' arts still made for, appreciated, and used by Fourth-World peoples within their own encapsulated communities function to maintain their separate identity, while those made for outside sale project an ethnic image determined to some degree by the alien purchasers' values. While some of the work produced for outside markets is of little artistic merit, Graburn points out that in what he terms 'reintegrated fine arts' outside inspiration may have a reinvigorating effect, as I think will be seen in one of the central Australian cases to be outlined in this essay.

Here, I want to consider the questions: (1) why it is that art provides an appropriate vehicle for the participation of hunter-gatherer communities in the market economy of the dominant society within which they find themselves encapsulated (Bailey, 1969: 149 ff.), and (2) how it is that such communities can preserve a viable culture out of which distinctive art-forms emerge.

The Cultural Context

In implying a distinction between traditional and contemporary art in central Australia, it is not intended to suggest that traditional art-forms have disappeared. Rather, the present context is one in which traditional forms, rooted in a persisting religion, have been supplemented by new commercial traditions. By means of the cash income, artists and their communities secure a degree of independence from state aid and the limited opportunities for employment offered by the dominant society (cf. Williams, 1976: 271–2).

I will examine the work of two central Australian groups: the Yankunytjatjara and Pitjantjatjara, who formed a traditional community, with their homeland stretching along the Petermann Ranges to Uluru (Ayers Rock); and the mixed community at Papunya, composed of representatives of the speakers of several Aboriginal languages drawn from country west and north of Alice Springs (see Map 1). All these people, from the Yankunytjatjara to the Warlpiri, share elements of a widespread traditional Aboriginal culture and today participate in the same ceremonial complexes, visiting each others' communities to celebrate rituals.

One of the hallmarks of central Australian Aboriginal culture is the distinctive art style. The essence of the style is the representation of the marks left by people and animals as they move across the landscape. Footprints are important, but there are other motifs, such as those illustrated in Fig. 6.1.

The commonest motif is made up of circles joined by straight lines, which typifies desert peoples' perception of their traditional way of life: camping and walking, camping and walking. Other subjects include hills, caves, vegetable foods, and stars: less obviously 'tracks' to us, but not to the artists.

As Munn (1973) recorded, figures may be drawn by people sitting in camp, telling stories. Women are especially fond of this, but men also do it when recounting legends. The figures are drawn in the sand with elegant movements of the hand, holding it edgeways on, or weaving it about from wrist to fingertip to utilize the hand's natural shape in as many ways as possible.

The art style also appears in ritual contexts, and Munn draws attention to the fact that the very simplicity of these motifs allows them to represent many things at once. They are ideally suited to depicting the transformations that ancestral heroes underwent during the 'Creation Period': the *tjukurrpa* or 'time of the law'. According to Aboriginal religion, both the landscape and society were shaped by the actions of ancestral heroes. These heroes established ceremonies and exemplified the law of social relations. In their travels they left camp-sites, tracks, and artefacts which became transformed into hills, creeks, rocks, and waterholes, many still today infused with the heroes' creative power. The process of initiation into the men's cults is largely concerned with the progressive revelation of knowledge: the simple narratives of myth are supplemented by complex song cycles, and paintings once said to have been done by 'some old people, one time' are revealed as the record of ancestral heroes (see Layton, 1985).

Munn wrote of Warlpiri art that the sacred paintings made by men, traditionally as ground paintings during ritual or on the dancers' bodies, are called *guruwari*, but that the word is also used of the fertilizing powers left by the ancestral heroes at sacred sites. Unlike painted motifs representing the

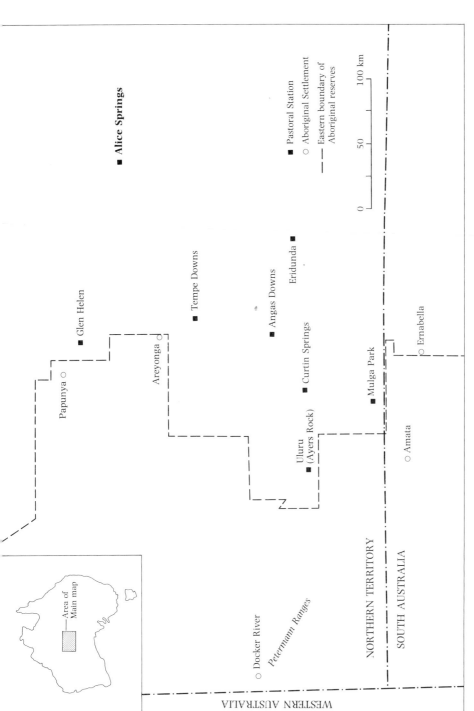

MAP 1. Northern Territory, Australia.

Person sitting down (buttocks and thighs)

 Possum tracks, with tail

 Finger marks made by man looking for witchetty grubs

 Fire, camp-site, waterhole

 Flowing water

 Kangaroo running

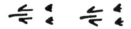 Kangaroo walking

 Camping and walking, camping and walking

FIG. 6.1. Typical motifs in central Australian art.

totemic ancestors, these powers are not 'conceive[d] . . . in any specific like-ness. They are simply a "strength" which infuses the soil' (Munn, 1964: 86). The features of the landscape which mark an ancestor's route—hills, caves, waterholes, and so on—are also sometimes called *guruwari*: these features are the transformed remains of the ancestor's camp-sites, footprints, weapons, and so forth.

The same painting may therefore represent both a snake hero, in the form of a wavy line, and the creek bed which marks his track. Concentric circles depicting a hero's fire also represent the waterhole which today marks the location of the hero's camp. By wearing a design, a dancer in ritual signifies his social allegiance.

It is important to distinguish between such related meanings represented in a single motif, and the meanings which potentially may be attributed to a single motif in different contexts. The first can be called the *multivalency* or *polysemy* of a motif; the second is in many cases simply *ambiguity*, engendered by the simplicity of the geometric forms (see Layton, 1977; Morphy, 1980).

Traditional art was, and is still, not executed for cash payments. Sacred designs, songs, and legends are primarily controlled by the clan in whose country the events described or depicted took place. Other individuals and groups hold secondary rights. Clans whose countries lie on the same dream-ing track share an interest in its songs and places. North of Alice Springs, it is the sisters' sons of clansmen who decorate men with their corporate design and prepare the dance ground. Enacting a ritual is a creative and political act in which the execution of paintings on the ground, in rock shelters, and on the bodies of dancers plays a central role (Bern, 1979; Layton, 1976). The abuse of designs—i.e. revealing them or their sacred meanings to women and children, or producing a design which belongs to someone else—is ultimately punishable by death.

Responses to Domination

Following Wolf (1982), it will be argued here that 'primitive' and 'peasant' societies respond differently to the domination of the West. 'Primitive' soci-eties may be defined as those which are small in scale, isolated, and relatively self-sufficient. They are exemplified by hunters and gatherers. While it may be hypothesized that this type of society retains traits characteristic of early modern human societies—i.e. from the Upper Palaeolithic (30,000 to 40,000 years ago)—modern hunter-gatherers have of course diversified and adapted as mankind has spread across the world. 'Peasant' societies, on the other hand, are those rural communities which belong to a wider political and economic system, which includes cities supported by tribute from the country-side. It is a type of society constructed on a larger scale, not insulated from outside events, and in which trade is a crucial ingredient. 'Peasant' societies are essentially a product of agriculture, and have therefore only existed during the last 10,000 years.

The expansion of European maritime trade from AD 1400 onwards, followed by colonial expansion, had quite different effects on 'primitive' and 'peasant' societies. Many, if not all, peasant societies in Asia and Africa were already linked into a trade network which ultimately ramified as far as Europe. As Europe moved from a peripheral to a central place in the activities carried out through that network, there was not necessarily (at first) any radical transformation: it was more like Edmund Leach's famous analogy of a sheet of rubber being stretched and pulled (Leach, 1961: 7) as the direction and intensity of trade changed. When Europe set out on colonial expansion, directly to control the states with whom it was trading, the indigenous political systems offered ready-made patterns of local government, on to the apex of which the colonial power could attach itself. Indeed this desire—to understand alien systems of government—was one of the main factors leading to the development of social anthropology as a practical research subject (Grillo, 1985).

On the other hand, the Industrial Revolution and the imposition of Western economic and political systems on the Third World often had dire effects on peasant societies. Bureaucracy recruits and funds its administrative hierarchy on principles different from those of the traditional systems of government it transforms. Ultimately, the rationale behind colonial expansion is to obtain food and raw materials and to open overseas markets for goods manufactured in the metropolitan country. In some cases, cash taxes were levied not simply to fund the colonial bureaucracy but, more basically, to make people sell their crops or labour to raise the money. Food, labour, and land became saleable commodities, and were no longer vested in households, descent groups, local labour pools, or small-scale systems of feudal distribution.

Primitive societies on the other hand, may be more resistant to colonial expansion and world trade. The fact that they have no identifiable system of government may (in favourable circumstances) allow them to operate 'invisible', egalitarian systems even when the colonial power believes them to be subjugated.

Because trade in subsistence goods plays little or no part in the economy of hunter-gatherers (or, indeed, of some pastoralists), they have nothing initially to offer the dominant society. Some live in environments too marginal for complex agriculture. This, in my view, is the reason why, when hunter-gatherers do enter the market, it is often by trading in the products of wild animals (particularly furs) or by selling the artefacts or art objects that constitute their few portable possessions. Both Inuit and north-west-coast American Indian communities entered commercial relations with the European market obtaining saleable furs through specialized hunting activities, and turned to selling art objects when the fur market declined (Brody, 1975: 22–3; Graburn, 1976c: 40–1, 58).[1]

Against the apparent resilience of hunter-gatherers, however, must be set factors stemming directly from the character of the 'primitive' economic and political system which make hunter-gatherer societies vulnerable to sudden and catastrophic change brought about by contact with Western colonialism (cf. Reynolds, 1982). Firstly, their low population density increases the impact of disease or abduction and limits their ability to put up physical resistance to invasion. Secondly, the marginal environments in which many living hunter-gatherer populations had been pushed even before the advent of European colonial regimes are susceptible to over-exploitation. Buffalo on the North American plains became virtually extinct in the twenty-five years up to the 1880s. The introduction of fur-trading in northern North American woodlands virtually extinguished moose and caribou between the 1850s and 1890s; the Ojibwa Indians were reduced to trapping fish and hare to survive (Rogers and Black, 1976, esp. 13–14). The low-latitude hunter-gatherers of central Australia depended principally on plant foods. They had their subsistence economy swiftly destroyed by the introduction of cattle-ranching: the cattle simply ate all the wild vegetable foods that provided 80 per cent of the Aboriginal diet. The Aborigines were reduced to dependence on government rations, and to work as stockmen and stockwomen. Their religion, however, survives, because it exemplifies their identity as a distinct culture, rejected by the dominant society (see Layton, 1986; Wallace, 1977).

Finally, the mobility of hunter-gatherers necessitated by the dispersed food supply makes it harder for them to assert visibly territorial rights, and hence they are more easily dispossessed. Once brought together on large settlements, wild foods accessible within walking distance are quickly exhausted. This is exemplified by the case of Yirrkala, in one of the richest areas of northern Australia. Within one year of its establishment, the resulting concentration of people in one place had the effect of exhausting the surrounding bush of wild foods. From the start, the mission attempted to find alternative means of livelihood for its Aboriginal population, in agriculture, and in arts and crafts to be sold for cash, thereby allowing people to buy in the mission-store goods produced elsewhere (Morphy and Layton, 1981).

Two Case Studies

PAPUNYA

Papunya, the first of the two central Australian cases I will consider, is one of a series of buffer communities set up by Church missions or the Federal Government along the western margin of European settlement. Although one

motive for their creation was to stop Aborigines drifting out of the bush
(particularly during the periodic droughts which afflict central Australia) and
crowding on to cattle stations or the margins of towns, government and
church policy was for a long time one of assimilation. Groups still living in
the desert were tempted or coerced on to settlements where it was intended
they would be prepared for integration into White society. The indigenous
political system continued to function undetected by White administrators and
teachers, and even traditional religious ceremonies continued to be held.

The geometric art of central Australia entered the commercial field in the
early 1970s. School children at Papunya were being taught European art and
craft techniques by a teacher named Geoff Bardon. When a project to
decorate the school with murals failed through the children's reluctance to
participate, Bardon and his Aboriginal teaching assistant decorated a small
area with traditional Aboriginal motifs. This aroused the interest of other
adults, who made contributions culminating in a large mural representing the
Honey Ant Dreaming, painted in mid-1971. Bardon came to appreciate the
problems which the men faced in choosing what to paint: they had to be
subjects which could safely be seen by women and children, and subjects
acceptable to the many different totemic groups living at Papunya (Bardon,
1979: 14). It was a context quite different from that of traditional, closed
ritual. At one point the large mural included 'realistic illustrations of ants and
bees, similar to the European manner', but Bardon seems to have encouraged
the men to replace these with indigenous U-shapes and other motifs.

When the murals were complete, the men who had made them began to
visit Bardon to ask for brushes, boards, and paint, simply so that they could
continue to paint Dreamings. Bardon was authorized to buy a collection of
these paintings for the school, and seems to have taken the initiative in
marketing others at Alice Springs (Bardon, 1979: 15). Hence the men became
aware of a new way of earning cash. Similar events occurred more recently
at another central Australian community, Yuendumu. These are described,
largely by the Aboriginal participants themselves, in the book *Yuendumu Doors*
(Warlukurlangu Artists, 1987).

Many early paintings contained detailed representations of body paint
and head-dress designs on ritual figures, sacred objects, and mythological
ancestors. As far as can be told, this seems to have been something specific to
the new art-form at Papunya. However, while such figures were acceptable if
painted in private, they were not acceptable on paintings which were going to
be displayed and sold: 'Other Aboriginal people saw the work on display and
were angered . . . Almost overnight, as it were, all detailed depictions of
human figures, sacred and other "dangerous" aspects were removed or
modified in shape' (Kimber, 1981: 8). Even if 'almost overnight' is only a
figure of speech, this change dramatically demonstrates the continued political
coherence of the community. There is an interesting contrast here with the

sequence of events at Yirrkala documented by Morphy (Morphy and Layton, 1981). In northern Australia, clans have greater political autonomy *vis-à-vis* the wider Aboriginal community, and several clans adopted distinctive strategies in response to the desire to conceal secret aspects of the art tradition. The most successful response, moreover, was to concentrate on silhouette motifs of animals, plants, and humans which lacked the multi-valency of geometric forms. At Papunya, lines, arcs, and hatching reminiscent of the designs on sacred objects were replaced by dots which, while they appear in some traditional, sacred paintings 'are rarely in themselves more than very generally significant' (Kimber, 1981: 8); they are like phonemes, not morphemes.

Early paintings from Papunya are illustrated in Bardon's book (1979), while later work is illustrated in *Mr Sandman Bring Me a Dream* (Crocker, 1981). Some of the paintings in Bardon's book include explicit figurative motifs readily decoded by the Western eye. *Children's Kadaitcha Dreaming*[2] by Long Jack Phillipus Tjakamara (Bardon, 1979: 32–3) depicts the 'Kadaitcha Man' who punishes breaches of Aboriginal law. The executioner has decapitated an offender with his boomerang; beside him is his ceremonial head-dress. *Man's Love Story* by Clifford Possum Tjapaltjari (ibid. 56–7; Fig. 6.2 here) depicts a pole on which hair string has been wound to help catch a girl through love magic. The pole seems to stand out of the picture in a stunning perspective which, as Bardon notes, is quite different from the two-dimensional, map-like conventions of traditional Western Desert art. Yet the man who sits by the pole is depicted with a conventional arc, and his dancing movements with a line of footprints. *Children's Water Dreaming with Possum* by Old Mick Tjakamara (ibid. 36–7; Fig. 6.3 here) also combines the two types of perspective. Water flows from one pool to the next along the creek bed, seen from above, while in the sand human footprints signify a boy looking for food. A possum runs parallel to him among trees on the bank. The possum is indicated by his track, whereas some of the trees are shown with trunks in a 'compressed "bird's eye" distortion that was characteristic of Aboriginal signs first departing from abstract symbols'. Yala Yala Gibbs Tjungarrayi's *Spider Dreaming* (ibid. 48–9; Fig. 6.4 here) is closer to Western Desert traditions. Concentric circles and radiating lines at the painting's centre depict both the spider's web and its representation on the ceremony ground. Men singing are shown as double arcs; a reference, I suspect, to the use of pairs of boomerangs to beat out the rhythm of the songs. The version of *Man's Water Dreaming* painted by Old Walter Tjampatjimpa (ibid. 24–5) shows the water spirit singing in his cave as a double arc, with water flowing in undulating lines from the waterhole before him on a simple background of dots. The same artist, writes Bardon, 'painted many [other] versions all around the same theme, far more elaborate than the example shown but these contain secret information' (ibid. 42).

FIG. 6.3. Old Mick Tjakamara, *Children's Water Dreaming with Possum*; 1973; acrylic on board; $17\frac{1}{4} \times 22\frac{7}{8}$ in. (45×58 cm.); courtesy Papunya Tula Artists. See also Pl. VI.

FIG. 6.2. Clifford Possum Tjapaltjari, *Man's Love Story*; 1973; acrylic on board; $17 \times 22\frac{7}{8}$ in. (43×58 cm.); courtesy Papunya Tula Artists.

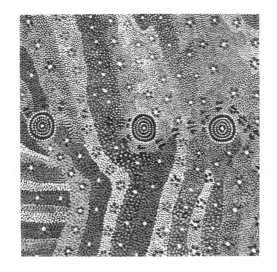

FIG. 6.5. Charlie Eagle Tjapaltjari, *Wallaby Dreaming in the Sandhills*; 1977; acrylic on board; $19\frac{3}{4} \times 19\frac{3}{4}$ in. (50 × 50 cm.); courtesy Papunya Tula Artists. See also Pl. VII.

FIG. 6.4. Yala Yala Gibbs, *Spider Dreaming*; 1971; acrylic on board; $15\frac{3}{4} \times 31\frac{1}{2}$ in. (50 × 80 cm.); courtesy Papunya Tula Artists.

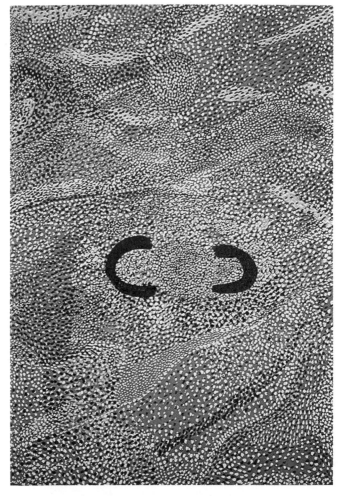

FIG. 6.6. Johnny Warrangula Tjaparula, *Old Man's Bush Tucker Dreaming*; 1972; acrylic on board; $17\frac{3}{4} \times 19\frac{3}{4}$ in. (40 × 50 cm.); courtesy Papunya Tula Artists.

The last two examples are more completely pointillist in style. Charlie Eagle Tjapaltjari's *Wallaby Dreaming in the Sandhills* (ibid. 58–9; Fig. 6.5 here) depicts lines of sandhills as curved bands of dots in shades of pink, orange, yellow, and cream. The wallaby's tracks move from waterhole to waterhole, running in the sandhills and pausing to drink where his tail and forefeet have rested on the sand. In Johnny Warrangula Tjaparula's depiction of *Old Man's*

Bush Tucker Dreaming (ibid. 26–7; Fig. 6.6 here), only the arcs showing where two men sit facing each other stand out from a dazzling background of yellow, red, and black dots.

By removing figurative elements and telling details, Papunya artists exploited the ambiguity inherent in the geometric-art style to produce aesthetically accomplished and characteristically Aboriginal art-works without further undermining the religious system that inspired them.

PITJANTJATJARA

The solution of the Pitjantjatjara, who entered the craft market a decade earlier, was more radical, in that it made almost no reference to the religious system. Yet the objects were attractive enough to Whites to give the Pitjantjatjara the economic independence they needed to return to the bush and keep alive their religious traditions.

The earliest White settlements in central Australia were established in the 1870s: Alice Springs on the overland telegraph line, and a few pastoral stations in the surrounding bush. As I have noted, cattle and sheep had a devastating effect on the semi-desert habitat. Major water sources were tapped with bores and tanks, while soaks and rock holes quickly became polluted by wandering stock. Plant foods were rapidly eaten out. Aboriginal foraging was directly affected by the lack of water and vegetable foods. Indirectly, it suffered because the small lizards and marsupial mammals which provided most of the meat supply were also losing their habitats. In the 1930s, central Australia had twenty-nine species of marsupial and eight types of rodent. By 1970, fourteen of these species were extinct.

Settlement spread west from the railway and overland telegraph towards Pitjantjatjara country during the 1930s.[3] In an attempt to alleviate its effects, church missions were established on land threatened by the spread of pastoralism. Ernabella, an early sheep station, was bought by the Presbyterian Church in 1936, and Areyonga was set up in 1943.

Unfortunately, the 1930s were also characterized by a major drought in the region further west which was the Pitjantjatjara heartland. Traditionally, people would have avoided drought by moving east towards the desert margin. This time, when they moved, they found the land occupied by White missionaries and pastoralists. They could not feed themselves, and the Whites were reluctant to let them move freely: the pastoralists because they feared their stock would be speared or driven from water; the missionaries because (with the honourable exception of the Presbyterians at Ernabella) they wanted to replace the traditional Aboriginal culture with a European one. In 1953, a schoolteacher at Areyonga described settlement as a planned step in 'the breaking down of the tribal spirit'. At Ernabella, however, the mission encouraged Aboriginal independence. The founders of the mission argued that it 'must have an industry, to provide work and help finance the cost of caring for the natives'. When Ernabella station was taken over by the mission, it held 1,950 sheep. In 1948, spinning, weaving, and dyeing wool provided the foundation for a successful craft industry. Because feral dogs (dingoes) threatened sheep flocks, the government paid a bounty of 7s. 6d. on each dingo scalp it received. Ernabella also encouraged Aboriginal bands to return to the bush on 'dogging' expeditions: the Australian equivalent (in some respects) of the North American fur trade.

After the 1930s, Aboriginal people moving in the area along the margin of pastoral settlement were still able partly to live off the bush. Despite the fact that Areyonga and Ernabella are 150 miles apart, people living in the two communities stayed in contact with each other.

The traveller Groom, at Areyonga in August 1947 while preparing to make an expedition to Uluru, met sixty Pitjantjatjara men who had come from Ernabella to arrange an initiation ceremony with the Pitjantjatjara at Areyonga (Groom, 1950: 115). Later, as he returned from Uluru, Groom met other men travelling north.

During the early years of settlement life, the collection of dingo scalps was one of the main sources of income which allowed people to buy the supplies they required to return to the bush. It was on 'dogging' trips that many people who are now adults first saw their parents' country.

During this period, Aboriginal groups were able greatly to increase their mobility by adopting camels for transport. Camels were brought to the region by early explorers and settlers, and for the Pitjantjatjara to learn how to handle them was a considerable adaptation. Not only did they use these animals for their own purposes, but White travellers like the anthropologist Mountford (1950) and the writer Groom (1950) were taken through the area by Aboriginal men with their own camel teams. When Rose was carrying out field-work at Angas Downs in 1962, he saw Aboriginal people use camels to travel to Areyonga, Ayers Rock, the Petermann Ranges, and Erldunda Station (Rose, 1965: 22). It was not until major floods in 1974 that camels were abandoned, and replaced by cars.

As tourism developed in central Australia during the 1960s, mobile parties of Aboriginal people became increasingly apparent to tourists and White authority. Selling artefacts to tourists replaced 'dogging' as the chief source of cash for these parties.

In 1964 an Aboriginal group was reported to have threatened some tourists in an attempt to sell them artefacts. One man attempted to jump on to the moving car. As the nervous driver accelerated, he had the impression that the man fell between car and caravan. A patrol officer was sent to investigate, but failed to discover any injured man, let alone a corpse. He did, however, find how widespread artefact sales had become. By the time of my field-work (1977–9), two classes of artefact were manufactured for sale. One consisted of traditional implements, some (like spears) reduced to the size traditionally made as toys; the other class consisted of carved animal figures. All the animals, and frequently the artefacts, were decorated with geometric patterns impressed with a heated piece of fencing wire. Although people sometimes carved animals which were among their totemic 'dreamings', and although some burnt-wire designs incorporate motifs from the traditional art style, neither was part of the pre-contact culture.

The two carvings illustrated in Figs. 6.7 and 6.8 are representative of this tradition. Both were carved at Uluru (Ayers Rock) during 1977 for direct sale to tourists, but were bought from the makers by myself. The brush-tailed possum was found in eucalypt groves growing close to water until the 1930s, when it was hunted locally to extinction for its fur, at a time when pelts could be traded with Europeans in exchange for food and clothing. The possum figures in the legends of its carver's country, Katatjuta (the Olgas). Using love magic, Wayuta, the possum, stole two girls from Uluru. The perentie lizard was carved by Nipa Winmati. Although Ngintaka, the perentie, is an important figure in legends of the region, he has no association with the legends of Uluru, which is Winmati's country, and this figure is a simple representation of the animal as a source of meat in hunting.

The origin of this tradition of wood-carving is hard to unravel. Brokensha, who has described the growth of European-organized craft production at Amata—a settlement created from Ernabella's overspill—is probably right to see the introduction of spinning and weaving by Ernabella Mission in the 1930s as one of the roots of contemporary artefact production (Brokensha, 1975: 68–9). According to Rose (1965: 93), burnt-wire decoration originated at Angas Downs in about 1960, at the suggestion of Arthur Liddle, the station owner, himself a man of Aboriginal descent.

It is consistent with government attitudes of the 1960s that the Welfare Branch failed to see in these groups camped by the roadside a strong attachment to Aboriginal culture; they saw simply a denial of conventional White values. The Aborigines were 'itinerant', 'loitering', or 'unemployed'. The assistant director wrote to tourist operators asking them to stop their customers paying Aborigines for artefacts or for taking photographs: 'the few shillings that the Aboriginals make in this way tends to undo the work of my officers'. Giving money to people had 'an adverse effect in our attempt to teach the natives the principle of work for pay and makes them parasites on society'. The same letter contrasts the 'unsanitary' nature of roadside camps with the facilities for health care, education, employment, and training on settlements. The advantage of an education which helps Aboriginal people deal with our culture is undeniable, but these groups were not simply begging by the roadside, they were often engaged in educating their own children in the traditions of Aboriginal culture. The following year one group was reported to be holding a ceremony at Mulga Park 'so that important tribal

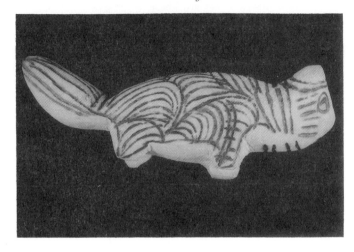

FIG. 6.7. Figure of a brush-tailed possum; carved at Uluru
(Ayers Rock) in 1977 by Ngapala Jack from the wood of the
desert poplar (*Codonocarpus cotinifolius*; *kaluti* in Yankunytjatjara)
and decorated with lines burnt on with a hot wire; 9 in. (23 cm.)
long; author's collection.

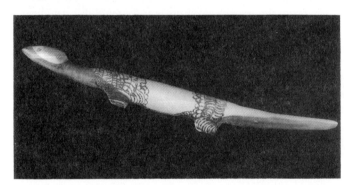

FIG. 6.8. Figure of a perentie lizard carved at Uluru (Ayers
Rock) in 1977 by Nipa Winmati from the wood of the mulga
tree (*Acacia aneura*; *kurrkurr* in Yankunytjatjara) and decorated
with lines burnt on with a hot wire; $27\frac{1}{4}$ in. (69 cm.) long;
author's collection.

beliefs and rituals could be passed on from the elders to the up-and-coming
influential middle-aged men', while the district welfare officer reported: 'it
seems that their main object of being in the area is to carry out rituals that are
important to them'.

In 1964 the Welfare Branch decided to stop refunding pastoralists for rations they issued to itinerant groups, but within a year it was clear that this would not stop people moving through the area. For instance, at one homestead that October, two hundred and fifty Aborigines gathered for a ceremony. The owner refused to supply them with rations, knowing he would not be refunded, but people survived by sharing the rations of the thirty-eight permanent residents, collecting bush food and buying supplies from the store with the proceeds of artefact sales. The patrol officer who records this comments that it will be 'very difficult to reduce the number of ceremonials held'. The district welfare officer commented:

In view of the fact that this Branch is not prepared to support them, they have maintained themselves by living off the country to some extent, but like many other people in the Territory these days, supplementing their other means of subsistence by exploiting the tourist industry. . . . They have developed a modus operandi . . . which in their experience gives them the most success.

He refers to the frequent efforts of patrol officers to get people to return to missions or government settlements, and remarks: 'In most cases he has found them to be a most agreeable group who have every intention of moving on "next Monday" but in actual fact they move when they are good and ready and return to the area as soon as they feel the need.' In 1966 a prolonged drought came to an end, and it is significant that since then people have relied less on artefact sales to support themselves. Their use of the cash economy was evidently an expedient they were happy to forgo when, as a patrol officer pointed out, the good rains had provided plenty of surface water and more game in the Aboriginal reserves bordering on the westernmost cattle stations.

Two events brought this period of movement along the margin of White settlement to an end. The first was the foundation of Docker River Settlement in Pitjantjatjara country in 1967. The second was a radical shift in government policy during the early 1970s. It was realized that the policy of collecting people together in settlements and missions had to a large extent failed.

Various Aboriginal groups had approached the Department of Aboriginal Affairs (the Federal body that took over from the Welfare Branch), saying that they wanted to leave settlements and move back to their own country, partly to maintain their traditional links with the land and partly to escape the pressures of life among groups with whom they would not traditionally have lived. This development was financed and encouraged by the Australian Government during the 1970s. Artefacts are still made on Pitjantjatjara settlements and at Uluru (Ayers Rock), but in many cases they are now sold in Alice Springs, Darwin, and even further afield through Aboriginal marketing organizations, rather than through direct exchange between the carvers and tourists.

The Critical Response

It may be acknowledged that the Pitjantjatjara carvings have to the Western observer less aesthetic appeal, and lack the depth of imagery and metaphor embodied in Papunya paintings. Yet while less successful (in our terms) as works of art, they were paradoxically more successful in preserving an autonomous, indigenous culture. Today the Pitjantjatjara are respected among other Aboriginal communities of central Australia for the tenacity with which they preserved their religious traditions. To understand the cultural context of the art—its meaning and purpose for the artists—it is necessary to look beyond purely artistic considerations, to the place of hunter-gatherer cultures in the modern world. The success of the artists' work cannot, however, be appreciated without also considering how it has been received in the wider Australian community.

Nelson Graburn suggested, in his introduction to the book cited at the start of this essay, that members of 'civilized societies' appreciate ethnic and tourist art for what it tells others about its new owner. The display of such works in the living room advertises the owner's encounters with exotic cultures and his aesthetic preference for the handmade over the mass-produced (Graburn, 1976*b*: 2).

Academic Australian reactions to the commercial success of central Australian art have been ambivalent. Some argue the work should be judged by Western artistic criteria, others that to be valued at all it must retain its exotic Aboriginality. Some critics have asked how far Aboriginal art can change, yet remain Aboriginal. Are, for instance, the use of acrylic paints or water colours, the incorporation of European stylistic techniques, and, indeed, the sale of art on a market symptomatic of the decline or dilution of Aboriginal tradition? Such critics still tend to regard Aboriginal culture as static.

The archaeologist and art historian Vincent Megaw has defended the right of Aboriginal artists to incorporate elements of European culture in their work, and urges that contemporary Aboriginal art be appreciated for its 'human value'. Megaw, however, objects to the White artist who, inspired by Aboriginal art, declared: 'To me, Papunya paintings are unique in the world in that they derive from a forty thousand year tradition but supersede modernism' (Megaw, 1986: 36). This, as Megaw points out, reassimilates Aboriginal art to old-fashioned theories of unilinear evolution. It is as if, having mastered art as religious icons, one might have expected Aboriginal artists to do the decent thing and work at the Renaissance and neo-classicism before attempting abstraction.

The anthropologist Eric Michaels has claimed that early European advisers at Papunya demeaned the art by assimilating it to a craft aesthetic. He contends that they encouraged the artists to achieve a 'well-crafted' appearance on the grounds that 'where evaluation is literally a problem of buying and selling, even the wholly ignorant can distinguish tiny, even strokes from bold broad ones and award a price accordingly' (Michaels, 1987: 136). Graburn's analysis of the failure of 'Cree Craft' as a form of tourist art in North America implies that Michaels has here oversimplified the evaluative process. Cree Craft failed precisely because it appeared too well-crafted to be the authentic product of an indigenous culture (Graburn, 1978). Nor does Michaels offer evidence to support his claim that advisers intervened in this way. None the less, Michaels is frank about his own intervention at Yuendumu during the subsequent development of the work portrayed in *Yuendumu Doors*. 'For me', he writes, 'these doors seemed to strike a chord with issues and images that were being negotiated in the art galleries of Sydney, Paris and New York' (Michaels, 1987: 135). Michaels recognizes that no outsider could 'read' the paintings with anything like the understanding of an initiated member of the artist's kin group. He considers that by offering a reduced gloss on some of the figurative meanings (as is done in this essay, Fig. 6.1), understanding is reduced to a superficial exercise in code-breaking. Yet Michaels considers that since the Yuendumu paintings were addressed to Europeans, aiming to tell them about the community's attachment to the land, he was entitled to intervene to advise the artists, in the light of his perception that their works 'have a unique place in contemporary painting . . . Something that was articulated as a "problem" in the Sydney work [at the Biennale show of 1983] seemed to me to be addressed, even solved, in the door paintings' (ibid. 139–40).

Despite Michaels's confidence, others have questioned the validity of interpreting Aboriginal paintings in terms of the Western category 'fine art'. The anthropologist Sue Kesteven has objected to the way that the monetary value of Papunya acrylics rose dramatically after they received approval from art galleries and festivals. Kesteven argues that Aboriginal culture possesses no category of 'fine art' as distinct from functional design, and that gallery owners have created 'Aboriginal fine art' to increase their profits as middlemen. It is certainly true that, if we consider parallels with our own culture instructive, we should not just consider Aboriginal paintings in relation to fine art, but also in relation to functional design, where simplicity of representation derives from the purpose for which the work is intended rather than poor draughtsmanship: road signs, for example, or Ordnance Survey maps. These too, may be admired for their skill in conveying messages in the idiom of particular cultures.

Another anthropologist has taken a different line. Peter Sutton works for the South Australian Museum, and some years ago acted as co-organizer of an exhibition of objects called *toas* (Jones and Sutton, 1986). *Toas* are mysterious sculptures, made by Aboriginal people of the Lake Eyre region at the turn of the century. European Australians with some local knowledge claimed in 1920, and again in 1938, that *toas* were a hoax in which their collector, the missionary Johann Reuther, had participated, perhaps to increase the value of his ethnographic collection (ibid. 23, 60). Jones and Sutton argue that *toas* may indeed (although unknown to Reuther) have been a short-lived but innovative response to a new, White market for Aboriginal artefacts created by the missionary's zeal for collecting material culture. They argue that *toas* none the less make genuine statements about man–land relationships. Further, the artists demonstrably drew upon traditional myth, artefact types, and art styles, even if some motifs seem to incorporate a European style learnt, perhaps, from H. J. Hillier, a water-colour artist resident at the mission. *Toas* exemplify 'the continuing metamorphosis and transformation of Aboriginal artistic traditions' (ibid. 61).

What, then, is their proper cultural context? In order to detach them from the contextual problem, the *toas* in the exhibition were presented against a plain black background, a decision which was criticized by the philosopher of art Donald Brook in a review of the exhibition. Brook (1986*a*; 1986*b*) claimed the organizers revealed what he termed a 'gemstone' theory of art: that by attractive display and lighting viewers would perceive beauty in objects they might otherwise have disregarded. But, Brook counters, *toas* are not 'found objects' like Marcel Duchamp's urinal; they were surely selected at least in part because of the role they were designed to play in Aboriginal culture. He asked: what was it about the *toas*' Aboriginal context of use that made them art for museum curators? It seems as if the roles of art critic and anthropologist have here been reversed.

Sutton (1986) replied that while he and Jones had not supposed the beauty of the *toas* inhered in the wood, gypsum, and ochre from which they were made, they had not wished to associate them too closely with their original context, as White Australian popular culture considers Aboriginal artefacts to be 'quaint, uninventive gewgaws, [and] pathetically simple contrivances'. Sutton follows Kesteven's view to the extent that he contends *art* is not an indigenous Aboriginal concept. *Toas* were, rather, objects of ceremonial attention. Aspects of their form and perceived symbolism fitted them to this role, and it is these same aspects which lead us to perceive them as art. However, 'There is no doubt', Sutton writes, 'that Aboriginal artists intend non-aboriginals to admire and buy their works.' He considers this goal is better achieved by focusing attention on the objects themselves.

One of the more encouraging effects of the resurgence of Aboriginal culture has been its effect on urban Aborigines. White prejudice has always militated against complete integration of Aboriginal people into the dominant community, and this has increasingly had the effect of turning Aboriginal people back upon the resources of their own culture as the foundation for their pride and self-identity.

One such artist, Lin Onus of Melbourne, has recorded his experiences living as a guest in a remote Aboriginal community in Arnhem Land. Onus sums up the experience of attempting to bridge cultures through art from personal involvement. In his painting *Gamerdi Dreaming* he has combined traditional motifs in the styles of north-eastern and western Arnhem Land (magpie goose, long-necked turtle, and fish), with the artefacts of European origin which facilitate bush life: the windmill, solar-powered two-way radio, and rifle. He writes, without apology:

surprisingly, through the bitterness comes other feelings, relief and joy, the knowledge that we have survived—damaged, yes, but not disintegrated. An artist is in a unique position, able to look into the past, the present and the future, able to keep the old traditions alive and to inspire others around them to create new ones . . . My people will be doing this as they always have done, quietly persevering and surviving, for surely we have another 200 years of hard work ahead of us.[4]

Notes

Field-work in the Uluru (Ayers Rock) area was carried out while I was employed by the Australian Institute of Aboriginal Studies, Canberra.

1 Impoverished or dispossessed cultivators (Graburn, 1976*b*: 19) and landless communities such as the ritual specialists in southern Sri Lanka studied by Simpson (1984) may respond in similar ways.
2 It should be noted that the titles given for these paintings are unlikely to have been assigned to the works by the artists themselves. More likely, they were probably assigned to the paintings by Geoff Bardon in response to what the artists said about them.
3 Further details of this period, and the archival sources for the material presented here, can be found in Layton (1986: chs. 5 and 6).
4 See *Australia: Art and Aboriginality*, p. 26.

References

Australia: Art and Aboriginality. Catalogue of an exhibition held at the Aspex Gallery, Portsmouth, UK, May–June 1987. Sydney: Aboriginal Arts Australia.
BAILEY, F. G. (1969). *Stratagems and Spoils: A Social Anthropology of Politics*. Oxford: Blackwell.
BARDON, GEOFF (1979). *Aboriginal Art of the Western Desert*. Adelaide: Rigby.
BERN, JOHN (1979). 'Politics in the Conduct of a Secret Male Ceremony', *Journal of Anthropological Research*, 35/1: 47–60.
BRODY, HUGH (1975). *The People's Land: Eskimos and Whites in the Eastern Arctic*. Harmondsworth, Middx.: Penguin.
BROKENSHA, P. (1975). *The Pitjantjatjara and their Crafts*. Sydney: Aboriginal Arts Board, Australia Council.

BROOK, DONALD (1986*a*). 'Without Wanting to Tread on Anyone's Toas' (review of Jones and Sutton, 1986), *Artlink* (Adelaide), 6/2–3: 4–5.

—— (1986*b*). 'Touching One's Toas: A Response to Peter Sutton', *Adelaide Review*, 33: 38.

CROCKER, A. (ed.) (1981). *Mr Sandman Bring Me a Dream*. Alice Springs: Papunya Tula Artists.

GRABURN, NELSON H. H. (ed.) (1976*a*). *Ethnic and Tourist Arts: Cultural Expressions from the Fourth World*, Berkeley: Univ. of California Press.

—— (1976*b*). 'Introduction: Arts of the Fourth World', in Graburn (1976*a*), 1–32.

—— (1976*c*). 'Eskimo Art: The Eastern Canadian Arctic', in Graburn (1976*a*), 39–55.

—— (1978). ' "I Like Things to Look More Different than That Stuff Did": An Experiment in Cross-Cultural Art Appreciation', in Michael Greenhalgh and Vincent Megaw (eds.), *Art in Society: Studies in Style, Culture and Aesthetics*. London: Duckworth, 51–70.

GRILLO, RALPH (1985). 'Applied Anthropology in the 1980s: Retrospect and Prospect', in Ralph Grillo and Alan Rew (eds.), *Social Anthropology and Development Policy*. ASA Monographs No. 23. London: Tavistock, 1–36.

GROOM, A. (1950). *I Saw a Strange Land*. Sydney: Angus & Robertson.

JONES, PHILIP, and SUTTON, PETER (1986). *Art and Land: Aboriginal Sculptures of the Lake Eyre Region*. Adelaide: South Australian Museum.

KESTEVEN, SUE (1983). Review of P. Loveday and P. Cooke 1983, *Aboriginal History*, 7/1–2: 196–200.

KIMBER, R. J. (1981). 'Central Australian and Western Desert Art: Some Impressions', in Crocker (1981), 7–9.

LAYTON, ROBERT (1976). 'Changes in the Style of AIAS Films', *Australian Institute of Aboriginal Studies Newsletter* (Canberra), 6/2: 26–32.

—— (1977). 'Naturalism and Cultural Relativity in Art', in Peter J. Ucko (ed.), *Form in Indigenous Art: Schematisation in the Art of Aboriginal Australia and Prehistoric Europe*. Prehistory and Material Culture Series No. 13. Canberra: Australian Institute of Aboriginal Studies, 33–43.

—— (1985). 'The Cultural Context of Hunter-Gatherer Rock Art', *Man*, n.s., 20/3: 434–53.

—— (1986). *Uluru: An Aboriginal History of Ayers Rock*. Canberra: Australian Institute of Aboriginal Studies.

LEACH, E. R. (1961). *Rethinking Anthropology*. London School of Economics Monographs on Social Anthropology No. 22. London: Athlone Press.

LOVEDAY, P., and COOKE, P. (eds.) (1983). *Aboriginal Arts and Crafts and the Market*, Darwin: Australian National University, North Australia Research Unit.

MEGAW, J. V. S. (1986). 'Contemporary Aboriginal Art: Dreamtime Discipline or Alien Adulteration?', *Bulletin of the Conference of Museum Anthropologists*, 18: 31–42.

MICHAELS, E. (1987). 'Western Desert Sandpainting and Post-Modernism', in Warlukurlangu Artists (1987), 135–43.

MORPHY, HOWARD (1980). 'What Circles Look Like', *Canberra Anthropology*, 3/1: 17–36.

—— and LAYTON, R. (1981). 'Choosing among Alternatives: Cultural Transformations and Social Change in Aboriginal Australia and French Jura', *Mankind*, 13/1: 56–73.

MOUNTFORD, CHARLES P. (1950). *Brown Men and Red Sand: Journeyings in Wild Australia*. Sydney: Angus & Robertson.

MUNN, NANCY D. (1964). 'Totemic Designs and Group Continuity in Walbiri Cosmology', in Marie Reay (ed.), *Aborigines Now: New Perspectives in the Study of Aboriginal Communities*. Sydney: Angus & Robertson, 93–100.

—— (1973). *Walbiri Iconography: Graphic Representation and Cultural Symbolism in a Central Australian Society*. Ithaca, NY: Cornell Univ. Press.

REYNOLDS, H. (1982). *The Other Side of the Frontier: Aboriginal Resistance to the European Invasion of Australia*. Harmondsworth, Middx.: Penguin.

ROGERS, EDWARD S., and BLACK, MARY P. (1976). 'Subsistence Strategy in the Fish and Hare Period, Northern Ontario: The Weagamow Ojibwa, 1880–1920', *Journal of Anthropological Research*, 32/1: 1–43.

ROSE, F. G. G. (1965). *The Wind of Change in Central Australia: The Aborigines at Angas Downs*. Berlin: Akademie.

SIMPSON, R. (1984). 'Ritual Tradition and Performance: The Berava Caste of Southern Sri Lanka'. Ph.D. thesis, Univ. of Durham.

SUTTON, PHILIP (1986). 'The Sculpted Word: A Reply to Donald Brook on Toas', *Adelaide Review*, 32: 8–9, 36–7.

WALLACE, NOEL M. (1977). 'Change in Spiritual and Ritual Life in Pitjantjatjara (Bidjandjadjara) Society, 1966 to 1973', in Ronald M. Berndt (ed.), *Aborigines and Change: Australia in the '70s*. AIAS Social Anthropology Series No. 11. Canberra: Australian Institute of Aboriginal Studies, 74–89.

WARLUKURLANGU ARTISTS (1987). *Yuendumu Doors Kuruwari*. Canberra: Australian Institute of Aboriginal Studies.

WILLIAMS, NANCY (1976). 'Australian Aboriginal Art at Yirrkala: The Introduction and Development of Marketing', in Graburn (1976a), 266–84.

WOLF, ERIC R. (1982). *Europe and the People without History*. Berkeley: Univ. of California Press.

7

Textile Design in Southern Lembata: Tradition and Change

RUTH BARNES

> One would be tempted to proclaim the Solor Islands as one of the least artistic and in their material culture most unimaginative areas in all of Indonesia, if there were not at least one field of craft activity . . . that is the *weaving*, and related to it, the *ikat*. (Vatter, 1932: 217)

The German ethnographer Ernst Vatter was the first to comment at length on the textiles woven in this particular group of islands in eastern Indonesia, and he was also the first to speak of the local weaving and ikat as a form of artistic activity.[1] Scattered throughout his book one finds comments on weaving in particular villages; patterns are sometimes mentioned by name, and textiles appear in specific social contexts, such as at dances and—most significantly and familiarly from other Indonesian societies—as part of the gift exchange associated with marriage. Vatter also includes one chapter that deals exclusively with the ikat textiles of the islands. However, Vatter did not attempt to interpret the designs in detail, but restricted himself to a description of what he saw and collected.[2]

The region which Vatter called the Solor Archipelago is now referred to in the ethnographic literature as Lamaholot and Kédang[3] (see Maps 2A and 2B). It is politically united under the regency of Flores Timur, and includes East Flores, Solor, Adonara, and Lembata.[4] Although the area was in early contact with European ships in search of the profitable sandalwood and spice trade of eastern Indonesia, it has until recently been largely neglected by scholars interested in aspects of maritime south-east Asian societies. Vatter's ethnographic travel account was complemented by the writings of the missionary Paul Arndt (1937; 1938; 1951), but neither author made it his concern to provide a close account and analysis of a particular community. Research of this sort is a matter of the last fifteen years (see Barnes, R. H. 1974; Barnes, Ruth, 1984, 1989a; Dietrich, 1986). Current anthropological, linguistic, and historical research may further add to our knowledge about the region.[5]

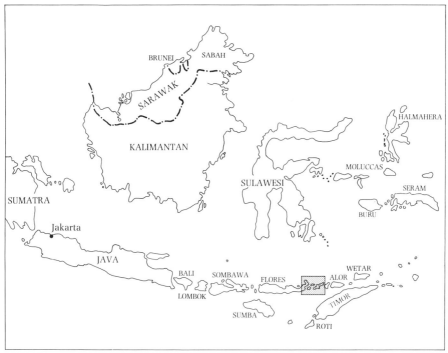

MAP 2A. Indonesia.

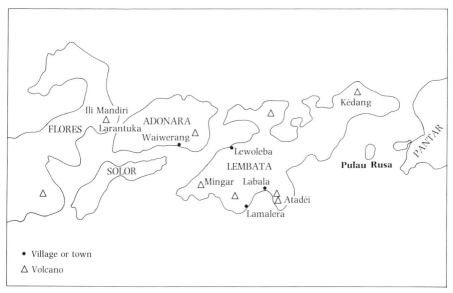

MAP 2B. The Lamaholot Islands.

Indonesia has long been famous for an unusually prolific and accomplished textile tradition. Throughout the islands, cloths are produced and worn not merely to dress and decorate the body, but to identify the wearer with a specific geographic region or social group. This can be expressed in the way of wearing the fabric, but also especially in the types of pattern used. Furthermore, textiles are often essential to certain ritual functions. They can play a crucial role in gift exchanges, especially in those associated with marriage and burial.[6]

The patterns and their arrangements might reveal much about the position textiles hold in a particular society.[7] They can also become evidence of cross-cultural influences and might be read as art-historical documents, an approach I have myself taken (Barnes, Ruth, 1984, 1989*a*). One of the earliest scholarly sources on ethnographic arts in Indonesia already attempted a similar interpretation, although the interest at the time was in an evolutionary development of design elements (Hein, 1890). What is still relevant today in this study is the importance Hein gave to the artistic ornamentation of everyday objects: he understood these to be decorated with an aesthetic sense which is associated with art, rather than relegated to 'crafts'. By now, several generations of researchers have been impressed with the visual presence of Indonesian societies. An early interest of Dutch scholars in describing the arts and crafts of their colony has resulted in basic works of reference which are still essential reading for the textile researcher (see in particular Jasper and Pirngadie, 1912; Rouffaer and Juynboll, 1914).

Yet it is only in the last two decades that social anthropologists and art historians have begun to take a detailed look at the role of cloth in Indonesia, and to attempt to establish a connection between function and design. Jager Gerlings's early study (1952) was based on museum research, rather than field-work, but nevertheless it pointed the way forward and raised many of the important questions. He related textiles and their patterns to a link between the living and their ancestors, a theme which was expanded and put into historical context by Schuster (1965). M. J. Adams's work (1969) on Sumba cloth was a turning-point for the interpretation of Indonesian textiles. She, like Hein eighty years before her, tried to combine an art-historical with an ethnographic approach. However, her emphasis was on the social context of textiles, and on an interpretation of patterns based on that context. Without necessarily agreeing with her analysis in all respects, we must credit her work with having had a great influence on a changing perspective on material culture.[8] In Indonesia, textiles have become a primary topic of interest, because of their prominent presence at certain rituals, because of their distinctive characteristics and iconography, and certainly because of their aesthetic appeal. I want in this essay to present aspects of a particular case-study of the ikat-decorated women's cloth of the village of Lamalera, a community that is part of the Lamaholot culture, yet has certain unique features.

Lamaholot Society

Traditionally, the Lamaholot region has had little political unity. Although indigenous rulers sometimes claimed suzerainty over large areas, occasionally extending across several islands, their real influence and power remained sporadic. Attempts by these local rajas to extract tribute from their nominal dependants frequently led to antagonism and warfare.[9] An early Portuguese report on the islands mentions a division into two opposed factions, the Demon and Paji (Basílio de Sá, 1956: 486; see also Arndt, 1938; Barnes, Ruth, 1984: 236). Their conflict is frequently referred to in the region; in western Lamaholot, in particular on East Flores, the two groups explain their opposition in mythological and political terms. On Adonara and Solor, the origin of the division is sometimes associated with a creation myth (Arndt, 1938). Alternatively, the Demon faction claim to be later arrivals to the area, who pushed the Paji, the original inhabitants, into more remote regions. Ceremonial war excursions and head-hunting were apparently parts of the continuing conflict. These raids were usually carried out by villages, and traditionally there existed no overall alliance between all Paji or all Demon (Barnes, Ruth, 1987: 18–19). Although local rulers emerged and Portuguese and Dutch colonial rule was largely implemented through them, the most effective political unit until this century was the village. The communities are divided into clans, and descent is patrilineal. The relations between clans are dominated by an asymmetric alliance system. Women change clans after marriage, although their original clan retains a special hold on them and, in fact, over their husbands and children.[10]

Throughout Lamaholot, marriage is associated with a gift exchange between the two clans involved. From the women's side, the prestations inevitably involve textiles. The man's clan in return should present an elephant's tusk. These tusks have been in the area since before European contacts. They were mentioned as most desired trade items by the first Portuguese who travelled through the islands (Basílio de Sá, 1956: 480). Beyond this general exchange requirement, local variations appear. Within one village the gift exchange is standardized. However, when moving from one community to another, differences quickly emerge which can be sources of major friction and distress; the relative values of tusk and cloth may vary, or the prestations from one place may be considered inferior to what one might expect at home. For example, the textiles offered vary greatly from one island to the next, or even between different parts of one island. Certain weaving centres that produce ikat cloths of (locally recognized) highest quality are in contrast to areas where few or no ikat textiles are made, and from where the gift of cloth is therefore considered to be inferior. In these cases, lengthy discussions between the clans involved will have to take place, but it is thought to be most important that an agreement is eventually reached and amicable relationships are established. The woman's clan, and specifically her brother or a person in the equivalent genealogical position, is considered influential for the spiritual and physical well-being of her offspring. Therefore, it is potentially dangerous not to be on good terms with that line of affines, the *opu-pukan*.

The indigenous economy is based on subsistence agriculture. The staple crops are maize and rice, the latter usually grown in dry cultivation. Most of Lamaholot culture is strongly land-orientated. Concepts of fertility are associated with the fields, rather than the sea. Many villages have origin myths claiming that the community, or even all of mankind, emerged from one of the region's volcanic mountains. But there are certain coastal communities which have long had contacts with areas outside the Lamaholot realm. One of these villages, Lamalera, has been the focus of my field-work. It is a community on the south coast of Lembata. Traditionally the village had few fields, but was inhabited by fishermen and weavers. The men go out to sea every day during the dry season (May to October), in locally built sailing-boats. Fishing is done from the boats with harpoons; it is exclusively a male activity. The catch, notably sperm-whale and giant manta ray, is cut up, dried, and traded by the women for agricultural products. Bartering the fish means strenuous journeys to the hills, returning with heavy loads of maize, tubers, bananas, and other seasonal products. On Lamalera's side, all aspects of the exchange are in the hands of the village's women.

Lamalera Textiles

Apart from trading, the women of Lamalera spend much of their time weaving (Fig. 7.1). The entire region of the Lamaholot is divided into areas where weaving and textile design are highly developed arts, and others where little weaving is done, or where it may even be prohibited by customary law (see Barnes, Ruth, 1987). Kédang, in the eastern part of Lembata, is an area where traditionally no weaving was done; still no loom may enter the old mountain villages, nor may cotton be grown there. Mingar, to the west of Lamalera, is another such region. Yet neither the people of Mingar nor of Kédang go naked; they have long depended for their textiles on those imported from other areas. Lamalera women, therefore, produce cloth which is only partly for their own use. They weave both everyday cloth and festive sarongs for special occasions, and they also make the type of sarong which is an essential part of the gift exchange at marriage.

All the textiles woven in Lamalera fall into one of the following categories: the man's sarong *nofi*, the woman's work sarong *kewatek biasa*, the shoulder-cloth *senai*, the woman's festive sarong *kewatek menikil*, the two-panel version of the woman's sarong which is suitable as bridewealth prestation, *kewatek nai*

FIG. 7.1. A Lamalera woman weaving a man's cloth, *nofi*; photographer: Ruth Barnes, 1979.

ruã, and the three-panel version of the bridewealth prestation, *kewatek nai telo*.[11]

The first two are cloths where patterns are created through the use of differently coloured threads, either in the warp only, which creates stripes, or in warp and weft, which gives a tartan-like design. The former is used for the women's work sarong, the latter for the men's cloth. All sarongs are sewn together to form a tube-like wrap-around. The third type of textile, the shoulder-cloth, is not an essential part of traditional costume, although it is often used by Lamaholot during dance performances. The cloths which will interest us here are the ikat-decorated textiles, all of which are women's cloths.[12] As is common in eastern Indonesia, the Lamaholot women are only acquainted with warp ikat, which means that the warp is set up on a frame, and the patterns are tied into the threads. The warp is then dyed, possibly retied, and dyed again with a different dye.

Ikat-decorated textiles are in the latter three categories of the above list. The *kewatek menikil* is a woman's sarong which is made to be worn on special days, for family or clan gatherings, weddings, or funerals (Fig. 7.2). The cloth always has some ikat design, which is most prominent at the border. It may be woven from locally grown, hand-spun cotton, or from imported, machine-spun

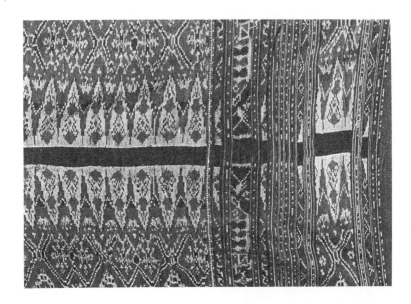

FIG. 7.3. The three-panel bridewealth cloth of Lamalera, *kewatek nai telo*, photographer: Ruth Barnes, 1979.

FIG. 7.2. A Lamalera woman displaying a festive sarong, *kewatek menikil*, photographer: Ruth Barnes, 1982.

thread. The dyes used in its production may be natural vegetable dyes, or they may be store-bought commercial colours, or a combination of both.

The *kewatek nai ruã* and *kewatek nai telo*, as cloth associated with marriage, must be made entirely of locally grown, hand-spun cotton (Fig. 7.3). The ikat designs have to extend over the entire surface of the cloth, and all colours must come from natural dyes which are procured locally. The basic colour must be a brownish red, achieved by dyeing the threads numerous times in chopped-up roots of the *Morinda citrifolia* tree. The ikat patterns tied into the warp threads are made up of, and restricted to, the colour triad black/red/white.[13] The source of black—which is in fact dark blue—is indigo. It is a firmly kept rule in the production of the bridewealth cloth that all material must be indigenous. Even the dye vats used when preparing the cotton threads have to be large, earthenware pots made in a nearby village.

The patterns found on the bridewealth cloth are transmitted from one generation to the next; certain patterns are said to belong to particular clans, and are only used by women who have established ties with the clan, through descent or marriage (Barnes, Ruth, 1989a: 74–7). The festive sarong, on the other hand, can include patterns which the weaver has either invented or has seen in cloth from elsewhere. If patterns are copied from elsewhere, European-type designs are favoured. Very rarely is a pattern adopted which is known to be part of a neighbouring weaving tradition. The Western designs, either religious or decorative, are associated with the prestige of the 'modern', the non-indigenous, and with change from a local tradition to a broader view. They emphasize a sense of incorporation into the present-day 'mainstream', as it is embodied, for example, in the Indonesian national State.

The indigenous patterns, however, have a different and equally important role: they identify the wearer as being part of a specific community, or possibly even more narrowly, as a member of a particular clan. Should we therefore identify the ceremonially important cloth with permanence, the festive sarong with change? There is certainly a difference between individual, often highly personal, creativity, as evidenced in the weaving of the woman's festive sarong, and communal creativity, i.e. the patterns which are trans-mitted through the community: individual creativity supports change, com-munal creativity supports tradition. To limit our analysis of the appearance of the different cloths to this division would, however, not say enough about Lamalera's particular weaving tradition. There exists, in fact, a great and subtle mix of change, reinterpretation, acceptance, and rejection of the out-side. Change and diversity are traditionally part of Lamalera.

A Village History

I want to elaborate on this last point. The initial impression of the village is one of great self-sufficiency, in a geographic situation which is removed from the easily accessible parts of Indonesia. The absence of roads restricts contact with the outside to transport via the sea, or on foot overland to the north of the island. The material evidence of traditional sea-going activities, the boats and their large sheds, creates a picturesque atmosphere which seems to belong to a different world altogether.

Yet the village has a peculiar and unique position in other ways than in its traditional livelihood. It has responded with unusual intensity to the educational possibilities which European missionaries have offered.[14] The Catholic mission which became active in the East Flores region early in this century made a quick and complete conversion in Lamalera; at the same time, the village population took advantage of the mission schools and the training offered through them. The first teachers in Lamaholot schools either came from Waibalun, near Larantuka, or from the far more remotely situated Lamalera. Similarly, the first Catholic priests and nuns from Lembata came from Lamalera. Training has by now produced numerous teachers, government officials on a local and national level, and a handful of very successful professionals, including a journalist working for a Jakarta daily newspaper, a doctor now practising in West Germany, a diplomat in Tokyo, and a powerful and influential general in the Indonesian army. It must be noted that advanced schooling is as available to the girls in a family as to the boys.

How does one explain the contrast between the strongly traditional culture which apparently emphasizes the indigenous and the readiness to adopt new possibilities and take full advantage of them? We might find an answer if we see the village, not from a European point of view, which stresses the obscurity of its position, but from the point of view of Lamalera's own account of history, and the role the community claims in it. Unlike most villages on Lembata, which are very strongly land-orientated, with an expressed fear of the sea, Lamalera was actually settled from the sea. According to oral tradition, the ancestors of the village originated in Sulawesi, and then travelled through the Moluccas, stopping off at Ceram, Ambon, east of Timor, and at a place called Lapan Batan east of Lembata. From there they were driven away by volcanic activity and a tidal wave. This event probably occurred at some time prior to the arrival of the first Europeans in the area; it is also recorded in the oral histories of other communities on neighbouring islands. When the ancestors of Lamalera came to southern Lembata they settled in Nualéla, a community not far from their present site. They arrived there as guests of the local villagers. With them they brought a knowledge of pottery; the local people in turn showed them how to forge iron for their harpoons.

Lamalera's oral history presents their arrival on the scene as a conquest of the external and foreign over the indigenous. The local population, according to Lamalera history, was so impressed with the superiority of the new arrivals that a transfer of power took place immediately: the indigenous ruler of Nualéla, who could claim the entire hinterland of southern Lembata for the

Raja of Larantuka and was a small king in his own right, supposedly transferred his political power to the new arrivals. There is no account of any hostility associated with the transference. As a fact of recorded, recent history, Lamalera held the title until and into the 1960s. It is improbable that the local inhabitants were quite so delighted and generous, but it is most significant that Lamalera presents the community's foundation in this particular way, emphasizing the importance of trade, which is interpreted as an exchange of knowledge. Trade, in this case, has far greater significance than the acquiring of useful goods. It was mentioned above that, according to Lamalera's oral history, their ancestors brought the technology of making pots into the host village. In return, the local villagers could show Lamalera's fishermen how to forge iron and make metal harpoons: hitherto, supposedly, they had used wooden ones.

This exchange is remarkable in so far as pottery-making is strictly a female activity, while metalwork is done only by men. I suggest that the opposition is intentional, and could be compared to the exchange that takes place at or following a wedding, in particular the exchange of textiles and elephant tusks. The use of a tusk as marriage prestation seems to be unique to Flores and the Lamaholot; more common in this type of exchange is the use of a metal gift from the man's group. Adams (1980: 220) mentions that in East Sumba 'a women's medium, textiles are typically contrasted with metal goods, associated with male activities'. She goes on to say that '[the] Sumbanese consider textiles, as they do women in a clan household, impermanent'. Of course a woman's position is impermanent, because she becomes incorporated into a different group at marriage. Metal objects, on the other hand, are considered to be permanent. A similar permanence can be attributed to the ivory tusk, in contrast to textiles in the Lamaholot view. As I have discussed elsewhere (Barnes, Ruth, 1989*a*: 78), cloths of particular value are said to change with the moon while they are stored in the clan houses: they unravel as the moon wanes, are totally disassembled at the time of the new moon, and then become complete again as the moon increases.

Furthermore, an inversion has occurred with the exchange mentioned above. The making of pots, like the making of cloth, is associated with the indigenous, the land. To shape, dry, and fire their earthenware nowadays, the potters of Nualéla must return to their original village site, which is different from their present location. Similarly, the textiles suitable for bridewealth must be made from locally grown cotton, dyed with dyes that are collected in the vicinity of the village. Metal and the tusk, on the other hand, are brought from the outside and are considered foreign. However, in Lamalera's story, as told above, the knowledge of pottery is brought by the outsiders, and the indigenous villagers pass on the craft of metalwork.

The ancestors of Lamalera successfully integrated with the local Lamaholot culture. They accepted the language and social structure of Lamaholot society, and the land-based aspects of their material culture are a variety of common Lamaholot themes. Fishing with harpoons for large sea animals, in particular sperm-whales, has no immediate local parallel. The village's traditional contact with the outside was via the sea: there was the link to important trading connections. This provides a likely reason for the position of very real superiority held over the inland population. The assumed political influence and its successful implementation should be seen in connection with it. Consequently, certain Lamalera clans who descend from the original founders speak of themselves as 'aristocracy' in relation to the mountain villages.

Textiles as Signs

I now want to look at the textiles of Lamalera against the background of local, oral history. In the local weaving traditions, certain characteristics are commonly found throughout Lamaholot. Although both men's and women's cloths are produced, the emphasis on critical evaluation and on differentiation into types, and statements on accomplishment are reserved for the woman's sarong. The complexity of creating the fabric's patterns prior to weaving is generally appreciated, and it is a skill which needs a considerable apprenticeship. It is the final aspect of textile production to be learnt, and it takes the longest to master. Women who become especially competent in it are well known in the village, and they are frequently sought out by people from the mountain communities in need of a ceremonial bridewealth cloth.

The Lamaholot bridewealth cloth is called 'red', *méan*. This refers to the colour of the textile, but *méan* also has a superlative meaning, in the sense of 'extraordinary, of great wealth' (Barnes, Ruth, 1989*b*). The fabric has to be decorated with ikat patterns which cover the entire surface. The cloth which is for mundane use, however, is dominated by indigo blue or black. It may or may not be decorated with ikat, depending on its intended use. The Lamaholot sarong is usually made up of two panels, although the seam is not visually apparent. The border is always emphasized; there the most prominent decoration is found. The bridewealth cloths of southern Lembata, however, show an important difference: they include a type which is made up of three panels. I have discussed elsewhere the composite nature of the three-panel cloths and the probable origin of their design (Barnes, Ruth, 1989*a*; 1991). In Lamaholot textile design, there exist two types of pattern: narrow designs which appear in bands; and wide patterns which, in southern Lembata, are always used in the central panel, where they are repeated to form a continuous design.

The first, narrow type of pattern is characteristic of all Lamaholot ikat cloths. Many of the designs which fall into the category have a pan-Indonesian distribution, and some of them already appear on pottery which has been found in archaeological contexts (Barnes, Ruth, 1989a: fig. 43). The second variety, however, has its source elsewhere: in Indian cloths which used to be sought-after import goods, brought into Indonesia by early traders. One particular kind of cloth interests us here: the *patolu* (pl. *patola*), a double-ikat silk textile from Gujarat (cf. Barbosa, 1921: 198). This kind of cloth is highly esteemed in its place of origin, and it was much in demand as an export article for several centuries. Europeans noticed the demand for *patola* in Indonesia, and they became interested in monopolizing its export and in controlling its distribution.

The *patola* brought into the Lamaholot region are used in two different ways. In the trading centres of coastal Adonara and Solor, which once had long-standing direct contact with non-Indonesian merchants, the Indian cloths are (or were until recently) part of the bridewealth gifts offered by a bride's clan. No red bridewealth cloth was woven in the communities; instead, the *patola* seemed to take their place. Elsewhere, the *patola* have been part of clan treasures, sacred possessions which must not leave the clan house. In Lamalera, the *patola* found in the village are kept as clan treasures and are never used as marriage prestations. However, they have had an unmistakable influence on the bridewealth cloths (Fig. 7.4). The patterns which are found in the central panels of the three-panel textiles *kewatek nai telo* have their source in *patola* (Barnes, Ruth, 1989a: 82–7).

The silk *patola*, as treasures, are seen as containing a great force, a wealth which is directly linked to the well-being of the clan (see Barnes, Ruth, 1991). It is dangerous for the treasures owned by a clan even to leave the physical confines of the ceremonial centre of the group, the clan house, and the notion that a *patolu* might leave the possession of the clan is considered with dread (Fig. 7.5). Yet the *patola* as clan treasures should not be seen in opposition to the marriage prestations. The latter are similarly associated with certain mystical qualities and are dominated by symbolic gifts: cloth and tusk. The tusk has no conceivable utilitarian purpose, although it is a primary manifestation of wealth. The cloth can be worn, but that is the exclusive privilege of old women, and is reserved for special occasions, connected, for example, with the building of a new clan house or the funeral feast of a very prominent person. To wear it at other times is considered improper and will bring bad luck. The textiles are usually carefully stored away, and are only seen at the time of the gift exchange. The important difference between a clan treasure and a marriage prestation is the mobility of the latter.

The most valued and artistically elaborate kind of cloth which is made in Lamalera, then, is beyond doubt a mixture of the indigenous and the foreign. The latter, foreign, influence is the result of an importation in the historical past. It is not possible now to say with certainty when the *patola* trade was initiated. Duarte Barbosa mentioned in 1516 that it was thriving in the Moluccas; the trade with the Lamaholot is mentioned in a source of the mid-

FIG. 7.4. Detail of a *patolu* kept as a clan treasure in Lamalera; photographer: Ruth Barnes, 1982.

FIG. 7.5. A Lamalera woman displaying a *patolu* cloth; photographer: Ruth Barnes, 1979. See also Pl. VIII.

FIG. 7.6. Central panel, *tukā*, of a Lamalera three-panel bridewealth cloth; photographer: Ruth Barnes, 1982. See also Pl. IX.

sixteenth century (Basílio de Sá, 1956: 480). It is likely to pre-date European contacts with Indonesia, but so far there is no conclusive evidence for the existence of the cloths in India, let alone their export, much earlier than the date of the first European sources.

The fact remains that in Lamalera the most strongly conventional type of textile, which has certain patterns and designs prescribed, combines the local with the foreign, and is likely to have changed its form under the influence of the *patola* trade. There are two probable reasons why the *patola* patterns were adopted into local forms of weaving. Indian silks were introduced into the area as extremely precious goods, and they became signs of wealth and superior connections. This aspect of the introduction of *patola* patterns is certainly prominently present in their display on Lamalera bridewealth cloth. The *patola* reference is placed in the central panel, called *tukā*. The centre is a place of honour.

The usual design of Lamaholot female cloth, which includes Lamalera cloth woven for a primarily utilitarian purpose, has two panels. These are mirror-symmetrical to each other, and the border is emphasized by placing there a wider display of ikat patterns. The three-panel bridewealth cloth (Fig. 7.6) is unique in its emphasis on the centre. By the addition of the wide central panel, the dyadic character of the Lamaholot textile gains a triadic aspect in the Lamalera version.

To return once more to the founding of the village, the following story is told. The prominent leader Korohama, who brought the original settlers to the village site, had three sons. The oldest stayed in his father's house and founded the clan Belikololong. The second son moved from the settlement on the hill side down to the beach, where the boats are kept. He thus established a two-part nature to the community which still exists: the beach and hill sites are physically and socially distinct to this day, although together they form one community. As 'guardian of the gate' (to the village), the descendants of Korohama's second son assumed a role of military leadership. The third, youngest, son received the political leadership from his father. He became the *kakang* of Lamalera, the local ruler who represented the Raja of Larantuka in southern Lembata. He built his house in the ceremonial centre of the village; he is said to have been the founder of the clan Lewotukang, a name which means literally 'the centre of the village'. The clan's ceremonial house is still considered to be in the village centre, although it is not so in actual fact. The village space is seen in dyadic terms, to which the political leadership adds a triadic dimension.

A parallel to the bridewealth cloth seems to exist here.[15] The patterns displaying an association with the prestigious Indian silk appear in the centre of the cloth, which otherwise consists of two end-panels arranged mirror-symmetrically to each other. A central display of power and importance is apparently intended. This is combined with a definition of affiliation to a particular clan, and possibly to its ownership of a precious Indian silk cloth. The original Indian silk cloth remains in the clan house, and supposedly brings wealth and well-being to the group associated with the house. It is owned by the clan. The bridewealth cloth made by the women descending from the clan reflects the wealth, by using some of its motifs, but reinterprets them and puts them into a position where they are surrounded by mainly indigenous patterns. These cloths, of course, are made to be offered as gifts: they are meant to circulate.

The form of these textiles is clearly prescribed, and is transmitted within the community. The particular quality of any one cloth, however, depends entirely on the skill and dedication of the woman who makes it. Actually, no two cloths are ever alike. Apart from the *patola* patterns, there are numerous locally developed patterns which are available for use in the outer panels of a bridewealth cloth. In Lamalera, none of these patterns is associated with a particular clan. They are undoubtedly of great antiquity in the area, and are variations on motifs commonly found in eastern Indonesia, all of which pre-date the arrival of imported Indian textiles.

Conclusion

This essay has discussed the most elaborate type of women's cloth from Lamalera. The three-panel textile must be seen, however, in the context of

F IG. 7.7. Detail of a shoulder-cloth, *senai*, made for the author in 1982; photographer: Ruth Barnes, 1982.

other cloths produced locally. Girls will start acquiring their technical knowledge of weaving, ikat-tying, and dyeing by working on the utilitarian cloth first, and most women spend their weaving career almost entirely on the production of these cloths. They learn to master the communally known patterns, the narrow band-type motifs as well as the motifs which are associated with certain *patola*. In addition, they have the freedom to experiment, and Lamalera festive sarongs are unusually lively in their display of foreign, recently introduced elements, chosen from various sources. There are letters to form initials of personal names, birds flanking vases, Christian motifs, and other copies of European images (Figs. 7.3, 7.7). There is no restriction, no limitation imposed on the weaver, as far as the designs are concerned. An example is the shoulder-cloth illustrated in Fig. 7.7, where the thread is hand-spun, the dyes are store-bought, and the design is a mixture of the traditional 'boat chase' motif, *téna tuba moku*, and a newly invented depiction of a boat encountering a whale.[16] Yet there are also certain restrictions of form which any ikat-decorated textile has to follow. All patterns have to be surrounded by narrow strips of distinctively coloured thread; in any sarong the border always has a prominent position. The making of the textile, finally, is bound by definite rules, both technical requirements and matters of symbolic significance.[17]

Tradition and change are aspects of both the utilitarian and the bridewealth cloth. The very nature of the prestation cloth shows that—although surrounded with the aura of ancestral prescriptions—it had to evolve in a particular way and take a certain form in order to express a particular message. It is a characteristic quality and strength of the community of Lamalera that change is selectively sought out and imaginatively adopted to fit the local requirements.

Notes

1 The term *ikat* is Malay, meaning binding, tying; cf. the verb *ikatkan*, *mengikatkan*, to tie, fasten, bind. It is used to describe the process by which a pattern is tied on the warp, the weft, or on both and is then resist-dyed before weaving begins. The reader is referred to Burnham (1981) for questions of textile terminology.

2 The objects gathered by Vatter during his 1928/9 expedition are now stored in the Städtisches Museum für Völkerkunde, Frankfurt.

3 Kédang, an area at the far eastern tip of Lembata, is linguistically different, but culturally related.

4 Lembata has been known under different names: Lomblen, Lomblem, Quella, Kawella, Levoleba, Lombatta. Lomblen was the name generally accepted under Dutch rule in this century. In the 1960s the name became officially Lembata, although the change has not been registered on many international maps.

5 My first stay on Lembata was from 1969 to 1971, when I accompanied my husband on his anthropological field-work in Kédang. In 1979 I spent 3 months in Lamalera, with the financial support of a postgraduate studentship from the UK Department of Education and Science. In 1982 I was able to return again for 6 months while working as a research assistant on a project funded by the UK Social Science Research Council. All research in Indonesia has been carried out under the auspices of the Lembaga Ilmu Pengetahuan Indonesia (LIPI). The spelling of Lamaholot words in this essay follows the conventions developed in Keraf (1978).

6 For descriptions pertaining to eastern Indonesia, see especially Adams (1969); Barnes, R. H. (1974); Barnes, Ruth (1989*a*); Fox (1977); Vatter (1932); Vroklage (1953). Elmberg (1968) gives an account of the ceremonial use of eastern Indonesian textiles in New Guinea. For a general discussion of textiles in their social context, Jager Gerlings (1952) and in particular Gittinger (1979) should be consulted. The latter is still the best introduction to the subject.

7 See Adams (1969, 1974, 1980); Fox (1977, 1980); Gittinger (1979).

8 However, her monograph (1969) was not based on field-work; it was only after its completion that she travelled to Sumba.

9 See e.g. the account of the often tempestuous relationship between Kédang and the head of the trading village Kalikur, who claimed leadership over the area, in Barnes, R. H. (1974: 11–13).

10 See Barnes, R. H. (1974, 1980) on the topic of kinship and alliance among the Lamaholot and Kédang. See also Barnes, R. H. (1974, 1977) for a discussion of the wife-giving clan as a source of spiritual and ritual power over the wife-takers.

11 I use the textile terms which are specifically appropriate in Lamalera. In other parts of Lamaholot names vary; e.g. the terms used for the bridewealth cloths differ from one area to the next (see Barnes, Ruth, 1989*a*: 96–122)

12 Lamaholot textiles which are decorated with ikat are almost exclusively made to be worn by women. One exception is a type of man's cloth from Ili Mandiri, East Flores, which has very narrow ikat decorations.

13 See Barnes, Ruth (1989*b*) for a detailed discussion of colour in Lamalera textiles.

14 See Barnes, R. H. (1986).

15 Adams (1980: 212) has discussed in a similar way the relationship between a village plan and the visual arrangements of an east Sumba cloth.

16 In reality, the boats always lower their sails when chasing whale.

17 See Barnes, Ruth (1989*b*) on the use of specific numbers in weaving.

References

ADAMS, MARIE JEANNE (1969). *System and Meaning in East Sumba Textile Design: A Study in Traditional Indonesian Art*. Southeast Asia Studies Cultural Report Series, No. 16. New Haven, Conn.: Yale Univ. Press.

—— (1974). 'Symbols of the Organized Community in East Sumba, Indonesia', *Bijdragen tot de Taal-, Land- en Volkenkunde*, 130/2–3: 324–47.

—— (1980). 'Structural Aspects of East Sumbanese Art', in James J. Fox (ed.), *The Flow of Life: Essays on Eastern Indonesia*. Cambridge, Mass.: Harvard Univ. Press, 208–20.

ARNDT, P. P. (1937). *Grammatik der Solor-Sprache*. Ende, Flores: Arnoldus-Drukkerij.

—— (1938). 'Demon und Padzi: Die feindlichen Brüder des Solor-Archipels', *Anthropos*, 33/1: 1–58.

—— (1951). *Religion auf Ostflores, Adonare und Solor*. Studia Instituti Anthropos 33. Vienna: Mödling.

BARBOSA, DUARTE (1921). *The Book of Duarte Barbosa*, ed. Mansel Longworth Dames. 2 vols. London: Hakluyt Society.

BARNES, R. H. (1974). *Kédang: A Study of the Collective Thought of an Eastern Indonesian People*. Oxford: Clarendon Press.

—— (1977). '*Mata* in Austronesia', *Oceania*, 47/4: 300–19.

—— (1980). 'Marriage, Exchange and the Meaning of Corporations in Eastern Indonesia', in J. L. Comaroff (ed.), *The Meaning of Marriage Payments*. London: Academic Press, 93–124.

—— (1986). 'Educated Fishermen: Social Consequences of Development in an Indonesian Whaling Community', *Bulletin de l'École Française de l'Extrème Orient*, 75: 295–314.

BARNES, RUTH (1984). 'The Ikat Textiles of Lamalera, Lembata within the Context of Eastern Indonesian Fabric Traditions'. D. Phil. thesis, Univ. of Oxford.

—— (1987). 'Weaving and Non-Weaving among the Lamaholot', *Indonesia Circle*, 42: 16–32.

—— (1989*a*). *The Ikat Textiles of Lamalera: A Study of an Eastern Indonesian Weaving Tradition*. Studies in South Asian Culture, vol. xiv. Leiden: Brill.

—— (1989*b*). 'The Bridewealth Cloth of Lamalera, Lembata', in Mattiebelle Gittinger (ed.), *To Speak with Cloth: Studies in Indonesian Textiles*. Los Angeles: Museum of Cultural History, Univ. of California, 43–55.

BARNES, RUTH (1991). 'Patola in Southern Lembata', in Gisela Völger and Karin von Welck (eds.), *Indonesian Textiles: Symposium 1985*. Ethnologica, n.s. 14. Cologne: Rautenstrauch-Joest-Museum, 11–17.

BASÍLIO DE SÁ, ARTUR (1956). *Documentação para a História das Missões do Padroado Português do Oriente, Insulíndia*, iv. Lisbon: Agência Geraldo Ultramar.

BURNHAM, DOROTHY K. (1981). *A Textile Terminology: Warp and Weft*. London: Routledge & Kegan Paul.

DIETRICH, STEFAN (1986). 'Kolonialismus und Mission auf Flores'. Ph.D. thesis, Univ. of Tübingen.

ELMBERG, JOHN-ERIK (1968). *Balance and Circulation: Aspects of Tradition and Change among the Mejprat of Irian Barat*. Etnografiska Museet Monograph Series No. 12. Stockholm: Etnografiska Museet.

FOX, JAMES J. (1977). 'Roti, Ndao, and Savu', in Mary Hunt Kahlenberg (ed.), *Textile Traditions of Indonesia*. Los Angeles: County Museum of Art, 97–100.

—— (1980). 'Figure Shark and Pattern Crocodile: The Foundations of the Textile Traditions of Roti and Ndao', in Mattiebelle Gittinger (ed.), *Indonesian Textiles*. Washington, DC: Textile Museum, 39–55.

GITTINGER, MATTIEBELLE (1979). *Splendid Symbols: Textiles and Tradition in Indonesia*. Washington, DC: Textile Museum.

HEIN, A. R. (1890). *Die bildenden Künste bei den Dayaks auf Borneo: Ein Beitrag zur allgemeinen Kunstgeschichte*. Vienna: Hölder.

JAGER GERLINGS, J. H. (1952). *Sprekende Weefsels: Studie over Onstaan en Betekenis van Weefsels van enige Indonesische Eilanden*. Koninklijk Instituut voor de Tropen Mededelingen No. 99. Amsterdam: Koninklijk Instituut voor de Tropen.

JASPER, J. E., and PIRNGADIE, MAS (1912). *De Weefkunst: De inlandsche Kunstnijverheid in Nederlandsch Indie*. The Hague: Mouton.

KERAF, GREGORIUS (1978). *Morfologi Dialek Lamalera*. Ende, Flores: Arnoldus.

ROUFFAER, G. P., and JUYNBOLL, H. H. (1914). *De Batik-Kunst in Nederlandsch-Indie en haar Geschiedenis*. Utrecht: Oosthoek.

SCHUSTER, CARL (1965). 'Remarks on the Design of an Early Ikat Textile in Japan', in *Festschrift Alfred Bühler*. Basler Beiträge zur Geographie und Ethnologie, Ethnologische Reihe, 2. Basle: Pharos.

VATTER, ERNST (1932). *Ata Kiwan: Unbekannte Bergvölker im tropischen Holland*. Leipzig: Bibliographisches Institut.

VROKLAGE, B. A. G. (1953). *Ethnographie der Belu in Zentral-Timor*. 3 vols. Leiden: Brill.

PART IV

The Anthropology of Aesthetics

8

From Dull to Brilliant: The Aesthetics of Spiritual Power among the Yolngu

HOWARD MORPHY

Content is a glimpse of something, an encounter like a flash.

Willem de Kooning

Introduction

In this essay I shall consider aspects of the aesthetics of Yolngu art. I am concerned primarily with a category of painting produced by men, but I place my analysis in the broader framework of the aesthetics of Yolngu ritual.[1] The Yolngu are an Australian Aboriginal people, renowned in the anthropological literature as the Murngin, who live in north-east Arnhem Land, a coastal area of northern Australia.

'Aesthetics' is a rubric term with no simple, universally acceptable, definition. It is easier to state the kind of things it is about than it is to provide a neat definition of what it is. Hence I will begin by briefly considering what I think an essay on Yolngu aesthetics should be about. Aesthetics is concerned with how something appeals to the senses—in the case of paintings, with the visual effect they have on the person looking at them. An aesthetic response concerns sensations or feelings that are evoked or caused in the viewer looking at a painting—a positive emotional response, one that can be associated with feelings of pleasure, but which is not necessarily interpreted as pleasure. An aesthetic effect may be additional to some other kind of property of an object, for example, its communicating functions or practical properties. The aesthetic effect may be complementary to some other kind of property of an object or necessary to its fulfilling some other function. For example, an object may be aesthetically pleasing in order to draw a person's attention to it so that some other function may be fulfilled or message communicated. An aesthetic effect may arise out of the way some other purpose of the object is achieved, for example, through the perfect functional utility of a chair, the simplicity of an idea, or the elegance of a solution to a problem.

Aesthetic properties are often properties of objects which require them to be seen in a particular way by viewers who, because of their background or personality, are able to appreciate them—a relationist perspective that may be reduced to: beauty is in the eye of the beholder and the light in which the object is seen (cf. Morawski, 1974: 23). In an extreme form, however, I reject this subjectivist position, for while an artist familiar with his or her audience may try to create an object which elicits a particular response from the audience, the creator of an object is never the complete master of its aesthetic potential. With the audience the artist thinks he or she knows, it is always going to be difficult to know if the intended effect has been achieved because of the difficulties involved in communicating the emotions. The artist may find an unfamiliar audience responding in unintended and unpredictable ways to quite different attributes of the object from those he was conscious of creating. Some have argued that it is precisely the potential of objects to be aesthetically or expressively productive beyond the control of their creator that makes them into works of art. Whitford (1981: 7) writes of the artist Egon Schiele: 'Only minor artists manage to say all they wish to and major artists frequently express things they did not intend to or were even unaware of.'

This essay will focus primarily on the aesthetics of Yolngu art for Yolngu people. I am not concerned with the aesthetics of Yolngu art for a European audience or market, though there is some overlap in response in the two cases, and European evaluations of different works of art can be related to Yolngu ones. However, although I am focusing on the aesthetics of Yolngu art for Yolngu, I am not concerned with Yolngu aesthetics in the strictest sense of the term. For by Yolngu aesthetics I would understand a body of theory about art which is reflexive and concerned with the theory of response to works of art and with art-critical practice. The Yolngu have neither aestheticians nor art critics in this sense. Indeed, even by using a looser definition it is arguable that the Yolngu do not have an indigenous aesthetics, in that there is little overlap between Yolngu ways of talking about objects that Europeans call art and Europeans' way of talking about the same objects. Yolngu are unlikely to say of a painting that it is beautiful or well balanced, or that it conveys a particular emotion relative to another painting. The terms Yolngu use when talking about art do have some overlap with those Europeans employ, but more often their critical focus seems different. Aesthetic motivations are seldom acknowledged by the Yolngu as a purpose behind the production of works of art. However, the Yolngu clearly are concerned to produce effects on the senses by which the success of the work can be judged and which Europeans would interpret as aesthetic effect. Indeed, I do not wish to exclude the possibility that Yolngu art may have certain expressive characteristics that are universal in their effect, and which have been utilized by artists of many different cultures throughout time. Such properties are properties of form that may have an effect on the senses in an analogous way to the effect of heat on the nerves—in other words, they do not have to be interpreted in order to have an impact. When interpreted, indeed, they may be understood in very different ways in different cultural contexts; and as aesthetic characteristics they may be evaluated differently in different traditions and in the context of different valuational criteria.[2] In the case of Yolngu art, at a general level what Europeans interpret as an aesthetic effect Yolngu interpret as a manifestation of ancestral power emanating from the ancestral past.

'Aesthetic' as I have employed the term implies the existence of a scale of judgement, or at least a standard that has to be achieved or properties that have to be created in an object if it is to be successful. In other words, some works can be judged failures as works of art. It also implies the possibility that some artists produce work that is in general considered to be better than that of other artists, and that they can hence be considered better artists. Both these propositions challenge conventional wisdom about Yolngu art which would have it that any, indeed all, Yolngu can paint, that no specialists are recognized, and that none is considered better than others.[3] However, it is this conventional view that is wrong. Some individuals are recognized as more skilful painters than others, and it is these individuals who are chosen to paint on ceremonial occasions in preference to others. The role taken by the individuals will, it is true, be justified on other grounds—for example, that as sisters' children they are the appropriate persons to do the painting, or that they belong to a mother's mother's clan, and mother's mother's clan members always do that particular kind of painting.[4] However, there are usually a number of other people, who fit the social specifications for performing the role equally well (if not better), who will never be seen producing a painting. These people's status is not diminished by the fact that they never paint, and they may well excel in other areas of ritual performance—for example, as leading singers or dancers.

The idea that the artist's skill is unrecognized by the Yolngu may have arisen partly because the individual appears to gain no status or reward for his role as an artist, and because his performance of that role is seldom attributed to any special skill he possesses. When asked directly, however, people readily acknowledge that some people paint better than others. By this Yolngu do not mean that they are more creative than other artists, for individual creativity is denied; rather, they refer to differential skill. Consistent with this, Yolngu, when criticizing a work of art, or explaining why a person does not paint, usually refer to a technical rather than a cognitive deficiency, as, for example, 'He knows all about painting, it's just that his hand shakes too much when he holds the brush'. (Unless, of course, a person has failed to learn the design correctly, in which case he has simply made a mistake which must be rectified.) Certainly, the ideology that individual creativity has no role in Yolngu art can be challenged and is indeed false, but as far as public comments are concerned, individual creativity has no positive role. If a person is said to have invented a design, then that is in itself a negative comment on it. Implicitly, however, artistic creativity is recognized, and those artists who are asked to paint on ceremonial occasions are frequently ones whom Europeans would label as creative.

Before considering the aesthetics of Yolngu paintings, it is necessary to consider what kinds of objects paintings are to the Yolngu: for if paintings vary cross-culturally, it is partly on the basis of the different meaning of these objects to members of different cultures. Their significance affects the way in which an object is seen and also what its emotional effect is interpreted as being: a ray of light may convey the awesome power of nature or, alternatively, be understood as the power of God.

Yolngu Paintings and the Creation of Bir'yun

Yolngu paintings are referred to as *mardayin miny'tji*. Neither word has a direct equivalent in English, but I will begin by considering the meaning of *miny'tji* as it overlaps in meaning with the English word 'painting'. *Miny'tji* can be roughly glossed as 'a painting' although, as we shall see, it is semantically more complex than this. The act of painting can be described by using either the phrase *miny'tji dja:ma* (painting work) or the compound verb *miny'tji-yarpuma* (jabbing or spearing paint). An artist can be described as 'a person having painting work' (*miny'tji-dja:mamirri yolngu*) or 'a person who jabs paint' (*miny'tji-yarpunhara yolngu*). These phrases refer to what I shall show to be two separate components of the meaning of the word *miny'tji*: design and colour. Thus *miny'tji* can be used adjectivally to describe anything that appears colourful, like the wings of a butterfly or a lump of yellow ochre used as pigment. *Miny'tji* can also be used to refer to any regularly occurring pattern or design, whether it is natural or cultural in origin. The pattern made by interlocking sections of a turtle's shell, the thin spirals engraved by insects on the bark of the scribbly gum, and the chequer-board pattern in black and white on the cone shell are all alike *miny'tji*, as are blazons on a car door and designs on a can of baked beans.

The distinction between natural and cultural designs must not be too rigidly conceived, as things which are called *miny'tji* are all believed to be the result of consequential action; *miny'tji* are meaningful designs (see also Stanner, 1960: 102). The design on the back of a turtle is seen as its design in much the same way as the design painted on a human body is seen as belonging to and representing a clan. A myth, for example, explains the origin of the pattern on the turtle's shell, how it was put there, and why it takes the form it does. Myths explaining the form of natural designs are analogous to those relating to cultural designs; indeed, natural and cultural designs are frequently

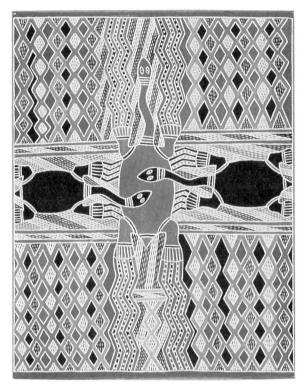

FIG. 8.1. Yangarriny Gumana, *Long-Necked Freshwater Turtle at Ga:rngarn*; 1976, Yirrkala; ochres on woven reinforced paper board; 20 × 25 in. (50.8 × 63.5 cm.); photographer: Howard Morphy; private collection. The painting represents the sea's flood-waters carrying debris of wood and logs along the river. Streamers of weed are attached to the limbs of the turtle.

seen as two manifestations of the same thing. The patterns on the back of the long-necked fresh-water tortoise (*minhala*), for example, are believed to have resulted from water-weed clinging to the shell of an ancestral being in the form of a tortoise, as it moved along the bottom of the river at Ga:rngarn. Ga:rngarn was also the place where Barama, one of the major ancestral beings of the Yirritja moiety, emerged from the ground. He, though human in form, also came out of the water with the water-weed clinging to his body and falling from his arms in streamers. The pattern of the weed on his body became the clan design of the Dhalwangu (Fig. 8.1). It is the same as shell designs on representations of the tortoise. The majority of designs are believed to have originated in a similar way, being naturally occurring designs isolated by their connection with a particular ancestral being. (Moreover, when it is realized that many ancestral beings were transformed from animals into men and from animate to inanimate forms, and that natural designs bear witness to the reality of these transformations, then the distinction between natural and cultural designs is largely irrelevant as far as Yolngu understandings are concerned.)

The word *mardayin* can be roughly translated as 'sacred law'; indeed, that is how it is referred to by Yolngu when speaking English. The *mardayin* consists of sets of songs, dances, paintings, sacred objects, and ritual incantations associated with ancestral beings. The *mardayin* refers to the actions of ancestral beings in creating the land and in instituting the practices of Yolngu life. Yolngu ceremonies involve the use of the *mardayin* to recreate ancestral events and the use of their powers to serve particular ends. To the Yolngu, the *mardayin* are not only the means of expressing ancestral events, but also part of the essence of the ancestral beings themselves. They provide a means of becoming directly involved with the ancestral past.

Ancestral designs are among the main manifestations of ancestral beings which can be reproduced by humans. The same design may take many forms: it may be produced as a sand sculpture, as a design in string, or in painted form as a body painting, bark painting or painting on a ceremonial post. Details of the design will vary according to the medium used and the space available.

Yolngu paintings are ancestral designs or manifestations in three senses. Firstly, the designs are ones that originally appeared on the body of the ancestral being they represent, and were designated by that ancestral being as part of the sacred law (or property) of the group of human beings who subsequently occupied the land with which the design is associated. Continued ownership of that land is thereafter conditional on maintaining the rituals associated with the land (see Morphy, 1988). Secondly, paintings encode meanings that refer to the events in the ancestral past that resulted in the creation of the landscape, including, of course, events that led to the creation of the design itself. Finally, designs are ancestral in that they are thought to contain the power of the ancestral being concerned and provide a source of ancestral power for use in ritual. The power of the design may be used for a specific purpose, for example, when painted on a coffin-lid it may assist the soul of the dead person on its journey to the lands of the dead. Or it may be used in a more general way to increase the fertility of the land or to strengthen the participants in a ceremony.

To summarize the argument so far, Yolngu paintings are ancestral designs which are the property of clans and which contain spiritual power. The functions of Yolngu paintings relate directly to these properties. Paintings are produced in ceremony as part of the recreation of ancestral events, as a demonstration of rights held by a clan in *mardayin* and land, and as a source of spiritual power. Aesthetic factors would seem at first hardly to enter the picture as far as the concept of paintings is concerned, or, indeed, in relation to their use. In the majority of cases, paintings that have taken many hours or even days to paint are covered up or destroyed within hours or even minutes of their completion. Coffin-lid paintings, for example, are carried out in a restricted context. Apart from the artists, hardly anyone appears to look at the painting except occasionally to see whether it is finished or not. Senior men with rights in the painting may occasionally look at it and offer instruction on a point of detail. Other men may occasionally offer assistance in finishing off the painting with cross-hatching, especially if time is getting short. As soon as the painting is completed, it is covered up with a sheet of cloth and will never be seen again. A body-painting's fate is usually similar. A painting that has taken eight or nine hours to complete may be rubbed out shortly after its completion in order that the person may return to the public arena. The majority of paintings like this are seen in their full glory for a fleeting second, and even then by a restricted set of people. It is inappropriate for women and uninitiated men to show too much interest in the ceremonial production of paintings. Although the majority of paintings are done in contexts that are only semi-restricted, where they could be observed by anyone who tried to look, people tend to avert their eyes. Hence much of people's experience of painting consists of images fleetingly glimpsed out of the corner of the eye.

On reflection, however, there is no reason why a painting has to be seen for aesthetic factors to be important in its production and in its effect. For example, a painting may only have to be known to be a type of object that is aesthetically powerful for it to achieve its purpose; it may not be necessary for it to be seen to be so. There are contexts in which paintings are displayed publicly and in which everyone has the opportunity to look at them. For example, mortuary poles that are erected in memory of a dead person have designs painted on them which are similar to those painted on coffin-lids. Their aesthetic effect is known, and hence the aesthetic effect of coffin paintings is, or may be, taken for granted. What this does suggest in the case of coffin paintings, however, is that gaining an aesthetic response from an audience is not part of the intention of the artist (as few people view the painting), and that the painting must be being produced for some other purpose. As far as the body-paintings are concerned, the aesthetic value of the art may be enhanced by the limited extent to which it is seen in its pristine state by the majority of people. Long, contemplative viewing is not the only way to appreciate a painting. The brief glimpse from the corner of the eye may, indeed, produce an aesthetic effect in harmony with the way Yolngu art is intended to be experienced and understood.

What, then, is the Yolngu artist trying to produce when he produces a painting in a ritual? What effect is he trying to create, and by what criteria is his work going to be judged? I would argue that the artist is guided by three objectives: to produce a correct design, to produce an ancestrally powerful design, and to produce a painting which enhances or beautifies the object it is painted on. The setting of the correct design is primarily associated with the first stage of painting, the drawing of the basic outline pattern which constrains the final form the painting will take. It is important that the design should be an acceptable representation of the ancestral design, in that other knowledgeable people are prepared to accept it as the correct form of the design. In outline form the design, although it is a sign of a particular ancestral being or set of ancestral beings, is relatively safe and free of ancestral power. At this stage the painting is referred to as 'dull' or 'rough'. The power and beauty of the painting are acquired through the painting process, and in particular are associated with the final stages of the painting. They are produced by qualities of the painting that are quite separate from correct form, though a painting that does not possess correct form could not, for the Yolngu, have other qualities.

In order to understand the aesthetics of Yolngu art, it is necessary to examine the painting process in some detail, particularly in relation to Yolngu understandings of the transformations that occur in the appearance of paintings as they progress.

Yolngu paintings are composed of a number of components of different types organized in a particular way. There is a base colour (Fig. 8.2), then various internal subdivisions, figurative representations, geometric background patterns, and cross-hatching.[5] For the purposes of this discussion, however, it is necessary to distinguish only between cross-hatching and the other components, which can be referred to as the underlying design. The underlying design is produced by outlining the figurative and geometric components of the painting in yellow ochre (or occasionally black) on a red background (Fig. 8.3).

The initial production of other components is played down in relation to cross-hatching. Thus artists assert that it does not matter if you draw the figurative representations roughly or the clan design quickly (as long as you do this correctly): 'you draw them roughly because you are going to cover them up' (Figs. 8.4, 8.5). In fact, the initial 'drawing' of a painting will usually be completed within an hour, with up to a week being spent in cross-hatching. Indeed, as the painting progresses it undergoes considerable transformation. Because cross-hatching always overlaps the outlines of figurative representations, their size is gradually reduced and the outline changed through the course of the painting. Thus the figures are initially drawn larger than they finally appear. Before cross-hatching, the painting looks dull, consisting of yellow and black on red, and it is often difficult to discern its structure. After cross-hatching, the successful painting attains a shimmering brilliance, and its separate components become clearly defined (Fig. 8.6).[6]

The transformation of a painting from a rough dull state to a clearly defined and bright state through the process of cross-hatching is clearly recognized by the Yolngu. The two main criteria employed in judging a painting, apart from the matter of its correctness, are its brightness and the clarity of its cross-hatched lines.[7] If the cross-hatched lines are too thick or if they run into each other, then the painting will be criticized as being 'too rough'; if there is a preponderance of black in the painting, then it may not be bright enough.

It is the quality of brilliance that is associated in Yolngu art with ancestral power and with beauty. I will consider its association with ancestral power first. The importance of the concept of 'brilliance' was first noted by the anthropologist Donald Thomson in his unpublished field notes (1937). The Yolngu word Thomson translates as 'brilliant' is *bir'yun*. *Bir'yun* can be termed an aesthetic property, as it operates independently of specific meanings encoded in a painting, although, as we shall see, it interacts with them. *Bir'yun* is a particular visual effect. Thomson (ibid. 5 Aug.) writes that the mundane or secular meaning of *bir'yun* refers to intense sources and refractions of light, the sun's rays, and to light sparkling in bubbling fresh water, as in:

gong	*ngayi*	*walu*	*bir'yu-bir'yun*	*marritji*
ray	its	sun	scintillate-scintillate	go
'the sun's rays scintillate'

Applied to paintings, *bir'yun* is 'the flash of light, the sensation of light one gets and carries away in one's mind's eye, from a glance at *likanpuy miny'tji*' (ibid. 4 Aug.). The *bir'yun* of a painting is the visual effect of the fine cross-hatched lines that cover the surface of a sacred painting: 'it's the sensation of light, the uplift of looking at this carefully carried out work. They see in it a likeness to the *wangarr* [ancestral past]'.

Thus *bir'yun* is the shimmering effect of finely cross-hatched paintings which project a brightness that is seen as emanating from the *wangarr* beings themselves—this brightness is one of the things that endows the painting with ancestral power.

In the past, paintings with fine cross-hatching were, in an unmodified form, restricted to closed contexts. These paintings were referred to as *likanpuy miny'tji*. Men painted with *likanpuy miny'tji* would have to have the design removed, or at least obscured, before returning to the main camp or public ceremonial ground. Most commonly the painting was modified by smearing the cross-hatched infill, reducing the fineness and separation of the cross-hatched lines to a smudge of pigment. They would be transformed back from a bright to a dull state. Thus, although some aspects of the form of the painting remained discernible, it had lost its brilliance (*bir'yun*) and, through losing this, had lost some of its ancestral power. It had lost, according to one of Thomson's informants, 'its likeness to the *wangarr*'.

There is, in fact, a category of paintings which has no cross-hatching. Such paintings are referred to as *bulku miny'tji* or 'rough' paintings. These consist

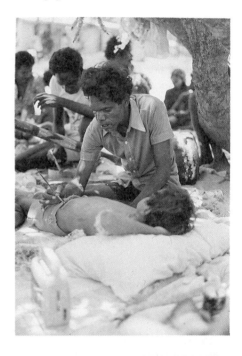

FIG. 8.2. A circumcision ceremony at Yirrkala, July 1974; photographer: Howard Morphy. The artist begins to outline a design on the initiate's body, which has already been painted with red ochre. See also Pl. X.

FIG. 8.3. A circumcision ceremony at Yirrkala, July 1974; photographer: Howard Morphy. A number of boys are having designs painted on their chests prior to their being circumcised. The painting is done to the accompaniment of songs. Sacred dilly bags decorated with rainbow lorikeet feathers are hung in the branches of the trees above the initiates' heads. See also Pl. XI.

FIG. 8.4. A circumcision ceremony at Yirrkala, July 1974; photographer: Howard Morphy. After the designs are outlined in yellow, cross-hatching begins.

FIG. 8.5. The artist Narritjin Maymuru finishing a painting, Canberra, October 1978; photographer: Howard Morphy. A brush of human hair (*marwat*) is gently drawn across the surface of the painting to produce the fine cross-hatched lines.

FIG. 8.6. Welwi Warnambi, *Dhuwa Moiety Wild-Honey Painting*; November 1974, Yirrkala; ochres on woven reinforced paper board; 20 × 25 in. (50.8 × 63.5 cm.); photographer: Howard Morphy; private collection. This painting captures the Yolngu aesthetic of brilliance and clarity. See also Pl. XII.

of the outline shapes of clan designs and are painted during the public phases of ceremonies. They are in many respects *likanpuy* paintings without the cross-hatching—in other words, paintings in their dull form or mode. This is explicitly recognized by the Yolngu. One of Thomson's informants described *bulku* paintings as being *mali nhangu likanpuy miny'tji*—shades or shadows of *likanpuy* paintings—whereas *likanpuy* paintings can be described as *mali wangarr*—shades of the ancestral world.

Bir'yun represents a generalized spiritual power associated with the *wangarr*, which all *likanpuy* paintings can potentially possess, irrespective of the clan or moiety to which they belong. Each painting, however, is more closely associated with one ancestral being or set of ancestral beings than it is with others, and, depending on the clan and ancestral being concerned, *bir'yun* may have more specific connotations. For example, Thomson records that the *bir'yun* of a Gupapuyngu clan *birrkurda* (wild honey) design expressed the light of fresh water and the light of eucalyptus in flower. He quoted an informant saying of it, *ngoy ngamathirri, ngoy kitkitthun*, which he translates as 'the light that makes the heart go happy, makes it smile'. Although a reasonable free translation, it is a little misleading, as *ngoy* refers to something more abstract than the heart, and is better referred to as 'the seat of the emotions', which Yolngu locate in the region of the gut. In myth, the wild honey ancestor is closely associated with fresh water and with eucalypt flowers that provide the nectar for Yirritja moiety bees. The meanings 'fresh water' and 'nectar' are encoded in elements

FIG. 8.7. Dula Ngurruwutthun, *Yirritja Moiety Wild-Honey Painting*; February 1975, Yirrkala; ochres on woven reinforced paper board; 20 × 25 in. (50.8 × 63.5 cm.); photographer: Howard Morphy; private collection. This painting is similar to that referred to by Thomson in his field notes. The diamonds represent the structure of the hive and various components of the wild-honey mythological complex (see Morphy, 1979: 153 ff.).

of the design. Hence the visual effect of the painting, *bir'yun*, is integrated with semantic aspects of the painting, enabling it to express characteristic properties of the *wangarr* being that it represents (cf. Fig. 8.7).

A second source of spiritual power, blood, is associated with similar qualities in ritual as the fine cross-hatched lines. In Warner's (1958: 274) description of blood-letting in the Djungguwan ceremony, it seems that both the process of blood-letting and the blood itself are associated with feelings of happiness and joy. The blood of initiates is drawn from the elbow (*likan*) and collected in a paper-bark basin. Warner (1958: 276) quotes an informant saying 'when [the initiate] gets up he'll be very quick and feel very light; and he will be very happy because the blood running out of him will make him that way' (cf. Munn, 1986: 191). Later the blood is used to paint sacred designs on the bodies of the participants, and white down is stuck on to the blood and highlights the design. The blood is now sacred blood, the blood of the *wangarr*. The blood is painted only on the initiated men, and it gives them strength: 'it makes us feel easy and comfortable and it makes us strong' (Warner, 1958: 277). But to women the blood is dangerous, for contact with it will cause sores, and it is too strong to be painted on the neophytes.

The language used to talk about the blood echoes the language used to talk about the qualities of the painting and its effect. In the blood-letting the feelings of lightness and happiness, perhaps induced in part by the loss of blood and the power of the occasion, are interpreted as ancestral power and are subjectively experienced as ancestral power by the initiate. *Bir'yun* is also interpreted as ancestral power, and the cross-hatched designs when painted on the body of the initate may become an objectification of those very feelings associated with blood-letting that the individual has come to interpret as the experience of that power. The visual effect of *bir'yun* is both a complementary source of such experiences and an objectification of related experiences which cumulatively create the felt reality of ancestral power.

In the majority of cases *bir'yun* is associated with positive emotions such as joyfulness (*wakul*) or happiness (*ngamathirri*). However, Thomson gives one example in which it appears to express negative emotions. This concerns the *bir'yun* of Ma:rna, the shark ancestor (Fig. 8.8). Thomson records that the *bir'yun* from paintings of the shark can also be referred to by a more specific term, *djawarul*. Djawarul is the proper name of a sacred well created by the *wangarr* shark, at the place where the shark was killed by Murrayanara. *Djawarul* refers to the 'flash of anger in the shark's eye—the blaze of anger of the shark killed by stealth'. The spirit of the shark is dangerous (*mardakarritj*), and was described as *miringu ma:rr*, 'the power of vengeance'. This is, of course, by no means inconsistent with Yolngu concepts of ancestral power. *Ma:rr* is a positive force associated with happiness, strength, health, and fertility, but it is also associated with death, and can always have a dangerous dimension. *Ma:rr* can be dangerous to anyone who is spiritually weak, to young people, to people suffering bereavement, to people recovering from serious illness, and, to an extent, to women as a category. It can also give strength to participants in an avenging expedition. If someone who is vulnerable sees a sacred object or painting, their sickness and eventual death may result. This is one of the reasons why paintings were, and sometimes still are, smeared before they are displayed in public, and why people avoid looking

FIG. 8.8. Ma:w' Mununggurr, *Djapu Clan Shark Painting*;
November 1974, Yirrkala; ochres on bark (*Eucalyptus tetradonta
Darwinii*); *c.*48 × 24 in. (122 × 61 cm.); photographer: Howard
Morphy. This is by the artist who painted the Marakulu
woman's coffin-lid (see pp. 200–1 below).

directly at paintings that are being produced. The 'flash of anger in the shark's eye' is a powerful image that captures this aspect of ancestral power; it reinforces some of the danger that surrounds that power, and contributes to its strength.

To summarize this section, Yolngu artists aim to create a particular visual effect in their paintings which is referred to as *bir'yun*. *Bir'yun* is thought of as a shimmering quality of light which engenders an emotional response. The response is associated with phrases that in the context of contemporary European art would be interpreted as being concerned with an aesthetic appreciation of the work as art, to do with feelings of lightness, joy, happiness, and power. In the Yolngu case, however, the emotional effect is interpreted as representing or being a manifestation of ancestral power. It is almost as if ancestral power is encoded in paintings by way of the emotional response it engenders in the viewer—a process that is probably widespread in religious art.

The Ritual Value of Brilliance

The aesthetics of Yolngu paintings is part of a more general aesthetics associated with Yolngu ritual and symbolism in which bright contrasts with dull and is associated with manifestation of the *wangarr*. The raw materials that are used to produce the surface finish on ceremonial objects or in decorating the human body, that is, red and yellow ochres, blood, pipe clay, rainbow lorikeet and cockatoo feathers, beeswax, and animal fats, all have properties of shininess and brightness. Frequently, within these categories particularly bright examples are considered most powerful, and are selected for use in preference to others. The most highly prized red ochre, and one that is traded throughout Arnhem Land, is a purple-coloured rock that produces a naturally burnished finish. It has the effect of providing a rich sheen to the painted surface. Other natural substances that are thought to be ancestrally powerful include blood and fat. These are both substances that, when applied to the human body in ritual, provide it with a sheen. The most prized fat is the rich yellow fat found round the liver and kidneys of animals such as shark and sting-ray, in the tail of goannas and kangaroos, and in the limbs of tortoises and turtles. Such fat, as well as being collected for ritual purposes, is a highly valued food resource that is thought to have restorative properties and to be a sign of health in the animal. Animals without fat may, indeed, be rejected as food. As far as the human individual is concerned, people who are plump and sleek are thought to be healthy, and may be thought to be endowed with spiritual power. Thomson (1975: 7) reports that to be too fat can be dangerous because it arouses fear and jealousy in others.[8]

The qualities of brightness are precisely those that are taken up when materials such as parrot feathers, red ochre, or fat are incorporated in Yolngu song and poetry, and their association with spiritual power is often referred to. For example, one of the key songs of Dhuwa moiety ritual refers to the Djan'kawu sisters hanging their dilly bags, decorated with the orange and green feathers of the rainbow lorikeet, in the branches of a casuarina tree, at the end of the day. The feathers are caught in the rays of the evening sun which intensifies their redness. As Ian Keen (1977) has shown, this particular song has many possible translations and evokes a series of complementary images and associations. One based on a translation by Wandjuk Marika is as follows:

> Rainbow lorikeet climbing the Djuta.
> Drying its feathers in the rays of the sun
> Children of the Djan'kawu ... shining[9]

Towards the end of the Djan'kawu sisters' journey is a place, Djiriniwuruma, on the mainland north of Milingimbi. There they laid down their dilly bags, which were transformed into a rock formation which, according to the Yolngu, radiates red and blue colours in the sunlight and produces coloured reflections in the waters of the swamps (Berndt, 1976: 164).

Within songs, and sequences of songs, it is possible to identify an underlying structure of content progressing from dark and dull to light and brilliant that is analogous to the transformation that takes place in the process of painting. A particularly good example is at the climax of the Goulburn Island series of songs that belongs to the Dhuwa moiety in north-east Arnhem Land. The Goulburn Island song cycle recounts the seduction of a group of western Arnhem Land women by the long-penised men of Goulburn Island. Their relationship was consummated amidst the cabbage palms beside a wide lagoon adjoining the Arafura Sea. The verses I quote follow on immediately from this idyll. The translated text is from Berndt (1976: 66) with some abridgements:

1

From those fighting clubs, assembled in rows come the Western clouds ...
Dark rain clouds and wind, rising up in the west ...
Clouds that spread all over the sky, spreading across the country
They spread all over the sky
Dark rain clouds they come rising up.

2

Thunder rolls along the bottom of the clouds, at the wide expanse of water,
Thunder shaking the clouds.
Large snake at the billabong edged with bamboo,
'I make the crash of thunder—I spit and the lightning flashes'.

3

The tongues of the lightning snake flicker and twist
Flashing above the people of the Western clans

All over the sky their tongues flicker.
Lightning flashes through the clouds, flash of the Lightning Snake.
Its blinding flash lights up the palm leaves
Gleams on the cabbage palms, and on the shining semen among the leaves.

Analagous transformations or movements from dull to brilliant, from dark to shining, occur within the ritual process itself. Many Yolngu rituals operate to enhance the spiritual power of individuals and the community. One of the ways in which this is done is by making people into sacred objects or representations of the *wangarr* by making them shine. The bodies of initiates are rubbed with ochre and fat and then decorated with feathers and *likanpuy* paintings. In such a state they become like the ancestral beings. Such a state is not achieved in a single ceremony but as a result of participating in a number of ceremonies during which the individual is progressively associated with the *wangarr* (cf. Keen, 1978: 229). For example, in the case of circumcision, the initiate will first take part in a ceremony in which his body is simply rubbed in red ochre. On subsequent occasions increasingly elaborate paintings will be put on his body until finally, at his circumcision ceremony, his body will be painted from his head to his knees with *likanpuy* paintings infilled with fine cross-hatching. The whole process will take place over a period of several years, and can be seen to involve a movement from dull to brilliant just like that which takes place with the production of a single *likanpuy* painting.

Aesthetics and Yolngu Ritual Performance

So far I have been dealing almost exclusively with the aesthetics of form; but aesthetics can also be concerned with content, with the way in which a particular idea is expressed, with the appropriateness of an image to a particular event.

Some aesthetic effects associated with particular genres, for instance catharsis in tragedy, are centrally concerned with content. Content is integral to the aesthetics of Yolngu ritual, as it is for reasons of content that the particular ritual component is chosen. The individual component has aesthetic qualities independent of context, but aesthetic effects also arise out of the way in which elements of the ritual are structured and joined together in a sequence in relation to the themes and objectives of the particular ceremony. In order to understand this aspect of the aesthetics of Yolngu art, it is necessary to look briefly at the semantics of ritual components and the way in which they are integrated within ritual performance.[10]

Components of Yolngu ritual are, as mentioned earlier, the *mardayin*: the songs, dances, paintings, incantations, and ritual actions that are associated with the actions of ancestral beings in the ancestral past that resulted in the creation of the landscape. The components can be used in many rituals of different types, in each case being joined with other components in ways that reflect the themes of the particular ceremony. For example, the same painting could be painted on a boy's chest prior to circumcision, on a coffin-lid for a primary burial ceremony, and on a memorial post for a Djungguwan ceremony (which is in part a regional fertility ceremony). In an abstract sense, the painting or any other ritual component has meaning independent of any context in which it is embedded. To use a concept of Schechner's (1981), a Yolngu painting is (in two senses) stored ancestral behaviour. First, it is an ancestral design that originated through actions in the ancestral past, and is indeed thought of as a manifestation of the being concerned. Secondly, the painting encodes meanings that refer to the ancestral events concerned, events which resulted in the transformation of the landscape in a particular locality. I will refer to the latter as the iconographic meaning of the component. In ceremonies, the iconographic meaning becomes the raw material for the creation of a metaphor or analogy that is appropriate to the performance of a particular ritual event. The purpose for which the painting is selected will affect which aspects of its iconographic meaning are emphasized and influence the way it is understood in the ceremony as a whole. To illustrate this point I will use an example taken from a mortuary ritual.

Yolngu believe that a person has two kinds of spirit: *birrimbirr* and *mokuy*. The *birrimbirr* spirit is the one associated with the *wangarr* ancestral beings, and on a person's death it returns to the ancestral domain. One aspect of it returns to the clan lands of the deceased, while another goes to one of the Yolngu lands of the dead. The *mokuy* spirit is an evil spirit or ghost; it must be driven away on a person's death or it will return to haunt the living.

One of the principal themes or objectives of burial ceremonies is the guiding of the *birrimbirr* spirit of the dead person back to the reservoirs of spiritual power in the clan territory. The journey of the *birrimbirr* spirit provides the ordering theme of the ceremony, and affects which ritual elements are selected and the order in which they are performed. In primary burial, the moving of the body from the place of death to the grave provides the framework for enacting the journey of the spirit from the place of death to the place where it will rejoin the clan's ancestors. The ceremony consists of a series of key events: making the coffin, painting the coffin-lid, carrying the coffin to the body, placing the body in the coffin, carrying the body to the grave, and finally burying it in the ground. Each of these events is, or can be, performed in a ritual way, accompanied by song, dance, and incantation. The ritual chosen is both appropriate to the event and associated with a stage of the spirit's journey. For example, when the coffin is moved to the body, a dance may be performed which represents the flood waters of the wet season tossing hollow logs along a water-course at a place half-way between the place of death and the final destination of the spirit. When the coffin is lowered into the grave, a dance may be performed that represents the *wangarr* beings at the spirit's journey's end. What happens to the body is an analogue for what happens to the soul. The coffin painting is incorporated within the structure, both in its purpose and through its integration with other ritual elements.

Frequently the coffin painting represents a central place on the journey of the *birrimbirr* soul. Ritual episodes which precede the nailing of the lid on the coffin refer to earlier stages of the journey, episodes which follow it represent the final stages of the journey. Sometimes the subject or content of the coffin painting may have little connection with the other episodes of the ritual except as a marker of a particular stage on the journey. On other occasions the content of the painting chosen may be interwoven, or connected with the content of subsequent episodes, to create a continuity of symbolic action that flows through the ceremony as a whole.

On one occasion a Marrakulu clan woman died at Yirrkala. Her spiritual home was at Trial Bay many kilometres to the south. Her mother's mother's group, the Djapu clan, were responsible for organizing the ceremony, and the painting chosen for the coffin-lid belonged to their clan. The painting represented the shark at Wurlwurlwuy, inland from Trial Bay (cf. Fig. 8.8). The iconographic meaning of the painting refers to a chunk of ancestral law that includes many ancestral actions and their consequences. The shark, as it rushed headlong inland from Djambarrpuyngu country in Buckingham Bay where it had been speared by an ancestral harpoon, created the river at Wurlwurlwuy. The shark was caught in a fish-trap at Wurlwurlwuy, but escaped by breaking it apart. The shark's body was transformed into various features of the environment including, for example, the trees that line the river bank. In the ceremony, many of those events were referred to in the songs that accompanied the painting of the coffin-lid. However, in the performance as a whole only certain events were singled out and represented in detail, events that became core metaphors for the two journeys that were to take place, the journey of the body to the grave and the journey of the woman's spirit to its spirit home. The shade in which the coffin was painted represented the fish-trap in the river. A trellis of sticks was built at the entrance to the shade representing the barrier wall of the fish-trap. When the body was placed in the coffin, it represented the shark caught in the fish-trap. The time came to move the body, and dancers acting as sharks held the coffin and burst out of the shade, smashing down the wall of sticks. The shark had escaped from the fish-trap and torn it to pieces. The coffin was then carried forward to the vehicle that was to drive it to the cemetery, in a dance that represented the rush of water released from behind the broken-down wall of the fish-trap. In the context of the mortuary ritual, the sequences of action were an analogue for the journey of the woman's spirit, the shark's breaking out of the fish-trap symbolizing the soul's struggle to leave the body and the struggle of the journey ahead. The energy of the shark and the power of the waters represent the power of the ancestral forces summoned to help the soul on its way.

The shark bursting out of the fish-trap functioned as the structuring performative metaphor that enabled the spirit's journey to be accomplished.[11] The principles of selection are concerned centrally with the appropriateness of the mythical episode to the ritual task that has to be accomplished and indirectly with those aspects of the human condition that the ritual is concerned with structuring. Thus in many respects they are equivalent to the aesthetic principles involved in the construction of Western drama. By this argument, the success of the ritual, in the subjective sense of engendering positive emotions in the participants, should depend on such factors as the success of the core metaphors, the extent to which they are integrated within an overall flow of ritual action, and the sense of coherence that the ritual has as a whole.

The same ritual episode can, of course, be associated with a number of different themes of a ceremony. In the burial ceremony for the Marrakulu woman, episodes associated with the shark not only were concerned with the journey of the woman's spirit but also had quite different connotations in relation to a second major theme of Yolngu mortuary rituals—the expression of grief and anger. Mortuary ceremonies provide a context for expressing anger towards anyone who is thought to be responsible for the death, whether through neglect or by sorcery. The shark provides an appropriate focus for these sentiments. The shark, like the mourners, had been wounded, he by a spear, they by bereavement, and he, like they, felt angry. The dancers who carried the coffin from the shade and who broke down the fish-trap had fighting bags gripped tightly in their mouths. The shark dance is a dance of aggression carried out after a member of a clan has been killed, prior to setting out on an avenging expedition. Performed in the mortuary ceremony, it has a cathartic effect, bringing out the emotions of anger and diffusing them or directing them outside the group. This aspect of the ritual is recognized explicitly by some Yolngu:

Before the body had been laid to rest, you are very angry. You feel wild, you break down, you are against the songs, the body, everything. If you just bite the dilly bag, hold yourself, make yourself still, you'll be settled down. But if you suspect someone has caused the deaths—then everyone bites the dilly bag, that's your connection, your power up from the dilly bag. You put into your mind all of your thoughts, and you connect everything to your power, and then you fight another man.[12]

In this respect the shark dance can be understood to be cathartic in the Aristotelian sense of 'arousing negative emotions in order to have some therapeutic effect on the audience's mental health, and thereby giving a pleasurable sense of relief, to reach a state echoed in Milton's phrase from *Samson Agonistes* "in calm of mind all passion spent"' (Beardsley, 1975: 64).

Conclusion

It is my hypothesis that *bir'yun* is an effect that operates cross-culturally. Its impact may be modified by environmental factors, by individual and cultural experience of different visual systems; the way it is experienced may vary on an individual basis according to certain neurophysiological factors; but basically it is an effect which transcends particular cultural contexts. The shimmering effect of the cross-hatching, the appearance of movement, the sense of brightness are all attributes of Yolngu art that can be experienced independently of any other knowledge about Yolngu paintings. They are attributes of Yolngu art as natural objects in much the same way as they are attributes of the sea glistening in the evening sun. However, Yolngu paintings are not natural products but cultural products, and the shimmering effect of the painting is integrated within the system of art as a whole to produce objects that are to be understood in a particular way. It is at this point that relativism enters aesthetics, for the way the *bir'yun* is understood by the Yolngu is quite different from the way a similar effect is to be understood, for example, in Bridget Riley's paintings. *Bir'yun* has a place in a Yolngu system of art that integrates it with other components, formal and semantic, in a unique system. The aesthetics of Yolngu art as it appears to the Yolngu cannot be apprehended directly by an outsider, but must be subject to the same process of translation that characterizes the work of anthropologists in general. However, I leave open the possibility that at the level of form and structure there is a component of the aesthetic that is relatively autonomous, and which consists of elements that can become incorporated in particular aesthetic systems regardless of time and space *and* for the same reason—that is, they produce effects that human beings find stimulating.[13]

In conclusion I will attempt to bring some of the threads of my argument together, focusing on aesthetic aspects of the shark painting. This painting possesses *bir'yun*, brilliance that is thought of as the power of the *mangarr* shark shining like a light from the painting.[14] The light is real in that it is an effect of the technique of painting; its interpretation is a cultural one. The interpretation of the brilliance, what it is understood to represent, is influenced by the images of the shark that are enacted in ritual and by what is known of the shark as an animal, its natural fierceness and power, enhanced by images of the wounded animal trapped in the fish-trap. In the ritual a series of expressive components, the brilliance of the painting, the effect of the music and the dancers, the clouds of dust they kick up, and the smashing down of the trellis of sticks, can all be related to a particular content, the shark ancestor in the context of myth and ritual. The components are effective independently (though in different ways to different people, depending on what they see, know, and experience of the particular events). *Bir'yun*, the shining effect of the painting, can, as we have seen, create sensations of movement, light, and joy. The well-chosen ritual episode can likewise, through its content, have a direct effect on the mental state of the participants, as was the case with the cathartic effect that the aggressive action of the shark dancers had on the feelings of the mourners. We can see how in such contexts the general expressive effect of *bir'yun* can become focused on a particular element of the content of a ritual, and how the two for a moment become interacting components of the shark ancestor. The relationship between form and content is a two-way one. The content gives a particular meaning to the flash of light or to the stamping feet of the dancers, yet the flash of light or cloud of dust in turn may emphasize or enhance a particular content, presenting it in a striking way that associates it with the emotions felt at the time. Such effects, feelings, and understandings, when, for example, they are associated with the shark ancestor, may enhance the latter's believability and, indeed, are interpreted as emanating from the shark, enabling people to experience its power. It is aesthetic effects in combination with cognitive understandings that give concrete form to an abstract conception, and enable people to use that conception for particular purposes.

In some respects my argument echoes Durkheim's (1954) and, more particularly, Radcliffe-Brown's (1964) theory of the role of the emotions in ritual. Radcliffe-Brown's analysis of Andamanese dancing came to conclusions which are similar to mine concerning *bir'yun*. He saw the rhythmic movements of the dancers directly creating feelings of pleasure and inner power that could be interpreted as religious feelings: 'the mental state of the [ritual] dances is closely related to the mental state that we call aesthetic enjoyment' (Radcliffe-Brown, 1964: 251). However, Radcliffe-Brown then went on to link this with a fairly straightforward Durkheimian argument. The Andamanese dance is a pleasure but it is also an obligation willingly undertaken: 'dance produces a condition in which the unity, harmony and concord of the community are at a maximum and in which they are intensely felt by every member. It is to produce the condition that is the primary social function of dance' (ibid. 252). Radcliffe-Brown made no attempt to analyse the cultural meanings of Andamanese dances.

Radcliffe-Brown's functionalist reductionism not only detracts from the original insight by oversimplifying the purposes and effects of ritual action, it also makes the specific content and form of the ritual action largely irrelevant. The analogy he draws throughout the section is between Andamanese dances and the waltzes of European ballrooms—an amusing dig at the Establishment, perhaps, but otherwise unhelpful. The Andamanese dances could consist of anything. What I hope I have shown in the case of the Yolngu is that the selection of ritual components for a ceremony is centrally concerned with matters of content as well as form. Both form and content are associated with aesthetic effects. The selection of dances and paintings is a creative act, undertaken to achieve a ritual purpose. The possibility of the act depends upon a belief in ancestral beings, but selection is also motivated by objectives that can be thought of as aesthetic—the successful ritual act is also successful theatre. The appropriateness of the images to the objectives of the ceremony may well enhance belief in the effectiveness of the ritual; but I certainly do not believe that the power of ritual can be reduced to aesthetic effects, or that such effects are produced in order to create feelings of social solidarity.

Notes

I carried out field-work among the Yolngu during 1973, 1974–5, and 1976. I am grateful to the Australian Institute of Aboriginal Studies and the Australian National University for supporting my research. An earlier version of this essay was written while I was at Oxford on study leave from the Australian National University. I thank Anthony Forge, Frances Morphy, Nancy Munn, and Luke Taylor for their help with various aspects of this essay. Access to Donald Thomson's field notes was facilitated by Judith Wiseman and the National Museum of Victoria. An earlier version of this essay, which won the 1987 J. B. Donne Prize for an Essay in the Anthropology of Art, was first published in *Man*, n.s., 24/1: 21–40. Permission from the Royal Anthropological Institute and the honorary editor of *Man* to reprint this essay is gratefully acknowledged.

Yolngu dialects of the Yirrkala area have 3 short and 3 long vowel phonemes. The short vowels are represented here by *i*, *u*, and *a*, and their long counterparts by *e*, *o*, and *a:* respectively. An *r* preceding another consonant denotes retroflexion of that consonant; between vowels it represents a retroflex continuant. The other 'r' sound in Yolngu dialects, which is an alveolar trill, is represented by *rr*. The digraph *ng* represents a velar nasal, the digraphs *dh* and *th* represent two phonetic variants of the lamino-dental stop phoneme, and *nh* denotes the corresponding nasal phoneme. The digraphs *dj* and *tj* represent the variants of the lamino-alveolar stop, and *ny* the corresponding nasal. ' denotes a glottal stop. For further details, see Frances Morphy, 1983.

1 Although in the past the paintings I write about were exclusively produced by adult men and rarely even glimpsed in unmodified form by women and uninitiated men, today the ritual context has opened out to a considerable extent and women have much greater access to them. Women today produce paintings for sale as part of the local art and craft industry, and in some rare cases have produced paintings in ceremonial contexts to which they had previously been denied access. (See Morphy and Layton, 1981 for a discussion of Yolngu responses to the marketing of their art; and for a detailed analysis of changing categories of Yolngu art, see Morphy, 1977.)

2 Morawski (1974) provides a good discussion of valuational criteria that is relevant to a cross-cultural study of aesthetics. I agree with Morawski (ibid. 174) that 'Aesthetic judgements concern emotions and conations and, even if they refer to some objective qualities, there is no possibility of verifying them by means of measurement operations'. Hence objectivity in evaluations must depend on 'universality'

which may be confined to one social group or culture or which may be spread across the whole of humanity.

3 This point of view is e.g. largely put forward by Mountford (1961: 8).

4 For a discussion of rights in paintings, see Morphy, 1978.

5 For a more detailed discussion of the structure of Yolngu art, see Morphy, 1977; 1989.

6 Jones and Meehan (1978: 27), in their excellent analysis of the Anbarra concept of colour, show how, in a neighbouring group, colour terminology is structured on the opposition between light and brilliant colours (*-gungaltja*) and dark and dull colours (*-gungundja*). They give many examples of the way in which these concepts are applied to objects in everyday contexts. It is clear from their analysis that degree of saturation is not in itself sufficient to determine the allocation of a colour to a particular class, since red is preferentially included in the *-gungaltja* category relative e.g. to greens and blues of the same hue. Brilliance is discerned in certain red objects, such as blood, sunset, and red ochre, and is not discerned in objects of other colours which have the same hues. Although Jones and Meehan do not make the point explicitly, the association between brilliance (*-gungaltja*) and manifestations of ancestral power is clearly revealed by their analysis.

7 In 1988 Bandak Marika, a Yolngu artist who has become a print-maker, discussed with me ways in which her art followed on from traditional Yolngu practice. She had been taught that in European print-making practice you begin with the lighter colours and gradually build up to the darker colours; as a Yolngu she could not do that, but had to begin her prints with the darker colours and end up with the lighter ones. She also said that in the successful Yolngu painting, when it was finished, everything became clear and well-defined, echoing the words that Narritjin Maymuru, a leading Yolngu artist, had used to me a decade earlier in discussing the process of Yolngu painting. He pointed out that towards the end of the painting process, when most of the cross-hatching had been completed and before the figures had been redefined with a thin outline, the painting often looked messy, but suddenly at the very end everything turned out all right and the painting became 'clear'. This simultaneous expression of clarity through shimmering brilliance lies at the heart of Yolngu aesthetics.

8 Thomson's 1975 article provides an excellent discussion of the Yolngu concept of spiritual force or *ma:rr*, in its various manifestations, supported by detailed Yolngu exegesis.

9 The translation comes from Ian Dunlop's film *In Memory of Mawalan* (1976). The film is of public phases of a Dhuwa moiety Nga:rra ritual that focuses on the journey of the Djan'kawu sisters. The film provides impressive illustrative material for anyone wishing to glimpse the power of Yolngu aesthetics. *Djuta* is the name for a species of tree and also for a sacred digging-stick.

10 A detailed analysis of the structure and semantics of Yolngu ritual is to be found in Morphy, 1984.

11 I use 'performative metaphor' in the sense developed by Fernandez (1972; 1977). A performative metaphor is a metaphorical idea that is performed through ritual action and by which certain objectives are said to be achieved. Fernandez sees performative metaphors operating on emotional states and altering them in a process similar to catharsis: '[People] come into a cult with some constellation of

feelings—isolation, disengagement, powerlessness, enervation, debasement, contamination—from which they need to move away. [Metaphors] by persuasion and performance—operate upon the minds of the member allowing him eventually to exit from the ritual incorporated, empowered, activated, euphoric' (Fernandez, 1972: 56).

12 This statement was made by Narritjin Maymuru following the burial ceremony of a child who died at Trial Bay in 1976. The burial ceremony was filmed by Ian Dunlop and is the subject of his *Madarrpa Funeral at Gurka'wuy* (1989). Narritjin's statement refers to the 'Yellow Ochre Dance' which is shown in the film (see also Morphy, 1984: 77 ff).

13 The idea that aesthetic values may be objective is quite compatible with aesthetic relativism: different valuations are not necessarily opposed subjective judgements, but can be complementary responses based on different understandings and perceptions of the same thing or different attributes of the same thing. Access to the aesthetic values of other cultures requires learning about them. McDowell has discussed this issue in an essay on objectivity and aesthetic value in which he writes (1983: 3): 'Our appreciating what we do need not preclude our supposing that there are different values, to which we are perhaps insensitive, in the artefacts of remote cultures—as if, when we take the value we find in the objects we appreciate to be really there in them, we use up all the room the world might afford for aesthetic merit to occupy. In fact it is remarkable, and heartening, to what extent, without losing hold of the sensitivities with which we begin, we can learn to find worth in what seems at first too alien to appreciate.'

14 *Bir'yun* is a manifestation of what using Munn's (1986) terminology we might refer to as a 'qualisign'. Munn's qualisigns are qualities (such as lightness or heaviness) that can be applied to different things across contexts, and which operate as signs. In the Yolngu case, it seems that lightness as a qualisign is associated with ancestral power, and that intense sensations of light are felt as manifestations of that power. Interesting confirmation of the experiential dimension of the dark–bright opposition and the association of light with ancestral power is provided by Chaseling's account (1957: 168) of a Yolngu sea voyage: 'Makarola told me that he had been overtaken by darkness when returning with his family after a day's fishing. A strong wind arose and the canoe was blown out to sea, waves half-filled it, and whilst wives and children baled frantically in the darkness, he toiled to keep the dug-out into the wind. Makarola then remembered his totem and called on it for help. He said that in that instant he saw a "bright light" which filled his head. By the light he was assured that they would be brought safely to land.'

References

BEARDSLEY, MONROE C. (1975). *Aesthetics from Classical Greece to the Present: A Short History*. Studies in the Humanities 13. Tuscaloosa, Ala.: Univ. of Alabama Press (first published 1966).

BERNDT, RONALD M. (1976). *Love Songs of Arnhem Land*. Melbourne: Nelson.

CHASELING, WILBUR S. (1957). *Yulengor: Nomads of Arnhem Land*. London: Epworth Press.

DUNLOP, IAN (director) (1979). *Madarrpa Funeral at Gurka'wuy*. Sydney: Film Australia.

——— (director) (1981). *In Memory of Mawalan*. Sydney: Film Australia.

DURKHEIM, ÉMILE (1954). *The Elementary Forms of the Religious Life*, trans. Joseph Ward Swain. London: Allen & Unwin (first published 1915).

FERNANDEZ, JAMES W. (1972). 'Persuasions and Performances: Of the Beast in Every Body . . . and the Metaphors of Everyman', *Daedalus*, winter 1972: *Myth, Symbol, and Culture*, 39–60.

——— (1977). 'The Performance of Ritual Metaphors', in J. David Sapir and J. Christopher Crocker (eds.), *The Social Use of Metaphor: Essays on the Anthropology of Rhetoric*. Philadelphia: Univ. of Pennsylvania Press, 100–31.

JONES, RHYS, and MEEHAN, BETTY (1978). 'Anberra Concept of Colour', in L. R. Hiatt (ed.), *Australian Aboriginal Concepts*. Canberra: Australian Institute of Aboriginal Studies, 20–39.

KEEN, IAN (1977). 'Ambiguity in Yolngu Religious Language', *Canberra Anthropology*, 1/1: 33–50.

——— (1978). 'One Ceremony One Song: An Economy of Religious Knowledge among the Yolngu of North-East Arnhem Land'. Ph.D. thesis, Australian National Univ., Canberra.

MCDOWELL, JOHN (1983). 'Aesthetic Value, Objectivity, and the Fabric of the World', in Eva Schaper (ed.), *Pleasure, Preference, and Value: Studies in Philosophical Aesthetics*. Cambridge: Cambridge Univ. Press, 1–16.

MORAWSKI, STEFAN (1974). *Inquiries into the Fundamentals of Aesthetics*. Cambridge, Mass.: MIT Press.

MORPHY, FRANCES (1983). 'Djapu: A Yolngu Dialect', in R. M. W. Dixon and Barry J. Blake (eds.), *Handbook of Australian Languages*, iii. Canberra: Australian National Univ. Press.

MORPHY, HOWARD (1977). '"Too Many Meanings": An Analysis of the Artistic System of the Yolngu People of North-East Arnhem Land'. Ph.D. thesis, Australian National Univ., Canberra.

——— (1978). 'Rights in Paintings and Rights in Women: A Consideration of Some of the Basic Problems Posed by the Asymmetry of the "Murngin System"', *Mankind*, 11/3: 208–19.

——— (1984). *Journey to the Crocodile's Nest: An Accompanying Monograph to the Film 'Madarrpa Funeral at Gurka'wuy'* (with an afterword by Ian Dunlop). Canberra: Australian Institute of Aboriginal Studies.

——— (1988). 'Maintaining Cosmic Unity: Ideology and the Reproduction of Yolngu Clans', in Tim Ingold, David Riches, and James Woodburn (eds.), *Hunters and Gatherers, ii: Property, Power and Ideology*. Oxford: Berg, 249–71.

——— (1989). 'On Representing Ancestral Beings', in Howard Morphy (ed.), *Animals into Art*. One World Archaeology 7. London: Unwin Hyman, 144–60.

——— and LAYTON, R. (1981). 'Choosing among Alternatives: Cultural Transformation and Social Change in Aboriginal Australia and the French Jura', *Mankind*, 13/1: 56–73.

MOUNTFORD, CHARLES P. (1961). 'The Artist and his Art in an Australian Aboriginal Society', in Marian W. Smith (ed.), *The Artist in Tribal Society: Proceedings of a Symposium held at the Royal Anthropological Institute*. Glencoe, Ill.: Free Press.

MUNN, NANCY D. (1986). *The Fame of Gawa: A Symbolic Study of Value Transformation in a Massim (Papua New Guinea) Society*. Cambridge: Cambridge Univ. Press.

RADCLIFFE-BROWN, A. R. (1964). *The Andaman Islanders*. Glencoe, Ill.: Free Press (first published 1922).

SCHECHNER, R. (1981). 'Restoration of Behaviour', *Studies in Visual Communication*, 7/3: 2–45.

STANNER, W. E. H. (1960). 'On Aboriginal Rites, 3: Symbolism in the Higher Rites', *Oceania*, 31/2: 100–20.

THOMSON, DONALD (1937). Field notes. Museum of Victoria, Melbourne.

—— (1975). 'The Concept of "Marr" in Arnhem Land', *Mankind*, 10/1: 1–10.

WARNER, W. LLOYD (1958). *A Black Civilization: A Social Study of an Australian Tribe*, rev. edn. New York: Harper.

WHITFORD, FRANK (1981). *Egon Schiele*. London: Thames & Hudson.

9

Predicates of Aesthetic Judgement: Ontology and Value in Huichol Material Representations

ANTHONY SHELTON

The 'eye' is a product of history reproduced by education.

(Pierre Bourdieu, *Distinction*)

In order to get clear about aesthetic words you have to describe ways of living. We think we have to talk about aesthetic judgements like 'This is beautiful', but we find that if we have to talk about aesthetic judgements we don't find these words at all, but a word used something like a gesture, accompanying a complicated activity.

(Ludwig Wittgenstein, *Lectures and Conversations*)

All discourse is institutionalized and historically specific. It is intimately related to particular social and economic relations at determinate phases of its existence which create and legitimate peculiar practices or techniques that reproduce both its intellectual and material conditions (Bourdieu and Passeron, 1977; Foucault, 1974). These practices and relationships confer respect and authority on the fields of knowledge which they institutionalize.

If we try to examine Huichol material representations from the perspective of an anthropological or art-historical discourse, we are confronted by a double paradox. First, the Huichol objects that are the subject of this essay do not correspond to any of the categories which ethnographic museums impose on material culture, and to consider them in such terms would bear no resemblance to their native conceptualization. Secondly, aesthetics, whether it refers to 'the science which treats of the conditions of sensuous perception' (i.e. as opposed to things thinkable or immaterial) or to 'the philosophy or theory of taste, or of the perception of the beautiful in nature and art' (*OED*), does not exist as an independent category of Huichol thought. Aesthetic judgements are predicated on a system of values, fixed, situated, and manipulated by rules which are, for the most part, culturally specific and historically determined. This view corresponds to Wittgenstein's notion that the meaning of acsthetics can only be derived from an examination of the different language games in which it features. It is precisely the context in which specific games place aesthetic terms that accords them their meaning at any one time or place. The competence of the manipulators of such games can be measured by their familiarity with the rules governing the use of categories, which in this case also indicates the level of their appreciation.

In the *Lectures* (1970), Wittgenstein notes that 'beautiful' is seldom used in ordinary language as an expression of pure taste. Usually it occurs as an interjection which is used to mean 'good'. Although the proximity of aesthetics to ethics in the English vocabulary is based on a technical misapplication of the term, its popular acceptance justifies taking this as its current meaning. What is at stake for Wittgenstein is the meaning of a word or concept as it is used in a common or special language game. For Bourdieu (1984), on the other hand, the distinction between different usages of an identical term corresponds to differences in family socialization and educational attainment which are used as markers of social class. Whereas Wittgenstein wanted to purify language by making it more precise, Bourdieu argues that not only are the very terms of discourse themselves politicized, but language is a site of class conflict which struggles to expropriate particular terms for its own ends and to impose its own view on the world.

What I shall try to demonstrate here is not that the Huichol have no word to denote aesthetics, but that, once we abandon attempts to force indigenous categories into supposedly precise and scientific Western terms, we may be able to describe broad fields of experience which correspond to historical and cultural experiences similar to those in the history of our own civilization. It is not enough to relativize the object of our subject; the subject must itself be treated with a similar epistemological scepticism.

In what follows, I shall use the analogy of Wittgenstein's idea of language games to describe the contexts and different strategies that certain categories of Huichol objects occupy and participate in. These categories of object will be seen to reiterate certain general themes which allow us to approximate their situational meaning in Huichol life and thought. However, to appreciate the criteria on which aesthetic judgements are based, one must describe their deeper symbolic meaning, that is to say, the relationship between one set of categories and those of another, which distinguishes the metaphysical and ontological foundations of their theory of beauty. As noted above, a theory of aesthetics is based on a conceptualization of perceptual experience which is closely related to fundamental ontological categories. The cultural reproduction of perception establishes the basis on which a system of aesthetic differences is founded and legitimated. The consideration of these fields will guide us in formulating some general statements concerning Huichol concepts of beauty.

The Huichol are an indigenous society whose core area is located in the north of what is today the State of Jalisco, the eastern part of Nayarit, and southern Zacatecas and Durango in north-west Mexico.

This essay will be primarily concerned with such traditional objects as ceremonial bowls (*xucuri*), arrows (*urú*), and woven materials (*itsari*). While among the most important, these are only some of the many objects that are used in ceremonial circumstances, and exclude such things as chairs (*uwéni*), beds (*itári*), and ceremonial capstones (*tepari*) which are also made for the use of a deity when summoned to the Huichol world. Arrows and bowls, like all traditional objects manufactured by the Huichol, have a mythical origin. The colours, patterns, decorations, and types of object which the Huichol make were originally requested by their different deities, who demanded they be given as offerings, and their power periodically renewed with libations of water and blood, in return for the deities' favours. The objects that will be discussed in the first and second sections of this essay are all used as offerings, inasmuch as they take part in acts 'of presenting something to a supernatural being' (van Baal, 1976: 161) or are used in important symbolic exchange relations between categories of people. The contexts in which such offerings are made will first be described, and there will follow an examination of the contracts so constructed between the human donor and the supernatural recipient. Section III will briefly examine the development of modern arts and crafts among the Huichol. While it will be noted that their elaboration corresponds to the overall argument concerning the loci of art production being focused at discrete junctures which mediate between distinct ontological categories, it is nevertheless important also to examine the wide differences between traditional objects and arts and crafts made for the external market, and to discuss the potentially disintegrative effects of the latter on the former.

I

Huichol deities can be divided into three categories. These are the solar deities, paramount among which are the Sun, Taweviékame; Kauyumarie, a deer person who is both trickster and culture hero, and who intercedes between man and the deities to create a communicative bridge between them; and an eagle woman, Tatei Werika Wimari, who is the guardian of the central region of the sky. The second category is composed of the water deities, senior of whom is Nakawé, Grandmother Growth, who is related to the earth; Tatei Yurianaka; and a large number of rain mothers, each associated with a cardinal direction.[1] The third category includes only the fire deity, Tatewarí. The first two of these categories are generally considered antagonistic, but because of the interdependence of the qualities each represents, all of which are required to secure the climatic variations on which agricultural activity is based, a third reconciliatory category, represented by the fire deity, is

FIG. 9.1. Huichol shaman's plumes (*muvieri*); collected by T. K. Preuss at Cerro Huaco, 1905–6; feathers mounted with fibre yarn on bamboo; 18¾ in. (48 cm.) long without shaft; Museum für Völkerkunde, Berlin, IV Ca 38062; photograph courtesy of Arnold T. Nelson.

necessary to mediate between them, enabling complementary relations to be established. Most of the ritual activity, at the level of household groups clustered around a district temple, is concerned with creating a balance between these two contrasting categories, which are associated with the dry season and wet season respectively: to implore the sun to soften his intensity, to supplicate the rain mothers to care for the maize, and then to restore the sun to his former condition so that the rains cease before flooding the earth's surface. Such activity is necessary for the maintenance of the agricultural cycle which is essential for the economic and social reproduction of Huichol society. The attitude of the deities towards man is summarized by Lumholtz (1902: 9):

the gods are angry with man and begrudge him everything, particularly the rain, which is of paramount importance to the very existence of the tribe. But when the deities hear the shaman sing of their deeds, they are pleased and relent, and they liberate the clouds that they have been keeping back for themselves, and rain results.

Chants or prayers are the primary means of communication used by man to supplicate the deities, and are conveyed by means of certain paraphernalia which are invested with supernatural powers. Such objects include the shaman's plumes (*muvieri*) (Fig. 9.1), which consist of one or two small feathers attached in an upright position to a wooden shaft with longer feathers suspended at its end (an eagle's claw, pieces of rock crystal, a snake rattle, or other attribute of the sun father may also be added), or by arrows, which may have a small embroidered or woven cloth attached to them, whose design signifies the thing or condition being requested. In place of such a small woven design, miniature snares to request luck in the deer hunt, strings of baked maize in the shape of serpents, or small sandals may be tied to their shaft (Lumholtz, 1902: 203, 205, 212). Each attachment has a specific significance intended to petition for a particular favour from the deity to whom it is addressed.[2] Different types of feather attached to *muvieri* relate them to specific deities. Macaw feathers are particularly favoured by Tatewarí, humming-bird by Kauyumarie, while hawk and eagle feathers, usually associated with the sun, may nevertheless refer to other deities as well (Negrín, 1975: 17). In the case of the water deities, half-yellow, half-white feathers are preferred by Tatei Rapaviyeme, while birds whose tail-feathers are half-white are favoured by Tatei Haramara (Mata Torres, 1980: 59). The arrow is conceptualized as a flying bird, and the designs painted on its rear shaft are described as its heart (*iyarí*). Zigzag designs signify lightning and connote the arrow's swiftness and force, while narrow straight lines refer to its path (*haye*).

The woven 'mats' (Fig. 9.2) attached to arrows are called *itári* (*náma* is the specific name given to square or rectangular 'mats'; cf. Lumholtz, 1900: 140), and serve as a resting-place for the gods. The woven or embroidered designs on these mats objectify prayers which are brought to the attention of the deities while they rest on them when visiting the localities where they have been left. A similar idea is present when small circular mirrors are tied to the arrows. These are called *nierika*, and 'are like the eyes of a deity' which enable him to see the communicant. As we shall later find, the ability to 'see' is a condition for sacred knowledge, and therefore also suggests the deity's possible awareness of the plea of the supplicant.

Arrows are offered the deities for a wide number of reasons and on many distinct occasions: as markers to identify the ground which a divinity is supposed to inhabit; to bring the rains; to request female fertility; as supplications for the increase of cattle, sheep, or other domestic animals; to cure illness; for success in weaving and embroidery; on construction of a new household building or after the renewal of a temple structure; for success in the ceremonial deer hunt; or even to cast a malignant spell on a victim. They are, therefore, the principal means through which communication is established with the deities. Together with plumes, they may be nailed to temple roofs to enable the deities to hear the prayers that are offered in their honour.

Votive bowls (Fig. 9.3) are also offered to all three categories of deity. They are made from a split gourd (*Lagenaria sisetaria*) and are decorated with beads, seeds, paper, coins, or yarn embedded in wax. The designs so produced identify the deity to whom the bowl is dedicated.[3]

FIG. 9.2. Five Huichol prayer mats (*itári*) dedicated to Tatewarí; collected by T. K. Preuss at Santa Barbara (except far right collected at Santa Gertrudis), 1906; fibre on wood; far left: 12 × 5 in. (30.5 × 13 cm.); Museum für Völkerkunde, Berlin, from left to right: IV Ca 32989, 34075, 32995, 34040, 34016; photograph courtesy of Arnold T. Nelson. See also Pl. XIII.

As offerings, votive bowls may be used less frequently than arrows. Usually they are kept in the temple (*túki*) or household shrine (*ririki*), or left at sacred sites during pilgrimages. The colours of bowls associate them with particular deities; blue with Tatei Rapaviyeme, black with Tatei Haramara, and red with Wirikuta (Mata Torres, 1980: 69). There may be a tendency for votive bowls to be more closely associated with the water deities, while arrows are thought more suitable for the solar deities. Zingg (1938: 635) noted the close association of bowls with water, rain, and maize:

Nakawé herself ordered clouds to cause the rain to fall in the votive bowls of the wet season goddesses, which leads the Huichol to say that if votive bowls are laid out evenly they will attract water from the sea. . . . Elsewhere in the mythology votive bowls are spoken of as being magically filled by water by a stream . . . gushing from a corn-ear.

In the mythology which describes the establishment of the maize ceremonies, Keamukáme planted a votive bowl in the ground and a stalk of corn sprouted from it (ibid.). Zingg also recorded that bowls are used by Nakawé to communicate with the rain mothers.

The centre of a votive bowl is often decorated with a concentric arrangement of beads, the colour of each band representing the colours most appropriate to the deity to which it is dedicated. Silver coins may be attached

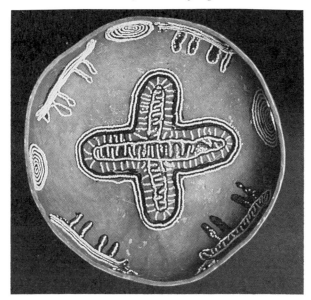

FIG. 9.3. Huichol votive bowl (*xucuri*) dedicated to Samatsima; collected by T. K. Preuss at Ranchería Los Baños, 1906; gourd decorated with beads on wax; $10\frac{1}{2}$ in. (27 cm.) diameter; Museum für Völkerkunde, Berlin, IV Ca 32790; photograph courtesy of Arnold T. Nelson.

in a diagonal line that runs from one side to the other (bowls entirely covered by beads are usually made for commercial sale). When placed in the temple, the deity to whom the bowl is dedicated enters it at its centre and rests during the rituals for which he or she has been summoned. Both mats and bowls, therefore, are used to accommodate the deities.

Votive bowls have one of the most highly charged symbolic significances of any Huichol offering. Not only are they related to the growth of maize, but the rains are said to be held in them in each quadrant of the sky realm.[4] The earth itself is conceptualized as a female womb (*uriepa*), envisaged as a bowl lying on a sea of water. Special types of decorated bowl which represent the lives of the household members are looked after by the family head and kept in the domestic shrine. Bowls are thus intimately related to the earth, the rains, fertility, and life, and while they are used as offerings to both solar and water deities, their symbolism is more closely connected with the latter.

Kauyumarie was the creator of many of these religious arts. According to one story, *nierika* are said to have grown from the left antler of a sacred deer person, while *muvieri* and gourds budded from the branches of his right antler. In another version, feathers were created when the sun spat into the sea. Kauyumarie then gathered them together, took them to the four cardinal regions, and made *muvieri* from them (Zingg, 1938: 647). Not only does Kauyumarie communicate the thoughts of the deities to men, but he also provides the instruments which allow the Huichol to reply to them. Elsewhere (Shelton, 1988) I have described the positions of and relationships between the five solar birds that govern each of the different segments of the sky and the five terrestrial deer that the sun made governors of the earth, and have illustrated how metaphorical associations between the plumage of the birds and the size and branching of antlers are used to establish relationships between the identities of the two sets of deities which occupy contiguous spatial domains. It is noteworthy that both these sets of deities belong to the solar class, and that both plumes and deer antlers, as well as the sacred paraphernalia which they gave rise to, are considered powerful instruments of communication. Thus the arrow is said to be a bird, inasmuch as it had its origin in deer antlers, which are themselves metaphorical feathers. However, the important distinction between them is that, while birds take the words of men to the gods, the deer carry the words of the gods to men.

The significance of these objects for communication between men and supernaturals is elaborated in prayer:

The flowers fly. The flowers turn.
They circle Burned Mountain.
And the deer and *itári* were born from the heart of Our Grandfather (Tatewarí).
The gods are speaking,
Yes, the gods are speaking to us and nobody can understand them.
Yet it is here you can see the arrow piercing the centre of the *itári*,
And the arrow understands the language of the gods.
Now, near to the arrow you can see the blue serpent (or humming-bird), Jaikayuave,
The interpreter of the gods, who knows the language of the arrow.
The rain is born from the *itári*, the rain is loosened
Sounding the message of the gods,
'Brothers, the time has arrived to make the arrow for the rain.'
The bowstring, Wikurra, appears to the notch of the arrow and the clouds rise again.
The gods of the four quarters take form.
They speak among themselves:
Wiricuta, Aurramanaka, Tatei Nakawé, Tatei Yurianaka, San Andrés all agree.
They rise into the air and fly around Burned Mountain.
On descending to the earth they see the arrow marking the place where the deer was
     born.
There lies the sacred *itári*,
Lying on the *itári* rests Our Brother Tomatz Kallaumari.

(Benítez, 1968: 137–8)

Before the Huichol were given arrows, they were unable to hear, let alone understand, the language of the deities. The arrow thus represents the relationship between them and their ancestors, and establishes the connection between the present age and its formation in pre-Creation times. The arrow is said to pierce the resting place of the deity, the *itári*. However, it is clear that the category *itári* embraces many things apart from the votive objects that I have discussed. It includes the centre of a sacred field cultivated outside a district temple, which will be discussed later, sacred sites or shrines, and even the sky realm (Tajeima), or the clouds which are manifestations of the rain mothers. The ability of the arrow to move swiftly between terrestrial and sky worlds further accounts for its identification with birds, which also mediate between the two worlds.

Muvieri, the instrument by which the shaman communicates with the deities, are arrows with bird-feathers attached to them which may account for their communicative efficacy. Apart from their association with the sun and Kauyumarie they are related to Tatewarí who first created fire from them (Zingg, 1938: 640). Together with other instruments used by the shaman, they are kept in a small, long, matted palm box called *tacuatsi*, which is likened to the body of the deer person, Kauyumarie. The diamond pattern woven into the cover and base of such boxes is said to represent the markings found on the back of the rattlesnake (ibid. 648), a symbol of the sun, which, like the *tacuatsi*'s association with Kauyumarie, reinforces the close bonds between shamans and the solar deities. The metaphoric associations between the body of Kauyumarie and bird plumage, closely connecting the two categories of deer and birds to arrows, constitute a symbolic complex clustered around the two-way communication between man and deities.

Votive bowls and arrows are also connected with agriculture, not only metaphorically, but also as part of the essential technology which ensures successful cultivation. Agricultural techniques and seeds were given to the Huichol by the water deities and, more specifically, by the senior goddess of growth, Nakawé.[5] Not only did she advise Watákame (Kauyumarie in the account recorded by Zingg), the only survivor of the mythical race of Hewi or Hewixii, to build himself a canoe and place within it seeds of maize, squash, and beans, but she guided him to the area where he should live once the floods had subsided, and taught him how he should plant and cultivate his fields.

Agriculture is the gift of the water deities, and cultivation involves their self-sacrifice. Cultivation is conceptualized as the cutting open of the womb of Tatei Yurianaka with digging-sticks in order to impregnate her with seeds. Offerings of votive bowls and other paraphernalia are made to her in exchange for her readiness to acquiesce to this, and to ensure that her womb remains fecund. The maize mother must be persuaded to lend her daughter for planting and later, at harvest time, agree to her sacrifice. Similarly, the rain mothers are beseeched to raise themselves from the four cardinal regions to the sky and, transformed into clouds, gather above the Huichol land before falling as rain serpents to nourish the earth. Finally, Nakawé herself must be acknowledged for the fertility she gave to the earth, and for establishing the order of agricultural process.

This cycle of production and reproduction can only be guaranteed if the deities are approached with humility and given the appropriate offerings that they stipulated in ancient times. Hence the production of votive bowls and arrows is necessary to placate their anger and win their favour, to ensure that they do not withhold the rains, and thus that agricultural activity can proceed. The very production of these objects, and the long pilgrimages undertaken to carry them to the shrines of the deities to which they are addressed, is a sign of the Huichol's continuous devotion to the rules of the world ordained by them. They constitute the instruments of a symbolic technology which is no less significant in achieving a prosperous harvest than the physical activities involved in cultivation. Bowls and arrows are therefore manufactured to be exchanged with the deities in return for the climatic conditions associated with the process of fertility necessary to benefit man.

The form, designs, and associations of Huichol arrows and bowls become clear when they are related to the symbolic technology on which the agricultural process is based. The votive bowl symbolizes the earth's womb which nurtures the maize and other seeds implanted in it. The metaphorical relation between the mythical bowl, and the maize that first sprouted from it, and the earth implanted with seed is explicitly recognized in the ceremony connected with sowing, Namawita Neirrara. As part of this ceremony, a bowl is placed in the centre of the sacred field (*naxa*),[6] to attract the gods so that they will care for the newly sown maize. A Huichol prayer describes the relation in the following way: 'In the place of the offerings is found the heart of the gods, the force of the gods, the words that contain the knowledge that the human mind could not have' (Mata Torres, 1974: 23).

Votive bowls and prayer arrows, as the products of artistic production, and rain, fertility, and light, as expressions of the agricultural process, therefore, are linked by a series of reciprocal relations that express the contract between the world of the ancestral deities and the domain of the Huichol. The creators of cultural products exchange their arts for the natural elements and processes which are in the keeping of their deities.

II

Decorated or ritual objects are not, however, restricted to exchange relations between human and supernatural beings. They also form part of an exchange of goods between wife-givers and wife-takers during traditional marriage ceremonies. Again, they intervene in a situation where a complementary communication is desired between distinct and potentially conflicting qualities.

During the pre-marital negotiations between the fathers of a boy and girl, and at the wedding ceremony itself, gifts are exchanged between the two families. The bride makes gifts of woollen belts (*xuyame*) and woven shoulder-bags (*kutsuli*) (Fig. 9.4.) while the groom responded traditionally with prest-ations of agave liquor, a votive candle dedicated to Nakawé (Benítez, 1968: 319), grey squirrel, or fish (Lumholtz, 1902: 93).[7]

Residence is usually uxorilocal, and the husband will often live in or near his wife's parents' home and contribute his labour to that productive unit during the first years of marriage. Later he may establish a household of his own near that of his family, or build his own house within its compound. An elder brother will eventually reside at his household of origin, and assume leadership of it on the death of his father.

The exchange that takes place between the families of wife-givers and wife-takers involves the transfer of fine weavings from the woman's side to the man's, while the candle and squirrel which are given to the wife-giver's family represent the man's abilities as a cultivator in transforming wild land (*acî*) into agricultural land. The votive candle and grey squirrel were offerings made by the first cultivator, Watákame, to Nakawé in appreciation of her teaching him the art of agriculture. These gifts express the man's relations with the solar deities, as the woman's weavings associate her with the rain deities.[8]

The long woollen sashes that the girl gives her future husband were traditionally woven in brown and white wool, although some coloured yarns are now also used, and commonly feature zigzag designs which have a poly-valent symbolism relating them to serpents, lightning, and rain. Like similar geometric designs, this motif acts as a prayer for rain (Lumholtz, 1902: 234). The designs on the shoulder-bags (Fig. 9.4), which the future bride also gives the man at this time, are much more varied, and include important solar symbols as well as others related to the water deities. I shall return to these later. By offering her future husband this apparel, the girl expresses her affiliation to the water deities, and thereby draws attention to her procreative qualities. Conversely, the prestations made by the husband's family to that of the wife-givers represent the son's agricultural labour which is temporarily placed at their service. Thus, the relationship between different gender categories in the social domain, and that which pertains between the solar and water deities and their human supplicant, are both marked by the exchange of distinct categories of object between the various contractees.

The complementarity achieved in the division of labour between men and women, symbolically stated in the prestations accompanying marriage, and between the human and supernatural domains, is reiterated in the manu-facture of art. Women usually decorate votive bowls and make bracelets (Fig. 9.5), necklace pendants, rings, and other beadwork decorations, as well as monopolizing weaving. All these activities were bequeathed them by

Fig. 9.4. Six Huichol shoulder-bags (*kutsuli*); collected by T. K. Preuss, 1905–6, provenance unknown; wool; Museum für Völkerkunde, Berlin; photograph courtesy of Arnold T. Nelson. These bags illustrate the use of stylized peyote and *toto* flower motifs to represent the four directions and the centre region. Note also the double-headed eagle, Tatei Wirika Wimari, depicted with a heart of peyote. See also Pl. XIV.

the water deities, and further create symbolic bonds between them. This theme is clearly present in the myth which relates the origin of weaving and embroidery.

In ancient times, the first Huichol woman, Wenima, did not know how to draw, weave, or embroider. She asked the advice of her father, who suggested that he take her to see the snake, Simalakoa, who might be willing to teach her.

Wenima followed her father into a dangerous and terrible part of the sierra, where he made a fork out of a branch. On approaching Simalakoa, he pinned her to the ground by capturing her head between the prongs of his fork. He then instructed his daughter to place needles into each of the five frets of the pattern that decorated the serpent's body. Then he told his daughter to spin the wool which she had brought with her around each needle and to remove the whorls and place them in her plain cotton bag.

The father then took Simalakoa in his hands and passed her over each part of Wenima's body which one day would be decorated by jewellery and textiles, saying: 'I pass you, Simalakoa, by the waist so that you teach her to make belts. I pass you over the neck so you will make necklaces. I pass you over the shoulders so you will make the straps of the bags. I pass you over the hips to make the *juiwamete* [small embroidered pouches worn over the belt]. I pass you over the wrists so you may make bracelets. I pass you over the fingers so that you can make rings, and I pass you over the head so you can make *kushira* [a thin headband]. Now look well at the frets painted on the body of Simalakoa, for they will teach you to weave the frets of the textiles.

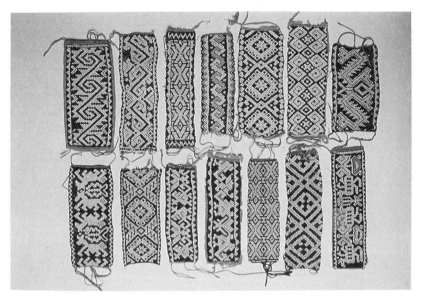

FIG. 9.5. Fourteen Huichol bracelets; collected by T. K. Preuss, 1905–6, provenance unknown; wool; Museum für Völkerkunde, Berlin; photograph courtesy of Arnold T. Nelson. Amongst the patterns here are lightning motifs, serpents, horses, birds, and stylized floral motifs representing the four cardinal directions.

When the man and his daughter returned home, they left the balls of wool in the temple and that night Simalakoa spoke to her and made her dream of the designs that she had seen. Simalakoa instructed her to ask her father to make two looms of brazil wood—a material sacred to the sun, a simple one, *teusika*, and a double loom, *imame*. In addition, she was told to ask him to make her a back-stitcher, *taushame*, and a spindle, *utzikiu*. When her father had completed making them, the girl fasted for ten days.

After five days she took a blue yarn, *yoakatzi*, and sat in front of the loom which was fastened to the ground, and wondered which of the frets that she had seen on the serpent's body she should weave first. Finally, she decided to begin with the fret nearest the head, and completed one of the frets every day until all five had been copied. Each night, Simalakoa appeared in her dreams to teach and advise her on her work. When the girl had finished the belt, Simalakoa asked if she might have it, so the girl's father tracked her down and tied it around her neck, while the girl thanked her.

(Benítez, 1968: 459–60)

Girls are taught to weave by their mothers, and the designs traditionally belonged to individual families. However, some women claim to have also dreamt their designs after fasting and having made offerings to a serpent deity with whom they have a special relationship, as in the story recounted above.

Women are ascribed their feminine identity by many of the activities and qualities that they share with the water deities.

Similarly, the male is connected with the manufacture of arrows and certain types of *itári*, such as gods' chairs and the sacred circular stones on which animals associated with a particular deity are carved. These techniques were inherited from the solar deity, Kauyumarie. Moreover, men are connected with the sacred fields attached to district temples. Cultivation of these fields by the temple authorities charged with caring for the votive bowls of the deities strongly characterizes the male domain. The dedication of both men and women to their particular art-forms is considered a sign of their devotion to the ancestral deities.

The different activities connected with the sexes also distinguish their particular qualities. Implicit in the division of labour between men and women, and between humans and deities, is that no one gender could maintain itself without reciprocal relations with the other. In this, too, the relation between solar and water deities concerned with the fertility of the earth is similar to that between males and females with regard to human reproduction. Women and water deities share similar transformative powers. These include transforming raw food into cooked, and creating weavings from raw material.

In the context of birth, Tatei Werika Wimari, one of the rain mothers, gradually moulds the foetus into a human form within the womb of the woman, just as maize grows from the womb of the earth. The later relationship between mother and child is also similar to that between the maize mother and the maize.

Transformatory qualities are also present in the myth which recounts the origin of women. The first Huichol woman had the ability to transform herself into a black dog. Only when the dog's master discovered the coat that she left behind after she had gone down to the river, and burnt it, did she lose this power and remain a woman. However, perhaps the most dramatic example of transformation is found among the water goddesses who, as part of the agricultural process, rise from their earthly lakes to become cloud serpents. The serpents cross the sky as lightning bolts which become entangled, causing them to fall to the earth as rain, and thus allowing them to return to their homes along the rivers, conceptualized as the earth's veins. These spectacular abilities of transformation distinguish women and the rain deities from men and the solar deities.

In contrast to the rain deities and women, the solar deities and men are related to the establishment of the social order and its governance. The sun assigned the deer gods to each of the earth's quadrants over which they hold governorship, while in the post-contact period Kauyumarie distributed the saints to their respective regions and defined their relationships with the Huichol by writing down the honours and offerings appropriate to each.

Huichol political and religious offices are reserved for men, and their authority derives directly from the solar deities.

These instances are sufficient to confirm the association of feminine categories with creativity and transformation, and the relationship of male attributes with the permanent and static domain of the solar deities. Men elaborate social institutions and materials but they do not fundamentally create them. Huichol cosmology, then, seems to embrace a dual metaphysic that will be the subject of section IV.

In the first two sections I have sought to explicate two domains in which certain objects participate. The use of arrows and votive bowls in exchange relations between the supernatural and human domains parallels that of the exchange of woven goods for candles, particular animals, and alcohol which occurs between females and males before marriage.

The objects and materials exchanged in each of these distinct contexts have similar symbolic meanings. The Huichol make offerings to the deities to procure the reproductive rains before they engage in production. Huichol women traditionally make prestations to men which symbolize their fecundity, and men make gifts to women and their families which signify their productive roles. The similarity between these two domains is, in very general terms, another example of what the comparativist Raglan (1964) called 'the marriage of earth and heaven', where the relations signified by the exchange of goods between categories of one domain closely parallel those of the other. These objects act as instruments of a symbolic technology which reaffirms the contracts between different categories and establishes complementary and reciprocal relations between unlike terms. They are a type of what Rivière (1969: 157) has called 'energy transformers'.

III

Huichol art and society are not impervious to changing historical contingencies which have their origin both within and outside the core area. Internal changes have modified the traditional wedding ceremony considerably since the time when it was first described by Lumholtz, but while the exchanges described in the last section are no longer made with the same frequency and regularity, the ideas which they represent still persist. More importantly, the Huichol have participated in many of the violent struggles that at times have dominated modern Mexican history, and which have sometimes been used as the pretext for land invasions by other groups, the break-up and forced abandonment of communities, attempts to concentrate the population in villages (often centred on a mission), and efforts to modify traditional forms of government and integrate them within the municipal system of local administration and authority.

A further source of change has been the policies of the Instituto Nacional

FIG. 9.6. Modern Huichol yarn painting depicting the story of the flood; 1981; yarn embedded in beeswax on wooden board; 24 × 24 in. (60.9 × 60.9 cm.); ex-collection Anthony Shelton; photograph courtesy of Arnold T. Nelson. In the centre is Nakawé, while the oval shape beneath her is the canoe that she told Watakame to build. Inside the canoe is Watakame himself, his female dog who was later transformed into the first woman, a snake, the bird that first spotted land once the waters started to subside, and the domesticated plants which Nakawé told Watakame to take with him. Beneath the canoe are a large fish and serpent. The picture is framed by an arched rain serpent whose body shed the rain which inundated the earth. See also Pl. XV.

Indigenista (INI), which established its presence in the area in 1960 and, between 1970 and 1974, administered 'Plan Huicot', a comprehensive development project designed to open up and transform the insular economy of the region. Although abandoned in 1974, the project and the INI's independent initiative have been sufficient to stimulate the development of a money economy in the Huichol area. Increasing regularization of land tenancy, the introduction of better strains of maize, the use of fertilizers and insecticides, the replacement of indigenous cattle by better breeds, and a successful campaign of vaccination have all encouraged the rural development banks to make loans to Huichol communities to help develop more efficient farming techniques aimed at producing a surplus for the external market. The growing dependence on outside agencies for loans, and the need to develop production for external markets in order to service them, has ended the region's economic and cultural autonomy in relation to metropolitan society. The flow of migrants to work permanently outside the core area has increased markedly during the past twenty years, and families are becoming increasingly dependent on seasonal work in the insalubrious tobacco, cotton, and citrus plantations of coastal Nayarit. The penetration of Western capital into the

FIG. 9.7. Tatei Otuanaka (Maize Mother); collected 1906 by T. K. Preuss from a shrine dedicated to Narihuama at Ranchería Las Guayabas; beads embedded in wax and mounted on wood; $5\frac{1}{4} \times 2\frac{3}{4}$ in. (13.5 × 7.0 cm.); Museum für Völkerkunde, Berlin, IV Ca 32636; photograph courtesy of Arnold T. Nelson. The cross running along the centre of the figure's body represents the four directions and the centre region.

Huichol homeland, and their increasing dependence on seasonal wage labour outside of it, has created a dual economy which threatens traditional subsistence patterns and the cultural forms elaborated around them. The partial incorporation and marginalization of the Huichol into the national and international market, together with the concomitant erosion of their cultural patrimony, has fostered the adoption of new attitudes, values, and tastes which have contributed to the rise of craft production as another means to achieve the satisfaction of those aspirations.

The best-known, and culturally most important, craft objects made by men outside the Huichol area are yarn paintings (*cuadros de estambre*, also known simply as *tablas*) (Fig. 9.6). These consist of brightly coloured, commercially produced yarns embedded in beeswax which has been spread over a plywood or fibre-board base. There has been a tendency to regard these tableaux as either a traditional art-form or as having evolved from a traditional form.

While the technique of attaching objects to the surface of other materials by embedding them in wax was and is well known, and is used to decorate votive bowls and small, square, or rectangular offerings with a wooden base (*nama*) (Fig. 9.7), I have been unable to trace any organic principle of evolution which would suggest a direct development from these older forms. The art discussed in the last two sections is quite distinct from the tableau work on at least four counts: materials, context of production, demand or market, and significance. While I hope to discuss Huichol crafts in more detail elsewhere, I shall nevertheless briefly describe these differences here in order to relate them better to the other domains of indigenous arts already discussed, and to extend my argument concerning the foci of artistic expression in this society.

Not all the materials employed in the manufacture of tableaux are used to make traditional religious or ritual objects, nor are they even found in the Huichol homeland. Neither plywood nor the more recently adopted and more commonly used fibre-board can be obtained in the sierra, and the yarns, although used for weaving, are only occasionally found as decoration on votive bowls. In most cases, wax is used to attach things such as beads, grains of maize, or coins to bowls or *nierika*, or sometimes, when shaped into small animals, is used as a decoration itself. Material for the external market and that for indigenous use are produced according to two different scales. Most objects intended for offerings are small, while tableaux are much larger and command a more extensive field which can be viewed and appreciated from a distance. Objects for external consumption are much more elaborately decorated than the ones used traditionally. Unlike tableaux, many votive bowls or *nierika* would only be sparingly decorated. This refinement is obviously aimed at attracting the external market, although if the elaborately decorated tableaux are compared with textiles in traditional use, it will be seen that the love of embellishment is not foreign to Huichol culture.

While votive offerings and objects for use in ritual are made in the sierra, tableaux are produced in urban areas such as Tepic, Guadalajara, and Mexico City, or along the coastal area of Nayarit. Because crafts are produced outside their mountainous homeland—the sierra, the sacred land created by the sacrifice of the Huichol deities, protected by and ruled over by them and embodying the ancestral knowledge that they bequeathed their people—it could be argued that they can never possess the same immanence or sacred character as the objects made of native materials within the sierra.

The first tableaux date from about 1951, when Alfonso Sota Soria exhibited a selection in Guadalajara (Negrín, 1979: 26). Since then, Miguel Palafox Vargas in Tepic and Juan Negrín in Guadalajara, as well as other anthropologists, have encouraged the development of the art, sometimes providing workshops where a master could train appentices. In the early 1970s, in an attempt to stimulate a rural economy, the INI encouraged craft production in the sierra, providing materials and a guaranteed (but low) price for finished products, which were then marketed through Government-sponsored craft stores. While this met with little enthusiasm and was soon abandoned because of lack of funds, the Franciscan missions successfully operate a similar system, and have their own shop in Zapopan on the outskirts of Guadalajara. A number of middlemen emerged in Tepic to commission particularly gifted artists to work for them and attempt to ensure a monopoly over their productions. Most tableaux fall into one of three categories; they either use foreign styles to depict non-Huichol subjects (e.g. portraits of Che Guevara and Zapata), use an indigenous style to create compositions which are nevertheless meaningless juxtapositions of Huichol symbols, or increasingly make narrative-style compositions which closely parallel Huichol myths collected by earlier anthropologists. This last category has been developed into a high art-form by sponsors who have encouraged individual Huichols to develop their own particular styles and identify their work by signing it, and to make repeated trips back to the sierra to keep in contact with the traditions that they are said to represent. This work has been marketed through national and international exhibitions, often staged in fine-arts museums rather than in ethnographic or natural-history museums.

While tableaux have been called *nierika* by various authors, like certain examples of traditional art, they have none of the religious uses of votive arts, nor are they part of the same religious economy. Their use is entirely defined by the market that has encouraged and developed their production. This market is quite unlike the internal religious economy which prescribes the rules for the offerings of votive arts, or its ethical counterpart, which is dependent on it and regulates marriage prestations, since the former is controlled from the outside. Nevertheless, as in the other two domains of objects previously described, tableaux and crafts are used in exchange relations which identify a particular ontological juncture which, in this case, mark the boundary between what, to the Huichol, is indigenous and non-indigenous society. They may serve both defensive and offensive ends. On the one hand, they promote a certain collective image of the Huichol by insisting on the continuum between rural and urban peoples and annulling their different economic conditions and ethical values by the projection of their religous system as a detached, homogeneous, and generalized abstract philosophy expressed through this art. The artistic products that contain this cultural fetishization, on the other hand, are made for external use and projected outside the indigenous community to confront the cultural symbolizations of the dominant society, thus reproducing and asserting the new values of the marginalized, urban Huichol. While some tableaux represent episodes from Huichol life, such as ceremonies or stages in the cycle of life and death (notably those by Ramon Medina), most of the narrative representations are focused on the creation of the world by the ancestral deities (as in the works of José Benítez Sánchez, Tutukila Carrillo Carrillo, Juan Ríos

Martínez, and Guadalupe González Ríos). The tableaux therefore assert the presence of the past in the present, and reproduce a particularly Huichol world paradigm. The meaning and significance of this paradigm may reasonably be expected to diverge significantly from that found in the core communities on at least four counts. First, the tableau is produced for circulation in a cultural milieu external to that of the Huichol, which has a radically distinct theory of knowledge (one which favours description and explanation rather than experience) and way of 'seeing' (which commonly emphasizes appearance rather than the underlying essence of a phenomenon). Furthermore, the metropolitan culture for which the tableau is intended possesses different criteria of evaluation, based on formal aesthetic principles distinct from Huichol concerns, which include making explicit the implicit reality behind their world. Second, the tableau represents a translation of experience from its normal expression through oral narrative to pictorial representation. Since the presentation of oral literature or written narrative is necessarily linear, and lends itself most easily to causally structured discourse, while pictorial representation permits linearity to be circumvented and the multiple and simultaneous relations of a field to be presented to consciousness, each mode of representation implies a specific style and allows the expression of a particular structure of events. Third, tableaux are exchanged in asymmetrical relationships rather than through a generalized and symmetrical reciprocity such as characterizes the other two categories of object which circulate internally. No permanent bonds are established between the producer and patron, and the artist is alienated from the final use to which his work will be put, and from the significance it will assume during its circulation in its new cultural network. Finally, and related to this last consideration, all Huichol crafts, and particularly tableaux, are luxury items made for conspicuous consumption. The values underlying such behaviour are foreign to the Huichol themselves, and conflict with their emphasis on humility and religious introspection. Consequently, tableaux would never be purchased by traditional Huichols.

Commercial arts and crafts are antipathetic to traditional Huichol values in other ways too. Because they are almost always more elaborate than traditional objects in indigenous use, the art objects made for foreign consumption may be thought of, even in indigenous terms, as more beautiful than those reserved as offerings for the gods. In a sense, therefore, as long as there is no enrichment of traditional arts (although some religious ceremonies are probably becoming more complex), the more elaborate the crafts for external use become, the more impoverished become the Huichol deities. If this argument can be sustained—and it is here only a suggestion—the impoverishment of the gods means a decline in their power and influence over the destiny of the Huichol world and its abandonment to the caprice of capitalist economy. The growing success of the few in producing art for art's sake, therefore, may coincide with successive stages of the general alienation of Huichol art from its subject, and the usurpation of the authority of the indigenous gods by some of their most avowed devotees.

At a less abstract level, craft production serves none of the integrative purposes of traditional art. The production of ritual objects and offerings for deities, and the use of textiles in prestations accompanying traditional marriage ceremonies, serves fundamentally integrative functions within the society, expressing and effecting the reconciliation of categories which were previously incompatible and contradictory. Craft production, however, while expressing another juncture, one that mediates between two radically different and culturally determined market situations, is (as we have seen) disintegrative, since it is controlled by an external value system. It represents a commoditization of Huichol culture according to terms foreign to it by a culture whose overpowering dominance assures the asymmetry of the exchange relationship in favour of the external market.

IV

Aesthetic judgements are based on values that may only be understood in the context of their relations to particular concepts of nature.[9] In the case of the Huichol, these are deeply embedded in the ontology that shapes their world view. Aesthetics concerns the judgement of a perceptual condition by the values particular to a society. Before examining these values themselves, we shall first describe some of the underlying concepts, to appreciate better the matrix of ideas on which they are founded, and which lies behind the inspiration of the objects which were discussed in the first and second sections of this essay.

In section II, it was suggested that the Huichol apprehend the world according to two divergent concepts of 'nature' demonstrated by the qualities and activities associated with men and women, and those connected with deities and humans. This is not unique to the Huichol; it is also found among indigenous peoples of the American south-west. For example, in his account of Navajo language and art Witherspoon (1977: 163–4) describes how females are associated with change, while males are related to a regularized cyclical quality held in stasis and representative of an unchanging 'reality'. Witherspoon has argued that the combination of these two diverse qualities which are represented by men and women in Navajo art 'seems to be able to combine the emphasis of order and balance found in classicism with the forcefulness, energy and expressiveness found in romanticism' (ibid. 173). Differences in the socially constructed characteristics of gender relationships manifest themselves not only in the materials but also in the pattern and stylistic conventions used in Huichol and Navajo art.

A common motif woven on shoulder-bags is the star-like design of the *toto*

flower (*Dasyirion wheeleri*) or peyote (*Lophophora williamsi*), which is represented radiating from a static centre in an increasingly complex, colourful,
and dynamic repetitious design. A similar combination of static and dynamic
elements is also found in the designs on votive bowls. The centre, the
emergence point of the deity to whom it is dedicated, is always the focus
of the design, around which other more complex and flowing motifs are
arranged. This balance is absent in the commercially produced tableaux in
which motifs are rarely clustered around a central design but have, instead, a
more fluid and dynamic quality with fewer formal elements.[10]

The presence of these two qualities reiterates the dichotomous picture of
nature already noted. It is detectable not only in the qualitative attributes
assigned to men and women, and represented by the centre/periphery
elements of motifs in textiles and votive bowls, but also in the significance
given to directional orientations, particularly in the opposition between east
and west.

The east is the birthplace of the sun and the direction of the mythical land
of the ancestors, Wirikuta, to where the peyote pilgrimage is made. Peyote was
'born' in the footsteps left by the sacred deer in the first times, and is identified
with the heart of the animal. It is the food that sustains the interior life of the
Huichol and enables them to see and communicate with their deities. It is the
hallucinogenic peyote, their spiritual food, which enables the Huichol to
perceive the world of essences which lies hidden behind the material
appearances of everyday 'reality'. Conversely, to the west runs the path to the
sea and the water deity Tatei Haramara, who is sometimes identified as the
mother of the maize children and is supplicated to bring the rains to ensure
their maturation. Maize is the food of the physical body, that which is material
and impermanent. The west is also the place where the senior water deity,
Nakawé, the goddess of growth, is said to have dismembered herself to
become transformed into wild fruits and vegetation.

As peyote is associated with the solar deities of the arid lands of the east,
maize is conceptualized as the daughter of a female water deity of the west. In
regard to this strict polarity, it is notable that communion with the deities in
preparation for, and during, the principal pilgrimage to the eastern land of
Wirikuta can only be achieved by denying the alimentary needs of the physical
body. Sexual abstinence, long fasts, and restrictions on the consumption of
salt and drinking of water precede the ingestion of peyote, marking the
transition from one ontological state to the other.

The polarity between these diametrically opposed regions clearly identifies
the east as the land associated with the interior essence of the objects which
present themselves to vision and which contain the kernel of reality underlying
the object world. The west is the converse: it is associated with the
appearance of the world, the phenomenal world amenable to the untutored
senses.

The articulation of these two orders according to a spatial structure includes the concomitant relations already described. The east is associated with the male sun deity; it is the area from where the food of the heart, *iyári*, is derived, food which enables the pilgrim to find the truth hidden behind object reality. This knowledge is considered eternal and absolute, planted there by the ancestral deities to inform the Huichol of the correct life-path they should follow. The west encompasses the contrary qualities. It is associated with the female water deities such as Nakawé or Tatei Haramara and evokes their transformatory nature. It is changeable, dynamic, related to procreation, birth, and the fertility that nurtures the maize to satisfy the body and sustain people in the phenomenal world.

The qualitative opposition between the east and the west, and the dualism it expresses between essence and appearance, is further elaborated in the concept of *iyári*. The Huichol translate *iyári* into Spanish as *corazón* which corresponds to the English 'heart'. This gloss, however, fails to give the full significance of this complex concept. It is used to refer to an essence inherent in all human beings which is considered essential to life, and which is present also within physical non-organic forms of phenomenal objects. *Iyári* is a component of the ancient fire deity Tatewarí, who is closely associated with shamanistic knowledge and who is the model for the Huichol shaman (*mara'akame*), who derives his powers from the deity. Both act as mediators, the first between the solar and water deities and the second between the world of the Huichol and that of their deities. The *iyári* of the fire deity is made of tobacco (*awákame*), a sacred substance restricted to ceremonial use which I shall return to shortly. *Iyári* also means 'sacred words' or knowledge, that is to say, knowledge of a distinct epistemological status which is largely restricted to shamans. The heart of the Huichol and the tobacco heart of Tatewarí should, therefore, be seen as expressions of occult knowledge. Consideration will first be given to the significance of this concept as it manifests itself in the physical body.

Iyári is an essence that is fixed inside the human being at birth and held in place by a sacred arrow. It comprises knowledge of the works of the ancestral deities in creating the world, their nature and relation to man, and the significance of the world and man's obligations in it. Such knowledge is not created or derived from experience and does not possess a human origin. It is the original wisdom of the deities. It is sometimes described as the 'thoughts' of the deities which were collected by the eagle mother, Tatei Werika Wimari, when they sacrificed their physical bodies to establish earth and sky and endow them with their features and the elements necessary to sustain life. Tatei Werika Wimari transmits this knowledge to the Huichol to enable them to know the way of their ancestors and remain loyal to them. However, although *iyári* is fixed into the bodies of Huichol children before birth, it is only through nurturing it by the ingestion of peyote (*hicuri*) and the denial of the physical necessities of existence that one becomes aware of it. These activities cause the growth and recognition of ancestral knowledge, and thus stimulate revelation of the 'true' nature of the world which lies hidden within material appearances: the order of the deities within the form of phenomenal objects. *Iyári* appears to have a different but related meaning when it is used to refer to non-organic phenomena such as mountains, cliffs, rocks, rivers, or lakes. Again, it refers to the real essence which underlies the appearance of an object, and is sometimes described as assuming the appearance of a serpent at its centre. This corresponds to the original appearance of the water-related deities who make up many terrestrial features.

The quality shared by both these uses of the concept—as a component of the essential life force of humans and as a true and intransmutable essence which lies at the centre of non-organic phenomena—is its absoluteness. In both contexts, such knowledge or essence is inherited from a world which pre-dates the formation of the present age in which the Huichol live. It constantly and surreptitiously conveys the past into the present, both to regulate the shape of experience and to renew it by applying traditional categories to new historical phenomena. In this way it extends its authority, and provides the means by which the deities intervene in the present. Further-more, when activated in the Huichol adept it becomes the means by which material appearances can be penetrated to reveal the 'true' reality which lies at their heart. This covert reality, hidden within the material presentation of the objective world in which the Huichol live, is the supernatural world of the ancestral deities. The present order of appearance is itself patterned by an ancestral order of intransmutable essences whose conceptualization strikes the imprint of the past forever on the perception of the present. Peyote, nurturing the *iyári* inherent in each human being, provides a means by which the Huichol can communicate with their deities despite the intransigence of their historical remoteness. In a certain sense these deities still live among the Huichol, at the centre of the mountains, rocks, rivers, and vegetation which surround them and in the force of the natural elements to which they are beholden.[11]

Tobacco, the heart of Tatewarí, may be considered the original manifes-tation of *iyári*. Fire can be conceived as a form of prayer. When the Huichol burn large areas of grassland and other areas of secondary growth, the smoke is described as a prayer for rain. The smoke is likened to clouds which cross the sky to the homes of the water deities, while the crackling of the fire is described as the voice of Tatewarí. As the rain is the message of the deities carrying their benediction in its fructifying action, smoke represents another form of communication, not from the deities to man, but a supplication from man to the deities. The significance of tobacco lies in its similar ability to produce voluminous smoke clouds when burnt, which may be thought of as the materialization of the ancestral thoughts of the fire deity, the original shaman who is the source of the Huichol shaman's power. Prayer as communication is not distinct from the object to which it is guided. Clouds and smoke can be *iyári* while, as we have already seen, material objects like bowls and arrows can be the depositories of rain and fertility and its manifestation as it pounds the earth.

The notion of *iyári* is closely related to the conception of sight (*irumari*). Ordinary sight, the perception of the world by untutored sense, has no depth and little meaning for the Huichol, since it is unable to penetrate appearance and reveal the essence which lies at the heart of the object. I have already described how sight is attained through the ingestion of peyote, but it is also sustained and effected through the aid of various external objects which are collectively called *nierika*. It is said that '*nierika* is like what we see in our mind and our mind is like Watetuapa' (Negrín, 1975: 33). Watetuapa is the pre-Creation world which the deities originally inhabited before they created the present world through their self-sacrifice. It exists today as the cavernous nether region inhabited by the ghoul Tukákame. The comparison of the mind with the ancestral world corroborates the relationships between *iyári* and ancestral thought and between *nierika* and ancestral vision. The similarity of the functions of *nierika* and peyote are also confirmed by their common origin. It will be recalled that the first *nierika* budded from the antlers of Kauyumarie, the same deity whose heart is peyote. *Nierika* include mirrors which are usually circular, and may be either attached to arrows or simply stored in the shaman's palm box, along with other sacred instruments, gods' eyes (*tsikuri*), which are made of rhombohedrons woven from different coloured yarns and mounted at the points and centre of two sticks made into a cross, and the circular or rectangular wooden or stone tablets decorated with yarn or beads embedded in wax representing deities. They are also known as 'faces of the gods' (*itari*), and represent the aspect of the object that they enable to be seen. As a category of objects, *nierika* have as their most inclusive attribute the ability to make visible those things which are usually hidden from sensory perception. They share with *iyári* the ability to secure revealed knowledge, but only in the more limited sense of providing a means for the appearance of a supernatural being.[12] The criteria of aesthetic judgements are derived from the realm of essences to which *iyári* is directed and which *nierika* makes visible.

More than simply devotional expressions or instruments for signifying the immanence of the sacred realm of the gods, the objects that we have discussed and their associated representational systems are also sources of power.[13] I have already described how certain objects are considered sacred, and how they are used in exchange relationships between men and deities to affirm a primordial contract which enshrines the reciprocal and mutual obligations between them. The exchange of objects compels both supplicant and the supplicated to comply with the terms of such contracts, which, if broken, threaten harsh sanctions, depriving the gods of their offerings and blood sacrifices and the Huichol of their sustenance. In the parallel situation of exchanges between wife-givers and wife-takers, objects encode the mutual obligations between the two partners sanctioned by district and community authorities.

While access to shamanistic office is open to all, mastery of the higher orders of shamanistic knowledge involves a long and arduous apprenticeship. This allows the control of sacred knowledge, which is considered necessary for all aspects of Huichol life, to be monopolized by a more restricted group of shamans who occupy senior positions. However, the shaman's power is potential rather than actual and is not overly exploited. While millenarian activity incited by shamans is not unknown in the area, most attempts by a shaman to exploit his power for his individual gain would be regarded as incompatible with devotion to the ancestral deities, and would encourage witchcraft accusations against him. Since, traditionally, design motifs and their combinations were taught to the Huichol by their deities and represent recognizable aspects of their 'thoughts', as well as manifestations of their presence and authority, invention and innovation are limited. Although few formal constraints are placed on the use of design motifs, sanctions strongly limit the behaviour of the artist and the uses to which his products are put. Transgression of these sanctions results in the pre-emption of the value and significance with which the Huichol would otherwise invest them. If the artefacts are not made sufficiently well, their maker may invite ridicule or punishment from the deity to whom they are dedicated. At the very least, he would certainly not be considered versed in sacred knowledge, and his work would be devoid of power.

For the Huichol, therefore, the source of inspiration lies not in idle con-templation of the world as it is perceived but in an acquaintance with the occult world of essences which is revealed through the activation of *iyári*. Inspiration is the gift of the deities, and consists in their permitting man to identify the original significance of the world and to apprehend the network of reciprocal obligations which binds him to his deities. Huichol art is not an art of this world, but an art in which is inscribed the essence of a deeper nature to which it only alludes.

Such a conception is not unique to the Huichol, and may constitute a more general characteristic of a category of thought common throughout much of Meso-America before the Spanish conquest. Westheim has described this vision of the world as 'mythical realism', and has suggested that it motivated the form and significance of pre-Columbian sculpture. In comparing it with Western art, he wrote (1972: 28):

Modern realism has as its end the reproduction of the visible; that of mesoamerican realism is to make visible the invisible. The artist in western civilisation believes he represents a nut by depicting its shell. In pre-Hispanic Mexican thought the shell of the nut is only an exterior aspect of little importance. The essential thing is the nut itself.

This section has attempted to detail the relationships between certain key conceptual categories which underlie the domain to which aesthetic judgements refer and which condition access to it. The existence of similar concepts among the people of the American south-west and related historical Uto-Aztecan peoples of central Mexico may indicate some general ontological principles once present throughout the area, but of which only few vestiges now remain.

V

It will be clear that any Huichol category of thought that at the outset may appear to have corresponded to what in the West is defined as aesthetics rests upon presuppositions exotic to the modern imagination. Huichol aesthetics has no existence independent of the religious and ritual contexts for which traditional objects were and are made, and which both provide the rules for their manufacture and use and supply the criteria for their evaluation. Aesthetics as a discourse does not exist, but aesthetics as an ethical codification of the use, significance, and purpose behind sacred and ritual arts pervades metaphysics and ontology.

Leach (1973: 227) has argued that art is nearly always associated with ambiguous, dangerous, sacred, interesting, mysterious, exciting, or sinful episodes which are restricted to ritual occasions. Art, he suggests, goes further than fulfilling normal expectations by entering into the forbidden or unexpected. And, because it touches upon taboo subjects, its elaboration and use will be most closely related and even restricted to the intermediate period of separation during ritual activity, which is clearly distinguished and kept apart from the normal round of social life. This argument clearly fits the Huichol data that I have presented here; and, indeed, if, in the absence of an indigenous category of 'art', the context and the emotional value which an object evokes can partly be used to define something as art, then I have no hesitation in describing those objects discussed here in these terms.

We have seen that certain objects serve to represent and evoke moral contracts between different categories during ritual or ambiguous situations which mark the junctures between different ontological and social domains, such as between the supernatural and human realms, as part of the wedding ceremony when the transition from being single to married is highlighted, or between Huichols and non-Huichols. These situations coincide both with the contexts in which Leach argued art would be used and with the values which are attached to them. Since the outcome of the supplicatory offering for the rain, of a marriage proposal, or the result of an encounter with a foreigner cannot be known in advance, they constitute situations full of ambiguity whose potentially opposing and conflictive nature is represented in the different categories of object that take part in the exchange. This uncertainty creates a tension among the parties involved, which in the case of offerings to a deity is both mysterious and dangerous and may be accompanied by intense pleas for forgiveness and by weeping. Marriages, on the other hand, are not considered consummated until the couple have accepted certain gifts from each other and have had sexual intercourse. Relations and friends gather around the house where the couple are sleeping, offering advice, joking, and encouraging consummation. The occasion is one of excitement, general interest, and sexual innuendo. The sale of crafts involves transactions with foreigners (*tewari*), outsiders who are never trusted and whose deviousness and cunning are legion. This negotiation is the most ambiguous of all. Its rules of engagement cannot be anticipated; they are capricious, sometimes incomprehensible and often only self-interested.

Having described traditional and commercial Huichol arts, the complex metaphysical notions with which the former are connected, and the ontology on which they are based, we are in a better position to discuss indigenous concepts of beauty. Since the world of appearances is subordinated to the world of essences, and is valued less than the latter as a source of truth and intransient certainty, objective judgement is based on occult rather than on visible criteria. In consequence, the realm of beauty lies in the manifestation of the essence of a thing, which is known through sacred sight. Among the Huichol of San Andrés, the beauty of an object or phenomenon is expressed in the term *xip'ane*, which corresponds to the Spanish *bonito*. As its opposite it is paired with *repu'ane*, *feo*, 'ugly'. Grimes and McIntosh (1954: 37) also give *vísi*, which seems to be used in a way similar to *xip'ane* to mean pretty or good. A beautiful thing is, therefore, a good thing, and, as we have seen, for it to be regarded as good it must be related to the ancestral deities. *Nierika*, votive bowls, and other ceremonial objects, as well as weavings, are most certainly beautiful because their manufacture is taught to the Huichol by the deities. However, arts and crafts which have no archetypal myth of origin or traditionally prescribed use or significance may be more ambiguous. Furthermore, the ethical basis of this beauty may be evaluated by its ability to objectify an aspect of the deity which it is meant to signify. Beauty is a form of revelation which explicates what is implicit and reveals that which is occult.

Among the most frequent Huichol expressions of beauty is 'clarity' (*claridad*),[14] which is used to describe the sierra in which they live. It is a sacred world, established, as I have recounted, by the ancestral deities, and is called the place of clarity (Benítez, 1968: 473). It is divided from the regions which lie around it by a curtain or frontier called Tukamerishe, 'the line of shadow', which is anthropomorphized as the god Reutari (ibid. 141). Within this boundary, the mountains, precipices, rivers, springs, and flora are all said to share this quality of clarity. Once, a Huichol standing next to me at the edge of a precipice, looking outwards to the consecutive ridges of mountains that unfolded as far as the horizon, described how 'pretty' (*bonito*) the 'clearness' of the sierra appeared. Whenever the Huichol leave the sierra, to undertake wage labour on the coastal plantations of Nayarit or live in the large cities to produce or sell their crafts, they lose 'clarity', which only returns to them once they re-enter their mountainous home. 'Clarity' does not refer solely to their perception of the objective environment, but also to their recognition and understanding of the essences underlying perceptual phenomena. When they leave their land, they also leave their deities, who are no longer able to protect and care for them. They become unable to see their deified land, and lose their *iyári*. Beauty is transcribed into the familiar landscape, since every object and phenomenon has a meaning as the metamorphosis of a deity and contains a significance particular to it which the initiate can read. If one is able to penetrate to the essence of the natural landscape, it is possible to enter the land of the deities, a realm of perfect parameters which coincide with aesthetic ideals. This world is described in the shaman's chants:

Here, say the songs, the gods were born. Thus says the peyote, the masticated flower. All say that an infinity of gods were born here and it is proven. My gods sing and they say that their path is in the Mountain with White Lines.

In the world of these divine flowers, all is wisdom, counsel, example and song. The whole landscape is transformed into dance and unknown horizons.

Oh divine flower, you were born amongst gods. In these lands you knew your world. You knew a people and this people reveres and respects you. Look to your world and your god, oh flower of the centre, oh flower of the divine priests. You [are] dispersed but everyone searches for you and finds you. Oh beautiful flower, flower of the gods, you will never again be deserted. Free from all evil mind, since you are followed always by good thoughts.   (Mata Torres, 1974: 44)

The chant refers both to the peyote and to the *toto*, a small white flower which grows alongside the maize and blooms when the maize is maturing. Like peyote, the plant is associated with the sacred knowledge of the deities. It is another manifestation of *iyári* and, therefore, a source of knowledge about their nature. The image of the flower cuts across the diversity and different categories of gods and emphasizes their unity and relationship to man. The flower is an image of the occult world, a representation of the order found in Wirikuta during the ancient times to which the world should correspond, and as such represents an ethically charged aesthetic imperative. The importance of the flower as a symbol of perfection and wholeness is shown by its popularity as a predominant motif in Huichol textiles, particularly on shoulder-bags. Following Lumholtz (1900), Villaseñor and Vanegas (1977: 155) list eighteen distinct stylizations of it in weavings. The flower's evocation of the world of essences is unmistakable, conveying the origin of the inspiration which lies behind their representation and the place to which the designs are addressed as a sort of prayer and offering.

'Clarity' is the gift of 'sight', and 'sight' is limited to the realm which the Huichol recognize as corresponding to the home of their deities. Clarity is, then, an essential component of the idea of beauty.

The world of essences, which 'sight' makes clear, is populated by many deities closely connected to birth, fertility, and regeneration, which the designs on votive bowls, different kinds of textile, and *nierika* commonly represent. Many of these themes revolve around sexual metaphors, which may be seen to be a chief concern of Huichol art, as well as providing the roots around which many connotations of beauty are clustered.

Further confirmation of this focus of aesthetic appreciation can be had from the exchange relations in which objects having such motifs partake. Huichol marriage preferences demonstrate the relationship between beauty and the ancestral world. A beautiful woman is one who has been well brought up and taught the correct ways of behaviour and ethics as they were given the Huichol by the deities. She must be hard-working, able to cook and weave, fertile, and committed in her devotion to the deities. Her archetype, as well as that of man, is established in myth. Such an idea of beauty, again a largely moral version of wider ethical concerns, emphasizes the woman's complementary role as a transformer and her reproductive capacities, as well as her ability to engage in a closely tied relationship by which she and her husband can approach the world of the ancestral deities. A beautiful woman is necessarily a good woman. Similarly, an upstanding man would be one who is diligent at his agriculture, proficient in his technical accomplishments, and devout in his religious obligations. This complementary relationship is essential, since a man cannot complete his shamanistic training until he is married, and his wife must also devote herself to the deities at the same time that her husband makes offerings and undergoes privations to receive ancestral knowledge.

The water deities, and particularly the rain mothers, are also associated with beauty, not just in the ethical sense by fulfilling their obligations to preserve life, but in the description of their homes and the elements connected with their cult. Tatei Rapaviyeme, the southern rain mother, dwells on the shores of Lake Chapala in southern Jalisco. She lives by an ancient fig tree (*rapa*), which has luxuriant green foliage covered by a moist, translucent sheen of dew which continuously drips from its leaves. Tatei Uteanaka, the protectress of fresh-water fish, lives in 'a beautiful house, beautiful as if seen on a clear night. It is a cave made of rock crystal and red, yellow and multicoloured tongues of flame', situated in the centre of the water (Benítez, 1968: 434). The home of Tatei Haramara is a rock which stands in the Pacific Ocean, just off the coast at San Blas, Nayarit. The sea is likened to a giant serpent, and the spray which is hurled against the craggy rock is said to be the many-coloured serpents which guard her house. The Huichol refer to all these places, and the other homes of their gods and goddesses at Tatei Matinieri and Rreunar in the east, as beautiful. With the exception only of the last-named shrine, the birthplace of the sun, all the other locations connected with beauty are steeped deeply in the imagery of birth, fertility, and life that are guaranteed by compliance with the terms of the ethical contract instituted by the ancestral deities. Tatei Uteanaka protects fresh-water fish, the form taken by the rain mothers after they have fallen from the sky as serpents, to return to their aquatic homes at the four cardinal points. The dew which always clings to the fig tree owned by Tatei Rapaviyeme represents not only the source of bountiful supplies of water but the soul, also conceived as a dew-drop fixed above the forehead. The serpents that guard the home of Tatei Haramara are the same as the lightning sky serpents, which represent the rain mothers as they cross the sky to fertilize the Huichol earth. Clouds, too, are much admired, and the many names given to the different formations were traditionally used as women's names. Beauty and goodness are thus intimately connected.

Leach (1973: 223) has suggested that art communicates at different levels, and is most effective at overcoming cultural barriers when its imagery depends on non-cultural forms, such as the human body, and when its meaning focuses on transcultural themes such as sexuality. Such images and meanings can be expected to be the most easily recognizable despite other cultural dissimilarities. While this argument is applicable to the present identification of such themes with art and concepts of beauty, it has nevertheless been possible to approximate the indigenous terms by which they are apprehended. Despite this, however, it must be agreed with Leach that even deeper and alternative meanings probably exist which lie undetected by the ethnographer's eye.

Aesthetic judgements are not confined to phenomena associated with the water deities. The fertility of the earth or Huichol woman is achieved only through the reconciliation of the water and solar or feminine and masculine categories; hence beautiful imagery is also ascribed to the sun. An example of such imagery has already been given in the prayer dedicated to the sacred flower. It is also evidenced in the close relationship between *iyári*, the sun, and Tatewarí. It is the resplendence of the sun that gives sight, and the heart of Tatewarí that permits the Huichol to penetrate the appearance of the world, and understand the distinct natures of the deities. As in other realms of Huichol thought, appreciation of the world is not possible without the co-operation of the different categories which compose it.

VI

Huichol art and aesthetics correspond to a site of intense emotional excitement. Devotional acts are made in an attitude of deep humility and reverence, when the supplicants express their own unworthiness, plead forgiveness, and acknowledge the benevolence and sanctity of their gods. During the recitation of sacred chants which tell of the sacrifices and privations that the deities underwent to create the world and provide sustenance, it is not uncommon for men and women to weep at being reminded of such selfless deeds. It is the high ethical regard in which these events are held that binds the Huichol to following the path of their deities and continuing the work that those deities began.

We have served all the gods that were born and now exist. We have complied to the letter with that which they have ordered us. We have conserved the offerings while we live. We have made uncountable journeys to find them and have them nearer.

We have followed your footsteps and cried at your absence. We have kept all your teachings. We love the religion that you have left us and understand your sentiments. Those do not cry who say they know nothing nor reclaim the past, which they no longer see in the present. Do not look with indifference to the being who takes us along the good path.

Think in this world to whom you owe what you are. Whether you know or not other lives and other generations, do not worry. Be content with what you are and with what you have.

Some day all the traditions that we have will be gathered by the gods. They will take them to the place of their dwelling, to the place of their birth. Everything will be left in darkness, but before this happens we will have brought to a head all that they ordered us.

We set a good example to our sons, since they too will have those to teach what is life and what is death. They will teach that after death there is another life, and in this life as well there is a duty to perform.   (Mata Torres, 1974: 43)

In summary, Huichol aesthetics is not concerned with an abstract concept of beauty, divorced from the ethical categories with which it is bound. However, while for the Huichol ethics and aesthetics may be compounded to constitute a single field of knowledge, the organization of its categories and the epistemology on which they are based are distinct from other aspects of contemporary Western aesthetics. Huichol aesthetics, unlike its contemporary Western counterpart, does not appear to make any distinction between signified and signifier. Its art is iconic in that it does not only represent the deities but becomes a manifestation of them and shares identical sacred qualities. Furthermore, Huichol art is profoundly religious, and its meaning is based on ideas of ontology and metaphysics that are exotic to our own thought. In these respects, its closest counterpart may be the art and ideas of beauty developed by scholasticism in medieval Europe (Eco, 1986).

I have described how, among the Huichol, traditionally produced decorative objects are used in exchanges between different domains and mark their distinct junctures. They signify, or actualize, the intangible things that are being exchanged: fertility and regeneration in one cycle, or productive and reproductive qualities and abilities in the domestic sphere of exchange. Commercial arts, however, form part of asymmetrical exchanges whose conditions express the economic and cultural dominance of the metropolitan society, rather than the aspirations of their producers. The situational meaning of the material and its form can be obtained from examining the structured contexts in which the objects participate. However, to penetrate the source of aesthetic inspiration and the values upon which appreciation and judgement are based, it is necessary to examine the fundamental ontological categories of their thought. For the Huichol, the world appears very different to that which confronts the Western observer. Outer reality is a trick, shifting, restless, deceitful, but constituted by essences from which the aesthetic dimension feeds. Aesthetics is about how the 'real' world is, but the real world, for the Huichol, is not the world that we perceive, and any attempt to explicate their aesthetic ideas cannot assume a shared body of perceptions about which objectively recognizable laws of form, position, and volume intervene to provide the criteria for beauty. For the Huichol, aesthetics is not concerned with passive reflection, but with an active attitude to maintain or adjust a system of ethics, inherited from their ancestral deities, which organizes the world and defines appropriate activities and relations within it.

In these remote regions which have conserved vestiges of cosmologies which maintain a continuity between culture and nature, art may still be invoked as a form of what Bateson called 'grace' (1973: 235). Art codes the world differently from language, and is not entirely reducible to a system of meaning which is constructed through secondary process. Unlike consciousness, which selectively encodes the world and expresses it through language, art shares with dreams, intoxication, religion, and poetry the ability to allude to a vast reservoir of the unconscious concerned with the intransmutable generalities of relationships and the 'interlocking circuits of contingency on which human survival rest' (ibid. 246–9). Twice distanced from the Huichol significance of art and aesthetics, first by the linguistic and cultural barriers that separate our world from theirs and second by the difficulty of translating from primary unconscious processes to the purposive secondary processes of language, we nevertheless can glimpse the broad and bold purview of the many and complex relations and obligations which pattern the existence of their world, and which express what Bateson has called 'wisdom' (ibid. 250). For the Huichol, art makes explicit the immanence of intransmutable essences underlying the appearance of the world, and aesthetics provides the criteria by which the success of such intervention is judged.

Notes

Field-work among the Huichol was carried out between Jan. 1979 and Mar. 1980 with a grant from the Social Science Research Council. I am grateful to Professor R.

Needham, Dr P. Riviere, Dr W. Merrill, and Mr M. McLeod, who read earlier drafts of this essay, and to Dr J. Overing and Ms O. Harris, who made valuable comments and criticisms on a later version read at the University of London. The final draft was prepared while I was a visiting fellow in the Department of Anthropology at the Smithsonian Institution (1989–90). I am grateful for the generosity of that institution, and for the encouragement and goodwill of its staff. All translation from Spanish texts are mine.

1 See Shelton (1988; 1989) for discussions of the Huichol pantheon and the relations between different deities.

2 The meaning of the symbolism of these designs has already been discussed in some detail by Lumholtz (1900; 1904) and Zingg (1938: 607–15), and will not concern us here.

3 Seler (1939: 11) considered these to be related to, and possibly derived from, the ancient Meso-American technique of mosaic work.

4 In a modern yarn painting by Jose Benítez Sanchez, *Invoking Our Mother the Rain*, the rain is depicted living under 3 gourd bowls.

5 The myth which tells of the acquisition of agriculture is recounted in Zingg (1938: 532–3).

6 These small fields, located around a district temple and cared for by temple officials, were traditionally divided into 5 areas, each reserved for a particular colour of maize, representing the 5 maize daughters specified in Huichol myth. Their mother, Tatei Haramara, and her sisters, the rain mothers, together with their father, whom Zingg (1938: 613) identified as Keamukáme, but who I was told was the sun, is invoked by the temple authorities to care for the maize children. It is not surprising that this field which becomes the home of the sacred family also bears the name *itári*.

7 Benzi (1972: 204) reports that the bride may also be given gifts of bracelets, earrings, vegetable dyes, and wool.

8 In ancient times, the squirrel stole the fire from the temple of the water deities and took it to the home of the solar deities, with whom he became associated. It is, therefore, an appropriate masculine symbol.

9 A concise expression of this view, which illustrates the historical evolution of the concept of nature in European thought, can be found in Collingwood, 1945.

10 North American peyote paintings, as illustrated by Jopling (1984), are much more naturalistic, and have been influenced by external Western conventions and styles which make them quite unlike those of the Huichol.

11 For the Huichol, the natural habitat has significance only through its mediation by myth. It represents a spatialization of temporality which consistently ties the present to the structure of the past.

12 Seler (1939: 10) compared these to the *tlachieloni* or *itlachiaya* used by the Aztec. These consisted 'of a disc borne on a stick, with a hole in the centre', and were associated with the Aztec fire deity and the nocturnal aspect of the sun, Tezcatlipoca. This similarity in form and association between solar deities and a fire deity, the source of shamanistic power, suggests that their uses were similarly conceptualized.

13 I do not refer just to power as a function of hierarchical ranking, but also to its

vertical distribution. This does not necessarily rest on the threat of coercion, but also offers a means of structuring relationships by moral compulsion.

14 'Clarity' here refers to the gift of vision bestowed on them by the sun. The light at sunrise is called *pari niube*, 'the speaking light of the sun'. *Pariya panatimie* is translated as 'here comes the clarity' or 'here comes the light of day' (Benítez, 1968: 534).

References

BATESON, GREGORY (1973). 'Style, Grace, and Information in Primitive Art', in Anthony Forge (ed.), *Primitive Art and Society*. London: Oxford Univ. Press, 235–55.

BENÍTEZ, F. (1968). *Los Indios de Mexico*, ii. Mexico City: ERA.

BENZI, M. (1972). *Les Derniers adorateurs du peyotl: croyances, coutumes et mythes des indiens huichols*. Paris: Gallimard.

BOURDIEU, PIERRE (1984). *Distinction: A Social Critique of the Judgement of Taste*, trans. Richard Nice. London: Routledge & Kegan Paul.

—— and PASSERON, JEAN-CLAUDE (1977). *Reproduction in Education, Society and Culture*, trans. Richard Nice. London: Sage.

COLLINGWOOD, R. G. (1945). *The Idea of Nature*. Oxford: Clarendon Press.

ECO, UMBERTO (1986). *Art and Beauty in the Middle Ages*, trans. Hugh Bredin. New Haven, Conn.: Yale Univ. Press.

FOUCAULT, MICHEL (1974). *The Archaeology of Knowledge*, trans. Alan Sheridan. London: Tavistock.

FURST, PETER T. (1978). 'The Art of "Being Huichol"', in Kathleen Berrin (ed.), *Art of the Huichol Indians*. San Francisco: Fine Arts Museum of San Francisco/New York: Abrams, 18–34.

GRIMES, J. G., and MCINTOSH, J. (1954). *Vocabulario Huichol–Castellano, Castellano–Huichol*. Mexico City: Instituto Linguistica de Verano.

JOPLING, CAROL F. (1984). 'Art and Ethnicity: Peyote Painting—A Case Study', *Ethnos*, 49/1–2: 98–118.

LEACH, EDMUND (1973). 'Levels of Communication and Problems of Taboo in the Appreciation of Primitive Art', in Anthony Forge (ed.), *Primitive Art and Society*. London: Oxford Univ. Press, 221–34.

LUMHOLTZ, CARL (1900). *Symbolism of the Huichol Indians*. American Museum of Natural History Memoirs 1 and 2. New York: American Museum of Natural History.

—— (1902). *Unknown Mexico*, ii. New York: Scribner's.

—— (1904). *Decorative Art of the Huichol Indians*. American Museum of Natural History Memoir 3. New York: American Museum of Natural History.

MATA TORRES, R. (1974). *El Pensiamento Huichol Través de sus Cantos*. Guadalajara (n.p.).

—— (1980). *El Arte de los Huicholes*. Guadalajara (n.p.).

NEGRÍN, J. (1975). *The Huichol Creation of the World*. Sacramento, Calif.: E. B. Crocker Art Gallery.

—— (1977). *El Arte Contemporaneo de los Huicholes*. Guadalajara: Univ. of Guadalajara Press.

NEGRIN, J. (1979). 'Les Huichols parlent la langue des dieux', *Courrier de l'UNESCO*, Feb., 16–27.

RAGLAN, LORD (1964). *The Temple and the House*. London: Routledge & Kegan Paul.

RIVIÈRE, P. G. (1969). 'Myth and Material Culture: Some Symbolic Interrelations', in Robert F. Spencer (ed.), *Forms of Symbolic Action: Proceedings of the 1989 Annual Spring Meeting of the American Ethnological Society*. Seattle: Univ. of Washington Press, 151–66.

SELER, EDUARD (1939). *The Huichol Indians of the State of Jalisco, Mexico*, trans. E. J. Thompson. Cambridge, Mass.: Carnegie Institution.

SHELTON, ANTHONY ALAN (1986). 'The Recollection of Times Past: Memory and Event in Huichol Narrative', *History and Anthropology*, 2: 355–78.

—— (1988). 'Huichol Natural Philosophy', *Cosmos: Yearbook of the Traditional Cosmology Society*, iv. Edinburgh: Edinburgh Univ. Press, 339–54.

—— (1989). 'Preliminary Notes on Some Structural Parallels in the Symbolic and Relational Classifications of Nahuatl and Huichol Deities', in *Cosmos: Yearbook of the Traditional Cosmology Society*, v. Edinburgh: Edinburgh Univ. Press, 151–83.

VAN BAAL, J. (1976). 'Offering, Sacrifice and Gift', *Numen*, 23/3: 161–78.

VILLASEÑOR, L., and VANEGAS, J. (1977). *Uicharica*. Guadalajara: Colegio Internacional.

WESTHEIM, PAUL (1972). *Ideas Fundamentales del Arte Prehispanico*. Mexico City: ERA.

WITHERSPOON, GARY (1977). *Language and Art in the Navajo Universe*. Ann Arbor: Univ. of Michigan Press.

WITTGENSTEIN, LUDWIG (1970). *Lectures and Conversations on Aesthetics, Psychology and Religious Belief*, ed. Cyril Barrett. Oxford: Blackwell.

ZINGG, R. M. (1938). *The Huichol: Primitive Artists*. New York: Strechert.

10

'Marvels of Everyday Vision': The Anthropology of Aesthetics and the Cattle-Keeping Nilotes

JEREMY COOTE

The current idea that we look lazily into the world only as far as our practical needs demand it while the artist removes this veil of habits scarcely does justice to the marvels of everyday vision.

(E. H. Gombrich, Art and Illusion)

Introduction

This essay is written out of a conviction that progress in the anthropological study of visual aesthetics has been hampered by an undue concentration on art and art objects. The cattle-keeping Nilotes of the Southern Sudan make no art objects and have no traditions of visual art, yet it would be absurd to claim that they have no visual aesthetic. In such a case as this, the analyst is forced to attend to areas of life to which everyday concepts of art do not apply, to attend, indeed, to 'the marvels of everyday vision' (Gombrich, 1977: 275) which we all, not just the artists and art critics amongst us, experience and delight in. It is my contention that such wide-ranging analyses will produce more satisfactory accounts of the aesthetics of different societies—even of those with art traditions and art objects. With this in mind, then, I present the cattle-keeping Nilotes of the Southern Sudan as a sort of test-case for the anthropology of aesthetics.

The Anthropology of Aesthetics

While it is generally recognized that aesthetics concerns more than art and that art is about more than aesthetics, anthropologists, along with philosophers and aestheticians in general, have tended to work on the assumption, made nicely explicit in the 'Aesthetics' entry in the *New Encyclopaedia Britannica* (Pepper, 1974: 150), that 'it is the explanation that can be given for deeply prized works of art that stabilizes an aesthetic theory'. In their accounts of the aesthetics of other cultures, anthropologists have concentrated on materials that fit Western notions of 'works of art', at times compounding the problem by making the focus of their studies those objects which are 'deeply prized' by the Western anthropologist, rather than those most valued by the people themselves. Moreover, what has passed for the anthropology of aesthetics has often been little more than talk about such 'art'; for many years, anthropologists' or art critics' talk, more recently, indigenous talk as systematized by the anthropologist.

While one doubts that works of art are ever deeply prized for their aesthetic qualities alone, it is probably true that in Western societies, and in others with highly developed art traditions, aesthetic notions are most perfectly manifested in works of art, and are given their most refined expression in that type of discourse known as the philosophy of art. But the aesthetic notions so manifested and refined are those of members of the art world, not necessarily those of the general population. For most of us—or, perhaps more accurately, all of us most of the time—our aesthetic notions have more to do with home decorating, gardening, sport, advertising, and other areas of so-called 'popular' culture. The presence of art having become almost a defining feature of Western notions of the civilized, anthropologists have been loath to say of any other society that it has no art. There is, it is true, probably no society that has no art-form at all, but there are certainly societies with no visual art traditions. A Western preoccupation with the visual has led both to the undervaluation of the poetic, choreological, and other arts, and to the widening of the definition of visual art so as to embrace all those objects or activities which have 'artistic' or 'aesthetic' qualities. So, for example, body decoration has been reclassified as art in recent years. While I have no fundamental objection to 'art' being defined in such broad terms, I find it more satisfactory to talk rather of the aesthetic aspect of a society's activities and products.

All human activity has an aesthetic aspect. We are always, though at varying levels of awareness, concerned with the aesthetic qualities of our aural, haptic, kinetic, and visual sensations. If art were to be defined so broadly as to encompass any human activity or product with an aesthetic aspect, then none could be denied the status of art. This seems to me unwarranted; the possible insight seemingly captured by such an argument is adequately caught by saying that all human activity has an aesthetic aspect.

I am encouraged in arguing for such a view by a trend that seems to characterize some recent anthropological and philosophical literature, a trend towards recognizing that aesthetics may be usefully defined independently of art. The anthropologist Jacques Maquet, for example, has argued repeatedly (e.g. 1979: 45; 1986: 33) that art and aesthetics are best treated as independent. Among philosophers, Nick Zangwill (1986: 261) has argued that 'one could do aesthetics without mentioning works of art! Sometimes I think it would be safer to do so.' And T. J. Diffey (1986: 6) has remarked how it is not just philosophers of art who require a notion of aesthetics; philosophers of religion require one too, and 'a notion of it as that which has no especial connection with art, but which, rather, is closer to perception'. Diffey regards 'aesthetic experience' as an as yet 'inadequately understood expression', as a term 'that extends thought, stretches the mind and leads us into new and uncharted territory' (ibid. 11). The task of philosophy, as he sees it, is to clarify and explicate what ordinary language has already 'inchoately discovered'. It is my view that rather than waiting for the clarifications and explications of philosophy, the anthropology of aesthetics should follow such ordinary language usage, disconnect itself from art, and get closer to perception.

I hope that what is meant by this admittedly vague contention will become clearer through the course of this essay. It might be thought too easy to have recourse to 'everyday usage', for probably any definition at all can be supported by judicious selection from the flux of everyday language. I am able, however, to adduce here non-specialist usages of 'aesthetic' and its cognates by three of the authors whose writings on the peoples of the Southern Sudan are drawn on in this essay. These authors do not discuss aesthetics as such, but make passing references which I find significant. Evans-Pritchard (1940a: 22) refers to 'those aesthetic qualities which please him [a Nuer] in an ox'. Elsewhere, Jean Buxton (1973: 7) tells us that 'marking and patterning are very highly estimated in the Mandari visual aesthetic', and John Burton (1981: 76) refers to a particular cattle-colour configuration as being 'the most aesthetically pleasing for the Atuot'. In none of these cases does the author explain what he or she means by the term. They can all be taken to be using the term in an everyday sense which they expect their readers to understand. I take them to mean by an 'aesthetic' something like 'the set of valued formal qualities of objects' or 'valued formal qualities of perception'.

The anthropology of aesthetics as I see it, then, consists in the comparative study of valued perceptual experience in different societies. While our common human physiology no doubt results in our having universal, generalized responses to certain stimuli, perception is an active and cognitive process in which cultural factors play a dominant role. Perceptions are cultural phenomena. Forge touched on this some twenty years ago when he wrote (1970: 282) concerning the visual art of the Abelam of New Guinea:

What do the Abelam see? Quite obviously there can be no absolute answer to this question: it is impossible literally to see through the eyes of another man, let alone perceive with his brain. Yet if we are to consider the place of art in any society . . . we must beware of assuming that they see what we see and vice versa.

I should argue that, more than just being wary of making assumptions, we must in fact make the attempt to understand how they see. The study of a society's visual aesthetic, for example, should be devoted to the identification of the particular qualities of form—shape, colour, sheen, pattern, proportion, and so on—recognized within that society, as evidenced in language, poetry, dance, body decoration, material culture, sculpture, painting, etc. A society's visual aesthetic is, in its widest sense, the way in which people in that society see. Adapting from Michael Baxandall's studies of Western art traditions (1972: 29 ff.; 1980: 143 ff.) the phrase 'the period eye', anthropologists might usefully employ the notion of 'the cultural eye'. It is a society's way of seeing, its repertoire of visual skills, which I take to be its visual aesthetic, and it is with this that I believe the anthropological study of visual aesthetics should be concerned. Such an anthropology of aesthetics will be a necessary comple-ment to any anthropology of art, for it surely must be essential to any anthropological consideration of art, however conceived, that an attempt is made to see the art as its original makers and viewers see it.

The study of aesthetics as it is taken here is to be distinguished from both art criticism and the philosophy of art. These disciplines are concerned with aesthetics, but not exclusively so. The evaluations of art criticism involve considerations of form, but also of content and meaning. The philosophy of art tends towards analysing the relations between art and such matters as the True and the Good, matters which are beyond the formal qualities of works of art. It is perhaps worth emphasizing that practices similar to those of Western art criticism and philosophy are to be found in other cultures. These practices are worthy of study in their own right. According to the terminology adopted in this essay, however, they are not the aesthetics of a society, but its art criticism or its philosophy.

The Cattle-Keeping Nilotes

The cattle-keeping Nilotes need little introduction here. This essay focuses on the Nuer, Dinka, Atuot, and Mandari of the Southern Sudan, concerning each of whom there is a substantial and easily accessible literature, while making passing reference to the closely related Anuak of the Southern Sudan and the more distantly related Pokot and Maasai of East Africa. The Nuer and Dinka in particular are well known to all students of anthropology.[1] What does perhaps require some explanation is their being taken together as 'the cattle-keeping Nilotes'. The million or so people who are referred to by the names 'Nuer', 'Dinka', 'Atuot', and 'Mandari' do not compose a homo-geneous society—but then, neither do any of the four 'peoples' themselves. There are, for example, variations in the ecological situation, economic life, degree of political centralization, and particularities of religious belief and practice both within and between these peoples.

However, they also share many social and cultural features, not least of which is the importance of cattle in their lives.[2] Cattle are not just a food source, but a central factor in all aspects of their social and cultural activities, being used to mediate social relationships through the institutions of bride-wealth and bloodwealth, as well as to mediate man's relationship with God through their role as sacrificial victims. Moreover, the Nuer, Dinka, Atuot, and Mandari share a common history,[3] live in geographical proximity, and have extensive interrelations across the 'borders' that might be supposed to exist between them.

The picture of Nilotic visual aesthetics painted here is an analyst's abstraction. It is founded on the current state of anthropological knowledge concerning the group of peoples which provide the ethnographic focus, peoples who are related linguistically, historically, geographically, and culturally. Further research may reveal significant differences between and amongst the aesthetics of these four peoples. It might, however, also reveal significant similarities between these four peoples and other Nilotic-speaking peoples. The analysis presented here is ahistorical. This is for the sake of convenience only. A full understanding of an aesthetic system must include the historical dimension. I hope to be able to deal with aesthetic change among the Nilotes elsewhere.

Nilotic Aesthetics

Little attention has been paid by scholars to aesthetics amongst the Nilotic-speaking peoples of Southern Sudan and East Africa.[4] In his thesis on Western Nilotic material culture, Alan Blackman (1956: 262–73) devotes a chapter to 'Aesthetics', but only to discuss representational art—or, more accurately, the lack of it. Ocholla-Ayayo's discussion (1980: 10–12) of 'Aesthetics of Material Culture Elements', in his account of Western Nilotic Luo culture, is a purely theoretical account of the abstract notion of beauty and its relation to value, appearance, use, and society, drawing on thinkers such as Santayana, without entering into a discussion of the particularities of Luo aesthetics as such. Harold Schneider's short but often quoted article on 'The Interpretation of Pakot Visual Art' (1956) is the best-known contribution to the study of Nilotic aesthetics, and is worth commenting on at some length.

Schneider defines his terms rather differently from how they are defined here. He defines 'art' as 'man-made beauty', but recognizes that what the Pokot themselves find beautiful should not be assumed by the analyst but has to be discovered. To do this, he analyses the meaning and use of the Pokot term *pachigh*, which his interpreter variously translated as 'beautiful', 'pretty', 'pleasant to look at', and 'unusual'. *Pachigh* is distinguished from *karam*, which means 'good', and which Schneider glosses as 'utilitarian'. The Pokot apply the term *pachigh* to non-utilitarian, aesthetically pleasing objects of the natural world or of non-Pokot manufacture, as well as to the non-utilitarian embellishments of Pokot utilitarian objects. Cattle, for example, are utilitarian (*karam*), but the colours of the hides are *pachigh* (ibid. 104). People are also *karam*, though a woman 'may have aspects of beauty such as firm round breasts, a light, chocolate-coloured skin, and white even teeth' (ibid. 104); and a fully decorated man may be referred to as beautiful but 'it is clear that they mean only the aesthetic embellishments' (ibid. 105).

Through his analysis of the term *pachigh*, Schneider is able to identify what it is that the Pokot find aesthetically pleasing, but he tells us little about *why* these particular objects and embellishments are considered *pachigh*. In recognizing that what is of interest is not a category of objects—art—but a category of thought—aesthetics—Schneider makes an important contribution—being 'forced' to, perhaps, by the very lack of Pokot art—but he tells us little about what characterizes this category of thought, merely listing those objects to which it is applied. While he refers in passing to contrast, which is discussed below—and to novelty, which I hope to discuss elsewhere—the discussion of aesthetic qualities, the very stuff of aesthetics, is not developed. It is on the aesthetic qualities which Nilotes appreciate, rather than on the category of objects in which these qualities are observed, that this essay concentrates.

For Nilotic-speaking cattle-keepers, cattle are the most highly valued possessions. This analysis of Nilotic aesthetics is, therefore, centred on cattle. The importance of cattle for the Nilotes is well known, and I do not propose to summarize the literature here. I wish to concentrate on the perceptual qualities of cattle as they are appreciated by their owners. These concern the colour configuration and sheen of the hide, the shape of the horns, and the bigness and fatness of the body including particularly the hump (see Fig. 10.1). These are discussed first, and then their ramifications into other areas of Nilotic life are traced.

Of primary importance for this discussion are the cattle-colour terminologies which are so characteristic of the cattle-keeping peoples of East Africa.[5] Nilotic languages in general have many terms to describe the colour configurations of cattle. Even people who no longer keep cattle or depend upon them materially may maintain cattle-colour terminologies. The Anuak, for example, who, according to Evans-Pritchard (1940*b*: 20), can only have been a pastoral people 'a very long time ago', still based their metaphorical praise-names upon cattle-colour configurations when Lienhardt studied them in the 1950s (Lienhardt 1961: 13 n.). Cattle-colour terms rarely refer to pure colours or shades of colours, but rather to configurations of colours or, in a loose sense of the term, patterns.

For the Western Dinka, Nebel (1948: 51) recorded twenty-seven terms, while for the Ngok Dinka, Evans-Pritchard (1934) recorded thirty. For the Nuer, Evans-Pritchard (1940*a*: 41–4) showed that there are 'several hundred colour permutations' based on ten principal colour terms multiplied by at least

FIG. 10.1. Dinka ox of the *marial* configuration; Bekjiu, near Pacong, Agar Dinka; photographer: Jeremy Coote, February 1981.

twenty-seven combination terms. In his 1934 article on Ngok Dinka terms, he promised that he would publish a full account of Nuer terms, a promise repeated in *The Nuer* (1940*a*: 44). The fact that the promised lengthy analysis, of what he noted in 1940 was a 'neglected' subject (ibid. 41 n.), has never appeared suggests how difficult such an analysis would be. Indeed, the application of the abstract terminology to real animals is not always straightforward for Nilotes themselves. According to Deng (1973: 96), 'the colour-patterns are so intricate among the Dinka that frequent litigation centres on their determination'. And Ryle has described (1982: 92)—in interesting terms, given the subject of this essay—how

When discussing the colour pattern of an animal—as they do for hours—the Dinka sound more like art critics than stockbreeders. For instance, when does *mathiang*— dark brown—become *malual*—reddish brown? If the animal has brown patches, are they large enough to make it *mading* or are they the smaller mottling that identifies *malek*?

Such discussions are a matter of both appreciation and classification, perhaps more akin to the discussions of antique-dealers or wine connoisseurs than to those of art critics.

It is not necessary to analyse these terminologies at length here. It is sufficient to identify briefly the principles underlying the perceived configurations. For Mandari, the colours red, white, and black have much symbolic importance (Buxton, 1973). With cattle, however, they are not so interested in pure colours; what is important is that an ox should be piebald or variegated. When a piebald is born, its owner is delighted and the beast is set aside as a display ox (ibid. 6). Similarly, Ryle has described (1982: 93–6) the 'hopeful expectation' that attends the birth of a new calf amongst the Agar Dinka. He relates how in one instance Mayen, the cow's owner, 'was ecstatic, beaming with pleasure and singing snatches of song, because the calf was a much desired *marial*'. It is the destiny of such well-marked male calves to become 'song', or 'display' oxen, being castrated when they are eight or nine months old. Animals with the most highly valued configurations are thus excluded from breeding. Ryle was told that one cannot anyway predict the occurrence of such colour patterns, 'and therefore there is no point in trying to breed for them' (ibid. 93; cf. Howell *et al.*, 1988: 282). For the Western Dinka Lienhardt (1961: 15) records how, when a male calf of a highly valued configuration is born, 'it is said that . . . the friends of its owner may tear off his beads and scatter them, for his happiness is such that he must show indifference to these more trivial forms of display'. If the dam that has produced the well-marked calf is a good milch cow, Dinka may find it hard to choose whether to keep the calf for stud purposes, knowing that it is likely to produce further good milch cows, or castrate it for display. They may hope that the dam will produce another, not so well-marked, male calf later, and castrate the one it has already produced. Mandari also choose their stud bulls from the progeny of good milch cows. All other things being equal, they will choose well-coloured ones; but, significantly, not the piebald or variegated but the plain black or red calves, trusting that these will produce offspring which are well-marked (Buxton, 1973: 6).

In fact, most cattle are not well-marked. Buxton noted that the majority of Mandari cattle are a nondescript white (ibid.), and my own experience would support this. Amongst the Agar Dinka to the west, the situation is much the same; greyish, off-white cattle are preponderant, as aerial photographs have demonstrated.[6] That they are relatively rare helps to explain why well-marked beasts are valued to such an extent that the Agar Dinka, for example, 'will trade two or three oxen of unexceptional colourings for one particularly desirable beast, if the owner is willing to part with it' (Ryle, 1982: 92). It follows that it is the cattle of less aesthetic interest, as well as those beyond breeding, which are marketed by those Nilotes, such as some Atuot, who have entered the incipient Southern Sudanese cattle trade (Burton, 1978: 401).

The sheen of the hides is also appreciated and valued. Though sheen is not a factor in cattle-colour terminologies, its appreciation can be amply illustrated by the amount of time and effort expended in the grooming of cattle, and by frequent reference to it in poetry and song. An Atuot song, for example, includes the words: 'the back of my ox is as white as the grazing in

F IG. 10.2. Dinka man with decorated song-ox; photographer: Survival Anglia, 1975.

the new grass'—the image, as Burton explains (1982: 274), being 'of morning dew glittering in the sunlight'. A song by Stephen Ciec Lam, a Nuer, refers to 'my sister's big ox/ whose glossy hide shines against the compound' (Svoboda, 1985: 32). Another by Daniel Cuor Lul Wur, also a Nuer, refers to an ox whose hide 'is like the sun itself: he is the ox of moonlight' (ibid. 19). And yet another by Rec Puk relates how 'Jiok's hide is as bright as moonlight,/ bright as the sun's tongue./ My Jiok shines like gold,/ like a man's ivory bracelet' (ibid. 11). In this last example, specific comparison is made between the white-on-black cattle-hide and the whiteness of the ivory bracelet shining against the black Nuer skin.

The training of ox-horns is practised by cattle-keeping peoples all over the world. Nilotes cut the horns of young display oxen so that they grow into shapes which their owners find particularly pleasing. They are cut with a spear at an oblique angle, and the horns grow back against the cut.[7] To describe such horn shapes the Nuer have six common terms, as well as 'several fancy names' (Evans-Pritchard, 1940*a*: 45). In combination with the cattle-colour configuration terms, these considerably increase the number of possible permutations to specify individual beasts—logically, to well over a thousand. As can be seen in Fig. 10.2, the horns may also be adorned with buffalo-tail hair tassels to accentuate the effect. When Burton (1982: 279) was carrying out his field-work among the Atuot, such tassels were exchanged at the rate of one tassel for six cow-calves. Cutting also thickens the horns, and large and heavy horns are especially characteristic of display oxen among the Mandari (Buxton, 1973: 7).

Appreciation of horns is expressed in song. A Dinka song, for example, tells of an 'ox with diverging horns,/ The horns are reaching the ground;/ The horns are overflowing like a boiling pot' (Deng, 1972: 84). The range of imagery is vast: Cummins (1904: 162) quotes a Dinka song in which an ox's horns are said to be 'like the masts of ships'—presumably referring to the masts of sailing ships which once plied the Nile and its tributaries. Horns are also sometimes decorated with ash, when oxen are exchanged in bridewealth, for example, the effect being to make them stand out more against the dull background of sky and landscape.[8]

In his discussion of the Nuer attitude to their cattle, Evans-Pritchard (1940a: 22) referred to 'those aesthetic qualities which please him [a Nuer] in an ox, especially fatness, colour and shape of horns'. And, according to him (ibid. 27), it is fatness which is most important, for 'colour and shape of horns are significant, but the essential qualities are bigness and fatness, it being considered especially important that the haunch bones should not be apparent'. He goes on (ibid.): 'Nuer admire a large hump which wobbles when the animal walks, and to exaggerate this character they often manipulate the hump shortly after birth.' This admiration of humps is shared by the Dinka and Atuot. A Dinka song (Deng, 1972: 81) has the lines: 'My ox is showing his narrow-waisted hump./ The hump is twisting like a goitered neck,/ Staggering like a man who has gorged himself with liquor;/ When he walks, the hump goes on twisting/ Like a man traveling on a camel.' Another Dinka song, quoted by Cummins (1904: 162), refers to an ox whose hump is 'so high that it towers above the high grass'.

The qualities of bigness and fatness are also referred to in songs. An Atuot song recorded by Burton (1982: 272) refers to the ox which is the subject of the song as 'the mahogany tree', thereby likening the size of the ox to the tree. Another Atuot song (Burton, 1981: 107) tells of an ox which is said to be 'so large like an elephant'. A Dinka song recorded by Cummins (1904: 162) tells of an ox which is 'so big that men can sit and rest in his shadow'. It should be stressed that bigness and fatness are not appreciated because they will lead to a better price at market, or to a larger meal on the death or sacrifice of the animal: cattle are primarily a feast for the eyes, and only secondarily a feast for the stomach.

Before going on to trace some of the ramifications of these elements of Nilotic 'bovine' aesthetics into the Nilotes' appreciation of, and action in, the world, it is worth making the attempt to understand why the particular perceptual qualities identified are so appreciated.

The appreciation of a large hump and of bigness and fatness are presumably at least partly explicable as indicators of healthy and well-fed beasts. And the same can presumably be said for the appreciation of sheen—it indicates a sleek and healthy hide; though it should be noted that sheen is perceptually exciting in and of itself, so its appreciation can be understood as a particular manifestation of the universal appreciation of brightness.

The appeal of horn shapes is not difficult to understand in the field. One quickly learns to appreciate the variety of trained and untrained shapes in a forest of horns in the cattle camp. Both the symmetrical and the asymmetrical curving shapes of Nilotic cattle horns have great visual appeal, especially when they are seen moving through space as the cattle move their heads, and when the arcs the horns make in the air are exaggerated by the swinging movements of the tassels. Fagg (e.g. 1973) has drawn attention to the frequent use of exponential curves in African art: the Nilotic appreciation of the curving shapes of cattle horns can be seen as yet another instance of this theme in African aesthetics.

As with horns, the appeal of particular cattle-colour configurations cannot be explained by reference to the healthiness or well-being of well-marked beasts. The majority of such beasts, though, are likely to have larger body proportions than other beasts, as the majority of well-marked beasts are castrated, and neutering encourages body growth. They also spend no energy in sexual activity and much less than uncastrated cattle in fighting; so their body growth is further encouraged and they remain physically unblemished. In general, more care is lavished on them by their owners, and one can expect this to have a beneficial effect on their health and well-being. Well-marked beasts are thus also likely to be big and fat, and vice versa. It would, however, be a strange argument which explained the appeal of well-marked beasts by the fact that they are healthier, when their being healthier depends upon their being well-marked.

As aestheticians stabilize their theories by explaining why highly prized works of art are so valued, the explanation for the Nilotes' appreciation of well-marked cattle might be sought in what they value most highly. For the peoples who are the focus of this essay, it is bold pied markings. For the Western Dinka at least, it is in particular the black-and-white configurations *majok* and *marial* (Lienhardt, 1961: 15). The former is most simply described as a black animal with a white chest, the latter as a black animal with a white flash on its flank. Black-and-white configurations provide strong contrasts. Buxton offered an explanation of the appeal of such contrasts, noting (1973: 7) that 'marking and patterning are very highly estimated in the Mandari visual aesthetic; and the strong contrast markings of black on white, red on white, or a combination of all three, stand out so strikingly in a landscape devoid of strong colour that the importance given to it can be readily under-stood'. Such an explanation can only be partial at best, but when one remembers that the vast majority of cattle are a nondescript white, the appeal of strongly contrasting black-and-white or red-and-white markings can be appreciated more readily.

The visual stimulation offered by both black and red markings amongst a herd of greyish cattle is not to be doubted. It might be expected, then, that it should be the pure black or red beasts which are most highly valued. This is not the case, for while the appreciation of well-marked beasts should be understood in the context of a dull and pale landscape and herds pre-ponderantly off-white in colour, it is the contrast of black and white or red and white in the single beast which provides the greatest aesthetic satis-faction. The individual beast, then, provides the locus for stimulating visual experience.

Aesthetics in the Wider World

Having introduced some elements of Nilotic aesthetics, it is possible to trace their ramifications in the Nilotes' appreciation of, and action in, the world in which they live.

The cattle-colour terms are associated with a wide range of phenomena apart from cattle. At its most simple, this involves the recognition of con-nections between, for example, the ox *makuac*—that is, an ox of the *kuac* configuration—and the leopard, *kuac*. In their poetic imagery, however, the Nilotes go beyond these relatively straightforward linguistic connections to more complex associations. Evans-Pritchard recorded (1940*a*: 45) some 'fanciful elaborations of nomenclature' among the Nuer where, for example, 'a black ox may be called *rual mim*, charcoal-burning or *won car*, dark clouds'. And amongst the Western Dinka, according to Lienhardt (1961: 13), a man with a black display ox may be known not only as *macar* 'black ox', but also as, for example, '*tim atiep*, "the shade of a tree"; or *kor acom*, "seeks for snails", after the black ibis which seeks for snails'.

It is not just that Nilotes make metaphorical connections between cattle-colour configurations and other phenomena; it is not just poetic play. In a real sense they see the world through a sort of grid or matrix of cattle-colours:

The Dinkas' very perception of colour, light, and shade in the world around them is ... inextricably connected with their recognition of colour-configurations in their cattle. If their cattle-colour vocabulary were taken away, they would have scarcely any way of describing visual experience in terms of colour, light, and darkness. (Lienhardt, 1961: 12–13)

This is not, of course, to say that they could not perceive the black ibis or the shade of a tree if it were not for the existence of black oxen, but it is to say that their visual experience and appreciation of the ibis and the shade is inseparable from their appreciation of the *macar* colour configuration in cattle.

Those cattle-colour terms, such as *makuac*, which are clearly related linguistically to natural phenomena, are no doubt derived from the term for the phenomenon and not vice versa. Presumably the Dinka called the leopard *kuac* before they called the spotted ox *makuac*. However, the *kuac* configuration in cattle is not called after the leopard because of some significance of the leopard as such, but because it is like the pattern to be found on *kuac*. Children will learn the names of cattle-markings, and apply them to natural and cultural phenomena, before they ever see the source of the name of the markings. A Dinka child will know what *kuac* means as a marking pattern, and will be applying it to cattle and to spotted cloth, for example, well before he or she ever—if ever—sees a leopard. The visual experience of young Dinka is focused on cattle and their markings, and the cattle-colour terminology is learned through listening to daily discussions about cattle. As Lienhardt (ibid. 12) writes, 'a Dinka may thus recognize the configuration in nature by reference to what he first knows of it in the cattle on which his attention, from childhood, is concentrated'. This fact is of greater significance than the possible historical origins of the terms.[9] That the Nilotes' visual perception of their natural and cultural world is thus shaped by their interest in, and experience of, the colour configurations of their cattle is amply attested, both by their complex cattle-colour terminologies and by the rich poetic and metaphorical elaborations of these terminologies by which associations are made between the most diverse visual experiences and cattle-colours. These associations are not by any means always obvious; part of the pleasure of composing and singing songs is in making creative connections which one's audience has to work at to comprehend.

That these associations are not made only in poetic contexts, however, is shown by Lienhardt's remark (1961: 19) that Dinka 'frequently pointed out to me those things in nature which had the *marial* colour-configuration upon which my own metaphorical ox-name was based'. One might expect a man to become particularly attuned to the colour-configuration of his own name or song ox, but, as Lienhardt's anecdote makes clear, this attuning is not exclusive; Dinka recognize and appreciate a wide range of colour-configurations. Agar Dinka friends called me Makur, explicitly referring to the dark rings around my eyes like the black patches round the eyes of the ox *makur*. Other Agar to whom I was introduced immediately grasped why I had been so called.

It is not just in their perception of their world, and their poetic expressions concerning it, that we can trace these elements of the Nilotic aesthetic. They can also be traced in the ways in which Nilotes act in the world. For example, they decorate their bodies with ash, the decoration being always (as far as I know) non-representational, but very commonly geometric.[10] Buxton tells us (1973: 401) that among the Mandari 'young people decorate their faces with white ash to imitate the facial markings of oxen and cows'. This is what one might expect to be the case for the Nilotes in general, though I know of no other report of such decoration as conscious imitation. The appearance of ash-covered bodies is, in any case, not unlike the colour of the majority of poorly marked, greyish cattle. Even if it is the case that when they decorate themselves with ash they are not consciously imitating the markings of cattle, it is surely not too much to assume that the appreciation of the markings of cattle and of the ash-covered bodies are similar, and that the former affects the latter.

More clearly, perhaps, the black-and-white animal skins, like that of the colobus monkey, which are part of 'traditional' Nilotic dress, can be seen as reflecting the contrasts appreciated in cattle-hides.[11] In recent years it has been possible for Nilotes to buy plastic accoutrements with which to adorn themselves; the man pictured with his ox in Fig. 10.2 is wearing a striking black-and-white plastic leopard-skin belt.

The contrasts that Nilotes appreciate in their cattle, and in the world around them, they also achieve in their decorative work. Mandari incise patterns on pots and gourds and blacken them with the heated point of a knife or spear, and contrasts are also made by rubbing white clay or ash into black or red surfaces. Black-and-white contrasts can also be seen in the frequent use of ivory bracelets in body decoration: as noted above, the whiteness of the ivory gleams against the wearer's black skin. Necklaces and bracelets made of indigenous materials such as wood and shell are also characterized by black-and-white contrasts.[12] It seems that contrast continues to be an important aspect of the aesthetics of beadwork, even with the immense range of hues now available in imported plastic beads.[13]

The forked branches erected in cattle camps, like the Agar Dinka example in Fig. 10.3, are decorated by the removal of alternate sections of bark to produce a banded, hooped, or straked effect.[14] In the 1980s, Mandari had access to acrylic paints, and took to painting the tall poles they erect in cattle camps. Instead of stripping alternate sections of bark to produce the desired effect, the whole bark was stripped off and alternate sections painted black and white, or, as in one example I saw, bright red and brilliant yellow.

The asymmetrical branching shape effected by horn-training can be seen in the tree branches erected as shrines amongst the Dinka, Mandari, and Atuot.[15] Although, as can be seen in Fig. 10.4, they also have a practical purpose, in that their shape makes them suitable to lean spears against and hang things from (Lienhardt, 1961: 257–60), it seems unlikely that shapes so reminiscent of the trained horns of oxen are accidentally so. One is encouraged to think that the resemblance is deliberate by the fact that the place marked by such forked-branch shrines is known amongst the Dinka as 'the head of the cattle-hearth' (ibid. 258); and Cummins (1904: 158) recounts a Dinka myth of origin in which it is said that where God lives there is a tree 'that is leafless with only two branches, one to the right and the other to the left like the horns of a bull'. For the Atuot, at least, 'the imagery of the spreading branches is consciously associated with the horns of a cow sacrificed on the occasion when the power was brought into the homestead' (Burton, 1979: 105 n.).

Whatever the case with forked-branch shrines, there can be no doubt that in other areas of life the representation of horns is conscious. Both symmetrical and asymmetrical shapes are imitated and represented. Some Nilotic scarification patterns can be seen as being based on cattle-horns; perhaps even the forehead marks of some Dinka and Mandari might be seen in this way.[16] Amongst Agar Dinka, at least, it is not unusual to see cattle-horn-shaped scarification on various parts of the body.[17]

After initiation, Nuer youths endure much pain and discomfort to imitate the horns of their oxen. They render useless their left arms by fixing a set of bracelets to them. This temporary deformation holds down their left arms as the left horns of oxen are trained downwards (Evans-Pritchard, 1956: 256–7).[18]

Lienhardt describes various ways in which Dinka imitate cattle in stylized action, remarking (1961: 16) that 'a characteristic sight in Western Dinkaland is that of a young man with his arms curved above his head, posturing either at a dance or for his own enjoyment when he is alone with his little herd'. Such posturing has been illustrated frequently and can be seen here in Fig. 10.5 where, as they dance at a sacrifice, Agar Dinka women raise their arms above their heads in imitation of the horns of cows.[19] This curving of the arms in imitation of cattle is, for the Dinka, 'one of the forms of "handsomeness" (*dheng* [or *dheeng*]), a bodily attitude which the Dinka consider graceful' (ibid. 16); it is 'a gesture of pride and triumph' (ibid. 269).

Evans-Pritchard (1940*a*: 38; cf. 1956: 251) colourfully describes how

when a Nuer mentions an ox his habitual moroseness leaves him and he speaks with enthusiasm, throwing up his arms to show you how its horns are trained. 'I have a fine ox,' he says, 'a brindled ox with a large white splash on its back and with one horn trained over its muzzle'—and up go his hands, one above his head and the other bent at the elbow across his face.

In one type of Atuot dance, 'men leap high into the air with their arms outstretched, imitating the girth and pattern of the horns of their personality oxen' (Burton, 1982: 268). Even when ox songs are sung in a sitting position a Dinka 'holds his hands up as the horns and moves his head and body in imitation of the ox' (Deng, 1972: 83).

Horn shapes are also found in Nilotic ornament. MacDermot (1972: pl. opp. p. 49) illustrates Thiwat, a Nuer man, wearing two leopard teeth fastened to a piece of leather around his neck, the resultant shape being very reminiscent of horns. Fisher (1984: 42) illustrates a Nuer wooden necklace with a central forked pendant 'shaped to resemble cows' horns'. She also

FIG. 10.3. Forked-branch post in an
Agar Dinka cattle-camp;
photographer: Jeremy Coote,
February 1981.

FIG. 10.4. Forked-branch shrine in
an Apak Atuot homestead, near
Aluakluak; photographer: Jeremy
Coote, February 1981.

FIG. 10.5. Agar Dinka dancing at a sacrifice; near Pacong; photographer: Jeremy Coote, February 1981.

illustrates (ibid. 54, 57) ivory pendants 'shaped like cows' horns' suspended from bead necklaces. And Ray Huffman (1931: fig. 3.6, opp. p. 17) illustrates a 'two-pronged wristlet'—in fact a ring—in which the shape formed by the prongs is again reminiscent of the horns of an ox.

It is not just horns which are imitated. In dance, it can be the whole animal, or groups of animals. In the same Atuot dance as that referred to above, young women imitate cows. Burton (1982: 268) describes it as follows:

a line of six or eight young women forms directly in front of the drummers. Here they perform a movement which attempts to imitate the slow gallop cows make as they saunter across a pasture. A girdle of colored beads reaching well above their heads sways back and forth, suggesting the manner in which the hump of a cow shifts back and forth when running.[20]

Deng (1972: 78–80) discusses a number of dances in which men and women act out the roles of bull, ox, and cow. And Lienhardt (1961: 17) describes a Dinka dance which is based upon 'the running of oxen with cows in the herd'. In considering fully the aesthetics of such dances, we should have to take into account more than just the purely visual; the major element is presumably the kinetic experience of the dancers themselves, though there are oral, and aural, elements too (ibid.). The visual appearance of cattle—the horns, the hump, and the general posture—are imitated as part of a more complete imitation the analysis of which is beyond the scope of this essay.

Nilotes have no developed tradition of figure sculpture or painting. There are, however, examples of modelling and drawing in which the aesthetic elements identified above are manifested. Through an examination of such models and drawings, we can deepen our understanding of the ideal forms in terms of which actual cattle are assessed and appreciated.

The making of clay, mud, or baked-earth models of cattle is a common occupation of Nilotic children. Generally speaking, the models are made by children for children's play, as is illustrated by the Dinka boy featured in a Survival Anglia film (1983) and in Fig. 10.6 here.[21] Amongst the Nuer, children play games with their oxen, 'taking them to pasture and putting them into byres, marrying with them and so on' (Evans-Pritchard, 1937: 238; cf. 1940a: 38), and Deng (1972: 60) tells of Dinka children making cattle camps using either shells or clay figures as cattle.[22] Such mud oxen may have their horns decorated with tassels in imitation of the real-life song oxen, as has the one at furthest left in the group illustrated in Fig. 10.7. They may also be coloured with ash or charred wood (Huffman, 1931: 65; Blackman, 1956: 273) in imitation of the markings of real animals.

In the examples illustrated in Fig. 10.7,[23] it is evident that what are emphasized and exaggerated are the hump, the horns, and the general fatness of the body: the head, legs, and hooves are of much less importance. A most satisfying example of such exaggeration, in which these features have been abstracted to produce a form which at first sight it takes a little imagination to see as a whole beast, are a group of five mud cows collected by Jean Brown among the Pokot in the 1970s and illustrated in Fig. 10.8. While not from a people within the particular focus of this essay, they are so striking that they are well worth illustrating here. In these examples, the aesthetically central aspects of the physical form of cattle—the fatness of the body, the hump, and the horns—have been brought together to produce a form which, though it bears little resemblance to the form of the animals themselves, is in itself aesthetically pleasing. That such models are made by children for children's play, or, as in the Pokot case, by mothers for their children, does not lessen their interest for an understanding of Nilotic aesthetics. They can be taken as an indication of what is aesthetically pleasing for the older brothers of these children, that is, for themselves when they grow up.[24]

Two-dimensional representations of cattle as illustrated in Fig. 10.9 are found on external hut walls amongst the Agar Dinka. Although there are reports of such mural drawings amongst the Nuer (e.g. Evans-Pritchard, 1937: 238; Jackson, 1923: 123–4), there are no published illustrations to provide comparative examples. They may be compared, however, with the figures of cattle incised on gourds by the Anuak as illustrated in Fig. 10.10. Here the cattle have triangular humps, and the colour configurations on their rectangular bodies are geometrically stylized.[25] They are more reminiscent of flag designs than the configurations actually found on cattle. If clay modelling reflects the Nilotic appreciation of the physical qualities of bigness and fatness, then the geometricized representations of cattle on gourds and walls can be seen to reflect the importance of colour configurations. That the bodies are rectangular and the configurations geometricized suggests that the cattle-colour classification represents a set of ideals which can be abstractly stated—or represented—even though real cattle only ever approximate to them.

Aesthetics and Society

So far I have discussed some of the qualities of perceptual experience recognized and appreciated by Nilotes. Little reference has been made to 'art', 'beauty', or 'the good', which are so often taken to be defining terms of the aesthetic. Nor has reference been made to those traditional concerns of anthropology, such as social organization and social structure, to which analysts have attempted to link aesthetics. The discussion of elements of visual appreciation in a given culture is an end in itself, contributing to an understanding of what it is to be a member of that culture. Nevertheless, I shall try to address, albeit briefly, some of the wider concerns often discussed in what has been taken elsewhere to be the anthropology of aesthetics. My concern is to bring out what I take to be the implications for the anthropology of aesthetics of the material presented above.

As for 'art', I have referred to body decoration, mural drawing, and clay modelling, all of which might well have been discussed under a heading of 'art'. I indicated my response to such an approach in the introduction to this essay. Such activities as body decoration and clay modelling have an aesthetic aspect, as all human activity does, and it is the aesthetic aspect of these activities which has been of concern in this essay. No good purpose would be served for the anthropology of aesthetics, as I understand it, in separating such activities as 'art', or in restricting any discussion of aesthetics to them.

As for 'beauty', it is hoped that the terminology adopted in this essay avoids the problems that beset attempts to use such vague terms in accounts of other cultures. An understanding of the aesthetic qualities which we have identified is, of course, relevant for any understanding of Nilotic ideas approximating Western notions of beauty. For example, Lienhardt (1963: 87) quotes a Dinka song in which the singer compares his own 'dazzling array'—glossed by Lienhardt as 'shining beauty'—with that of the ugliness of 'a big coward' to whom a girl in whom the singer is interested has been promised by her father: 'This dazzling array is a poor man's truculence, ee/ [That her father] gives her to that big ugly coward to play with, ee/ This dazzling array is just

Fɪɢ. 10.6. Dinka boy modelling a mud cow; photographer: Survival Anglia, 1975.

Fɪɢ. 10.7. Nuer mud toy cattle; collected by E. E. Evans-Pritchard in the 1930s (all but one, far right, labelled 'Anuak', though they are almost certainly all Nuer); maximum height $5\frac{1}{2}$ in. (14.0 cm.); Pitt Rivers Museum, Oxford (d.d. Evans-Pritchard 1936).

Fɪɢ. 10.8. Pokot mud toy cattle; collected by Jean Brown in the 1970s; largest $4\frac{1}{3} \times 3\frac{3}{4}$ in. (11.0 × 9.5 cm.); Pitt Rivers Museum, Oxford (1978: 20.194–8).

FIG. 10.9. Agar Dinka hut-wall drawings of a young man with two tasselled oxen (*majok*, left; *makuac*, right); near Pacong, Agar Dinka; photographer: Jeremy Coote, February 1981. The human figure is approximately 9 in. (23 cm.) high.

FIG. 10.10. Anuak gourd bowl, incised with figures and decorative designs; collected by E. E. Evans-Pritchard in the Southern Sudan in the 1930s; $7\frac{7}{8}$ in. (20.0 cm.) high, $14\frac{1}{8}$ in. (36.0 cm.) max. diameter; Pitt Rivers Museum, Oxford (1936.10.79).

truculence'. The words for 'dazzling array' and 'ugly' are, in fact, the cattle-colour terms *marial* and *malou*. As noted above, *marial* is one of the most highly valued black-and-white configurations signifying a black ox with a white splash on its flank. *Malou* is a grey ox, the implication in this context being dullness—*lou* is the Dinka name for a large bustard, probably the visually uninteresting kori bustard (*Ardeotis kori*) (Nebel, 1979: 52, 56). That *rial* combined with *nyin*, 'eye', is the Dinka term for 'to dazzle' gives some indication of the Dinka conceptualization of the visual stimulation of the *rial* black-and-white configuration (ibid. 76). In some contexts, 'pied' and 'beautiful' might be virtually interchangeable: Deng (1972: 63) quotes a song in which some young girls are said to wear 'pied and beautiful beads'.

But what is aesthetically pleasing and what is beautiful are not necessarily the same thing. A better appreciation of Nilotic ideas concerning beauty can be achieved through a discussion of indigenous concepts, such as the Dinka notion *dheeng*, mentioned in passing above. In a discussion of the virtues and dignity of a 'gentleman', Deng (1972: 14) glosses the term as follows:

dheeng . . . is a word of multiple meanings—all positive. As a noun, it means nobility, beauty, handsomeness, elegance, charm, grace, gentleness, hospitality, generosity, good manners, discretion, and kindness. The adjective form of all these is *adheng*. Except in prayer or on certain religious occasions, singing and dancing are *dheeng*. Personal decoration, initiation ceremonies, celebration of marriages, the display of 'personality oxen', indeed any demonstration of an esthetic value, is considered *dheeng*. The social background of a man, his physical appearance, the way he walks, talks, eats, or dresses, and the way he behaves towards his fellowmen are all factors in determining his *dheeng*.

In the context of this essay it is the perceptual qualities contributing to *dheeng* which are of significance, and some of these, as they relate particularly to cattle, have been identified. But it is clear from Deng's discussion that for the Dinka there is more to 'beauty' than meets the eye.

It is also in the notion of *dheeng* that aesthetics and morality are linked. What is morally good is expected to display valued aesthetic qualities, and what displays valued aesthetic qualities is expected to be morally good. It is recognized, however, that this is far from always being the case. A Dinka man is *adheng* if he has social status, whether ascribed or achieved, if he is virtuous in his relations with others, or if he is physically attractive. Ideally, these three aspects should go together, but Dinka recognize that they do not always do so.

Some of the recent literature in the anthropology of aesthetics attempts to relate aesthetics to social organization or social structure. As presented here, Nilotic aesthetics seems rather to be a contingent product of these cattle-keepers' experience of the world which they inhabit, and to have little to do with any social facts. In his account of the aesthetics of the Fang of Gabon, Fernandez (1971: 373) claims to identify basic principles of opposition and vitality at work in Fang society and culture: 'in both aesthetics and the social structure the aim of the Fang is not to resolve opposition and create identity but to preserve a balanced opposition'. This is achieved in the social structure, he argues, through complementary filiation, and in their ancestor statues through skilful aesthetic composition. Should it not be possible to make such a profound summation concerning the material presented in this essay?

To some extent, one's answer to such a question depends upon one's intellectual temper. No doubt many would find it intellectually satisfying to relate the high value of piedness to the segmentation of Nilotic political structure and to the divided world of Nilotic cosmology. The combination of black and white, or red and white, in the pied ox, the argument might run, is valued because it fits with the principles of the social organization and religious thought. It is probably the case that an intellectually diverting picture of the anthropological material concerning Nilotic aesthetics could be constructed along such lines. But what would it mean? That social structure and cosmology are products of aesthetic principles, or that aesthetic principles, and cosmology, are products of social structure, or that they are all products of underlying principles? For anyone wishing, despite these ontological puzzles, to make links of this sort, there are some suggestive facts in the ethnography to which one might point. They do not, however, stand up to closer inspection.

There is, most famously, the Nuer leopard-skin priest, amongst whose duties it is to resolve conflicts between disputing factions, and to act as an intermediary between man and God. Is it not, therefore, most suitable that he is the *leopard-skin* priest? The leopard-skin is pied, and combines within itself the opposites of black and white. However, the priest is not usually known by this title by the Nuer themselves. The more usual title can be translated as 'earth (or soil) priest'; as Evans-Pritchard (1956: 291) points out, 'the leopard-skin title is taken only from his badge [of office] whereas the earth title is derived from a symbolic association with the earth of deeper significance'. He is, therefore, not in fact a leopard-skin priest, but a priest of the soil who wears a leopard-skin as a badge of office. There is no hint that the Nuer regard a pied skin as suitable, *qua* its piedness, for a priest who is in an intermediate position and whose duty it is to resolve disputes. There is no reason to suppose any more profound reasons for the wearing of the leopard-skin than the symbolic associations of the leopard itself, which are beside the point here, and that it is a visually attractive and bold material symbol.

While Nilotes do not, in general, picture God to themselves,[26] Lienhardt relates (1961: 46) how some Western Dinka conceive of Nhialic, God, or Divinity, as being pied:

Some people claim to have had visions of Divinity. Two youths, at different times, told me that their mothers had once seen Divinity . . . In one vision Divinity was seen as an

old man, with a red and blue pied body and a white head. In the other he appeared as
a huge old man, with a blue-green body (the colour of the sky) and again a white head.
Other Dinka who have heard of such visions seem usually to be agreed that in them
the body of Divinity is strikingly pied, but with a white head, a mark of age and
venerability.

The blue-green body, it is worth noting at the outset, is not pied blue and
green, but a single blue-green colour—the colour of the sky, *nhialic*, in which
Divinity is conceived as living. The red-and-blue pied configuration is not
found in cattle, but represents one of the strongest perceptual contrasts. It is
an extreme form of piedness. Among the Atuot, similarly, one of the powerful
spirits of the sky, the power of rain, is 'usually referred to by its ox-name
awumkwei', and according to Burton (1981: 76), 'this color pattern is the
most aesthetically pleasing for the Atuot; it signifies a boldly marked black and
white animal, with a fully white head and red nose'.

That Nhialic and Awumkwei should be thought of as pied is not surprising,
given how much the Dinka and Atuot value such configurations. The high
aesthetic value of pied configurations, whether in cattle or elsewhere, is
sufficient reason for Divinity to be though of as pied, when Divinity is thought
of as displaying any perceptual qualities at all.

Lienhardt (1961: 46) goes on to explain that 'white oxen or oxen boldly
marked with white are especially appropriate for sacrifice to Divinity'. Significantly, it is not the piebald which is especially suitable, but the white
ox—or, in the case of the piebald, one that is marked with white. Similarly
for the Mandari, Buxton's careful and sophisticated analysis of their colour
symbolism (1973: esp. 385–94) makes it clear that, despite the high aesthetic
valuation of variegated beasts, they have no symbolic importance and no
especial place in sacrifice over and above their being cattle like any other. The
appropriateness of different colour configurations for sacrifice to different
divinities—or Divinity—amongst the Dinka, however, is exemplified in a
number of cases in Lienhardt's study. In particular, the black-and-white
configurations in cattle are especially suitable for sacrifice to the free-divinity
Deng, which is particularly associated with celestial phenomena such as rain,
thunder, and lightning. It is, however, not the piedness as such which makes
beasts of black-and-white configurations suitable for sacrifice to Deng, but
rather the imaginative connections between the quality perceived in the black-
and-white ox and the quality of the lowering skies: 'the black-and-white
configurations in cattle . . . impress themselves upon the minds of the Dinka as
does the lightning in dark, overcast skies which signifies the activities of Deng'
(Lienhardt, 1961: 162). The symbolic action is thus inexplicable without an
understanding of the workings of the Dinka imagination, and our appreciation
of the workings of the Dinka imagination involves, I should argue, an appreciation of Dinka aesthetics.

Conclusion

Cattle provide the primary aesthetic locus of Nilotic society. This is a given of their pastoral life-style and the well-documented centrality of cattle in their lives. The particularities of the Nilotic aesthetic relate to their deep appreciation of the physical qualities of their cattle and their ideals of bovine form. Their appreciation of cattle-colour configurations can be understood in the context of the environment in which the cattle are perceived, and as a particular instance of the universal appeal of contrast, manifested here in the appreciation of black-and-white and red-and-white beasts in herds of mostly off-white, greyish cattle. Elements which have their origins in this 'bovine' aesthetic can be traced through the ways in which Nilotes perceive, appreciate, enjoy, describe, and act in their world.

The underlying assumptions of this essay are that, all other things being equal, people act in the world to maximize their aesthetic satisfaction, and that an awareness of this aspect of human activity may help us to understand what we might otherwise seek to explain with reference to social structure, cosmology, symbolism, etc. I do not imagine that I have established beyond doubt the worth of these assumptions here, but I hope that I have provided at least an insight into how the Nilotes of the Southern Sudan take pleasure in the lives they lead, as well as into some of the marvels of their everyday vision.

Notes

This essay is based primarily on literary research, although, thanks to the British Institute in Eastern Africa and the Social Science Research Council, I was able to visit Agar Dinka and Apak Atuot country in 1981 and Mandariland in 1982. I am grateful to Survival Anglia and the Pitt Rivers Museum, Oxford, for permission to reproduce photographs. For comments on earlier drafts of this essay I am grateful to Gerd Baumann, Nigel Fancourt, Wendy James, Godfrey Lienhardt, John Mack, Andrew Mawson, Howard Morphy, Michael O'Hanlon, John Penney, and Simon Simonse.

1 For the Nuer, see Evans-Pritchard (1940*a*); for the Dinka, Lienhardt (1961); for the Atuot, Burton (1987); and for the Mandari, Buxton (1973).
2 See, for the Nuer, Evans-Pritchard (1940*a*: 16–50); for the Dinka, Lienhardt (1961: 10–27); and for the Mandari, Buxton (1973: 5–11).
3 This includes the war currently being waged in the Southern Sudan, in which Nuer, Dinka, Atuot, and Mandari have been involved as combatants, victims, and refugees.
4 In his comprehensive overview of the literature on 'African Aesthetics', Van Damme (1987) mentions only one work on a Nilotic people, Schneider (1956) on the Pokot. Klumpp (1987) includes a brief discussion of Maasai aesthetics. There are a number of works which discuss body decoration, material culture, and so on

amongst Nilotic peoples; this literature contains material relevant to the study of aesthetics, but rarely discusses aesthetics specifically.

5 See e.g. Turton (1980) on the Mursi.

6 For illustrations, see e.g. Ryle (1982: 17, 26–7, 34–5, 139); Howell *et al.* (1988: 287, 288, pls. 21, 22); and Fig. 10.1 here, in which the 'background' of off-white cattle is an accidental feature of the photograph. The veterinary officer Grunnet (1962: 7) claimed that 60% of Dinka cattle were 'greyish white or dirty white'.

7 On Nuer practice, see Evans-Pritchard (1940*a*: 37–8; 1956: pl. xiii, opp. 256); for the Dinka, see Lienhardt (1961: 17), and the illustrations in Ryle (1982: 65, 94–5), and in Howell *et al.* (1988: 205, pl. 18); for the Atuot, see Burton (1981: fig. A, opp. 36); and for the Mandari, see Buxton (1973: 7, pl. 1, opp. 6).

8 For an illustration, see Ryle (1982: 39).

9 The fact that similar patterns are highly valued by geographically contiguous peoples who do not keep cattle—such as the Uduk (James, 1988: 28–9)—suggests that these elements may have been part of Nilotic aesthetics even before the Nilotes became cattle-keepers. This is, however, irrelevant to an understanding of the appreciation of such patterns by Nilotic cattle-keepers today, which is founded in their daily experience of their cattle.

10 For illustrations, see e.g. Ryle (1982: 62–5).

11 See e.g. the photograph of a Dinka wearing a colobus monkey skin and other finery in Howell *et al.* (1988: 205, pl. 18).

12 For illustrations, see e.g. Fisher (1984: 42).

13 Schneider (1956: 105) noted the importance of contrast in Pokot beadwork, and Klumpp (1987) has discussed the importance of both contrast and complementarity in contemporary Maasai beadwork. I hope to discuss Nilotic beadwork at length elsewhere.

14 See also e.g. the post illustrated in Buxton (1973: pl. 2, opp. 78).

15 For the Dinka, see Lienhardt (1961: pl. vi, opp. 176); for the Mandari, see Buxton (1973: 54, fig. 1; pl. 7, opp. 371; and app. ii at 419); for an Anuak example, see Evans-Pritchard (1940*b*: pl. ivb, opp. 40).

16 For illustrations, see, for the Dinka, Fisher (1984: 48, 50, 52); for the Mandari, Caputo (1982: 366).

17 For illustrations, see Ryle (1982: 7, 18, 70–1).

18 For an illustration, see Evans-Pritchard (1956: pl. xii, opp. 234).

19 For other illustrations, see, for the Dinka, Deng (1972: 18); Ryle (1982: 15, 58–9); Lienhardt (1961: pl. 1, opp. 16); and the various sequences including dances interspersed throughout the film *Dinka* (Survival Anglia, 1983), especially the sacrifice sequence.

20 For illustrations of such girdles, or corsets, see Fisher (1984: 50, 51); Howell *et al.* (1988: 205, pl. 18).

21 Lienhardt (1961: 264), however, found mud models of bulls hanging in a shrine he visited.

22 Lienhardt (1963: 82) also refers to children playing at cattle-herding with snail-shells. I do not know what form these shells have, but I should not be surprised if they resembled in some ways the schematized cattle forms represented in the abstracted Pokot examples in Fig. 10.8.

23 These examples are in the Pitt Rivers Museum, Oxford, and were collected by

Evans-Pritchard. All but one are inscribed as having been collected among the Anuak, but it is almost certainly the case that they were all collected among the Nuer.

24 In his discussion of Dinka arts, Caravita (1968: 366) suggests that painting and sculpture remain undeveloped and marginalized because they are the work of people, that is, women and children, who are marginalized within Dinka society.

25 Huffman (1931: 69) remarks that the figures drawn by Nuer children and those incised on gourds by Nuer women always have rectangular bodies.

26 Evans-Pritchard (1956: 123) says that 'Nuer do not claim to see God', while, according to Buxton (1973: 19), Mandari say 'Creator has not been known or seen', and among the Atuot, according to Burton (1981: 138), '"God the Father" is never said or imagined to exist in any physical form'.

References

BAXANDALL, MICHAEL (1972). *Painting and Experience in Fifteenth-Century Italy: A Primer in the Social History of Pictorial Style.* Oxford: Oxford Univ. Press.

—— (1980). *The Limewood Sculptors of Renaissance Germany.* New Haven, Conn.: Yale Univ. Press.

BLACKMAN, A. A. (1956). 'The Material Culture of the Nilotic Tribes of East Africa'. B.Litt. thesis, Univ. of Oxford.

BURTON, JOHN W. (1978). 'Ghost Marriage and the Cattle Trade among the Atuot of the Southern Sudan', *Africa,* 48/4: 398–405.

—— (1979). 'Atuot Totemism', *Journal of Religion in Africa,* 10/2: 95–107.

—— (1980). 'The Village and the Cattle Camp: Aspects of Atuot Religion', in Ivan Karp and Charles S. Bird (eds.), *Explorations in African Systems of Thought.* Bloomington: Indiana Univ. Press, 268–97.

—— (1981). *God's Ants: A Study of Atuot Religion.* Studia Instituti Anthropos 37. St Augustin, Germany: Anthropos Institute.

—— (1982). 'Figurative Language and the Definition of Experience: The Role of Ox-Songs in Atuot Social Theory', *Anthropological Linguistics,* 24/3: 263–79.

—— (1987). *A Nilotic World: The Atuot-Speaking Peoples of the Southern Sudan* (with a foreword by Francis Mading Deng). Contributions to the Study of Anthropology, No. 1. New York: Greenwood Press.

BUXTON, JEAN (1973). *Religion and Healing in Mandari.* Oxford: Clarendon Press.

CAPUTO, ROBERT (1982). 'Sudan: Arab–African Giant', *National Geographic,* 161/3: 346–79.

CARAVITA, GIANNI (1968). 'L'arte dei Dinka', *Africa* (Rome), 23/3: 350–69.

CUMMINS, S. L. (1904). 'Sub-Tribes of the Bahr-el-Ghazal Dinkas', *Journal of the Royal Anthropological Institute,* 34: 149–66.

DENG, FRANCIS MADING (1972). *The Dinka of the Sudan.* New York: Holt, Rinehart & Winston.

—— (1973). *The Dinka and their Songs.* Oxford Library of African Literature. Oxford: Clarendon Press.

DIFFEY, T. J. (1986). 'The Idea of Aesthetic Experience', in Michael H. Mitias (ed.), *Possibility of the Aesthetic Experience.* Martinus Nijhoff Philosophy Library 14. Dordrecht: Nijhoff, 3–12.

EVANS-PRITCHARD, E. E. (1934). 'Imagery in Ngok Dinka Cattle-Names', *Bulletin of the School of Oriental and African Studies*, 7/3: 623–8.

—— (1937). 'Economic Life of the Nuer: Cattle', *Sudan Notes and Records*, 20/2: 209–45.

—— (1940a). *The Nuer: A Description of the Modes of Livelihood and Political Institutions of a Nilotic People*. Oxford: Clarendon Press.

—— (1940b). *The Political System of the Anuak of the Anglo-Egyptian Sudan*. London School of Economics Monographs on Social Anthropology, No. 4. London: Lund, Humphries.

—— (1956). *Nuer Religion*. Oxford: Clarendon Press.

FAGG, WILLIAM (1973). 'In Search of Meaning in African Art', in Anthony Forge (ed.), *Primitive Art and Society*. London: Oxford Univ. Press, 151–68.

FERNANDEZ, JAMES W. (1971). 'Principles of Opposition and Vitality in Fang Aesthetics', in Carol F. Jopling (ed.), *Art and Aesthetics in Primitive Societies: A Critical Anthology*. New York: Dutton, 356–73 (first published 1966).

FISHER, ANGELA (1984). *Africa Adorned*. London: Collins.

FORGE, ANTHONY (1970). 'Learning to See in New Guinea', in Philip Mayer (ed.), *Socialization: The Approach from Social Anthropology*. ASA Monographs, No. 8. London: Tavistock, 269–91.

GOMBRICH, E. H. (1977). *Art and Illusion: A Study in the Psychology of Pictorial Representation*, 5th edn. Oxford: Phaidon (first published 1960).

GRUNNET, N. T. (1962). 'An Ethnographic–Ecological Survey of the Relationship betwęen the Dinka and their Cattle', *Folk* (Copenhagen), 4: 5–20.

HOWELL, PAUL *et al.* (1988). *The Jonglei Canal: Impact and Opportunity*. Cambridge: Cambridge Univ. Press.

HUFFMAN, RAY (1931). *Nuer Customs and Folklore* (with an introduction by D. Westermann). London: Oxford Univ. Press.

JACKSON, H. C. (1923). 'The Nuer of the Upper Nile Province', *Sudan Notes and Records*, 6/1: 59–107; 6/2: 123–89.

JAMES, WENDY (1988). *The Listening Ebony: Moral Knowledge, Religion, and Power among the Uduk of Sudan*. Oxford: Clarendon Press.

KLUMPP, DONNA REY (1987). 'Maasai Art and Society: Age and Sex, Time and Space, Cash and Cattle'. Ph.D. thesis, Columbia Univ., New York.

LIENHARDT, GODFREY (1961). *Divinity and Experience: The Religion of the Dinka*. Oxford: Clarendon Press.

—— (1963). 'Dinka Representations of the Relations between the Sexes', in I. Schapera (ed.), *Studies in Kinship and Marriage: Dedicated to Brenda Z. Seligman on her 80th Birthday*. Royal Anthropological Institute Occasional Paper No. 16. London: Royal Anthropological Institute, 79–92.

MACDERMOT, BRIAN HUGH (1972). *Cult of the Sacred Spear: The Story of the Nuer Tribe in Ethiopia*. London: Hale.

MAQUET, JACQUES (1979). *Introduction to Aesthetic Anthropology*, 2nd edn. Other Realities 1. Malibu, Calif.: Undena Publications (first published 1971).

—— (1986). *The Aesthetic Experience: An Anthropologist Looks at the Visual Arts*. New Haven, Conn.: Yale Univ. Press.

NEBEL, ARTHUR (1948). *Dinka Grammar (Rek-Malual Dialect) with Texts and*

Vocabulary. English text rev. by C. W. Beer. Museum Combonianum 2. Verona: Missioni Africane.

—— (1979). *Dinka–English, English–Dinka Dictionary: Thong Muonyjang Jam Jang Kek Jieng, Dinka Language Jang and Jieng Dialects*. Museum Combonianum 36. Bologna: Editrice Missionaria Italiana (first published 1954).

OCHOLLA-AYAYO, A. B. C. (1980). *The Luo Culture: A Reconstruction of the Material Culture Patterns of a Traditional African Society*. Studien zur Kulturkunde 54. Wiesbaden: Steiner.

PEPPER, STEPHEN (1974). 'Aesthetics', in *New Encyclopaedia Britannica: Macropaedia*, i. Chicago: Beaton, 149–63.

RYLE, JOHN (1982). *Warriors of the White Nile: The Dinka*. Amsterdam: Time-Life.

SCHNEIDER, HAROLD K. (1956). 'The Interpretation of Pakot Visual Art', *Man*, 56: art. 108, 103–6.

SURVIVAL ANGLIA (1983). *Dinka. The Vanishing Tribes of Africa 3*. Film. Norwich: Survival Anglia.

SVOBODA, TERESE (trans.) (1985). *Cleaned the Crocodile's Teeth: Nuer Song*. Greenfield Center, NY: Greenfield Review Press.

TURTON, DAVID (1980). 'There's No Such Beast: Cattle and Colour Naming among the Mursi', *Man*, n.s., 15/2: 320–38.

VAN DAMME, WILFRIED (1987). *A Comparative Analysis Concerning Beauty and Ugliness in Sub-Saharan Africa*. Africana Gandensia 4. Ghent: Rijksuniversiteit.

ZANGWILL, NICK (1986). 'Aesthetics and Art', *British Journal of Aesthetics*, 26/3: 257–69.

INDEX